Drilling Down

MW00622712

Turning Customer Data into Profits
with a Spreadsheet

Drilling Down
Turning Customer Data into Profits with a Spreadsheet

Third Edition

Copyright 2004 Jim Novo

ISBN 1-59113-519-2

Manufactured in the United States of America.

Booklocker.com, Inc.
2004

Drilling Down

**Turning Customer Data into Profits
with a Spreadsheet**

Jim Novo

Acknowledgements

Without the support and input of my wife Barbara, you would not be reading this book, and there would be no Drilling Down software. 'Nuff said.

I'd also like to thank Alex Romanov and Wade Downs, two friends from Home Shopping Network who helped to develop these techniques and along with my wife, forced me to massage my ramblings on these topics into a book the average person can read and understand.

Thanks to Richard Hoy and Angela Hoy, for starting this whole book thing in the first place and making it come true through Booklocker. Visit them at http://www.booklocker.com.

Bud Paxson and Roy Speer, the founders of the Home Shopping Network, deserve more credit than they have ever received for pioneering 24 x 7 interactive retailing, business operations, and customer service. Despite the limitations of technology at the time, they provided customers real-time interaction, community, and the first taste of being "in charge," all in one service. Thanks to them for believing our small group could find profitable marketing and customer service answers for the new interactive world, and for also seeing past our failures to the future.

And thanks to my Mom and Dad, for helping to shape my life.

Table of Contents

Preface ix

Introduction xi

About Jim Novo xiii

Chapter 1 Jonesin' for Some ROI 1

Chapter 2 Customer Profile or Customer Model? 7

Chapter 3 Data-Driven Marketing and Service Drivers 10

Chapter 4 Customer Marketing Basics 15

Chapter 5 Customer Marketing Strategy: The Friction Model 20

Latency Metric Toolkit

Chapter 6 Trip Wire Marketing 26

Chapter 7 The Hair Salon Example 32

Chapter 8 The B2B Software Example 39

Chapter 9 Turning Latency Data into Profits 45

Recency Metric Toolkit

Chapter 10 Predictive Marketing 55

Chapter 11 The Ad Spending Example 66

Chapter 12 Turning Recency Data into Profits 74

Chapter 13 The Online Retail Example 81

RFM Scoring Toolkit

Chapter 14 Cash Flow Marketing 98

Chapter 15 A Tweak for Interactive Customers 107

Chapter 16 No Customer Database? How to Set Up a Spreadsheet
    to Score Customers 112

Chapter 17 How to Score Your Customers..121

Chapter 18 The Commerce and Content Examples: Turning Scoring
    Data into Profits..130

Chapter 19 Case Study: Non-Profit Scores 192% Increase in ROI
    using RFM Model...141

Advanced Data-Driven Marketing Toolkit

Chapter 20 Using Customer Characteristics and Multiple Scores........143

Chapter 21   Customer LifeCycles: Tracking Scores Over Time 152

Chapter 22 Customer LifeCycle Grids: High Performance
    Behavior-based Modeling...161

Chapter 23 Straight Talk on LifeTime Value 176

Chapter 24 Lifetime Value, I'd Like to Introduce You to the CFO......186

Chapter 25 Fellow Drillers at Work..197

Definitions and Background Information 197

Customer Loyalty and Retention 213

Customer Segmentation and LifeTime Value.......................................219

Professional Services 241

Ad-Supported Content / Subscription Models.....................................244

Online / Offline Retailing and Catalogs...252

Distribution / Operations / Channel Management 274

The ROI of Online Branding Efforts 290

Chapter 26 Predicting Campaign ROI: Set Up 298

Chapter 27 Predicting Campaign ROI: The Model 304

Chapter 28 Predicting Campaign ROI: Fine Tuning 312

Chapter 29 Expense and Revenue You May Not be Capturing:
Subsidy Costs and Halo Effects 319

Chapter 30 Some Final Thoughts: Seasonality, CRM, Behavioral
Inertia, Data-Driven Program Outlines 325

APPENDIX: Software Download and ReadMe 333

Preface

Drowning in data but have no information? Confused by ROI, LTV, RFM and all the rest of the alphabet soup involved in using customer data to increase profits? You know you should be "Drilling Down" and creating "customer profiles," but how is it done? Drill how deep, and look for what?

Drilling Down pulls back the curtain on the "how" of Data-Driven marketing and service concepts, the enabling knowledge behind CRM, database marketing, frequency marketing, loyalty marketing, relationship marketing, 1-to-1 marketing, permission marketing, and so forth. Learn the basic techniques of Data-Driven marketing / service and you will know how to use your data to attack any of these approaches, while customizing them for your business.

You will learn the hands-on fundamentals of teasing out and evolving the essentials of highly profitable marketing and service programs using customer data, without using fancy hardware or software. Do it yourself with a spreadsheet! Drilling Down is not another "consultant fluff book," where the promise to deliver actionable ideas is not kept. You will get the whole "how do I actually do it" story in this book.

The book puts forth an easy to follow real world framework for designing your own marketing and service programs using customer data. The core ideas are based on a process and techniques proven under circumstances where there was no previous history to follow for guidance, and require no specialized skills other than knowledge of your business. This framework allows those with little customer data experience to create a structure for marketing and service decision-making. Instead of going about business in a haphazard way, always wondering, **"Who** should I pay attention to? **When** should I pay attention to them? **How** should I design the program?" the reader will be able to make these marketing and service decisions based on the customer data they have on hand.

If you work in a larger company trying to figure out the mysteries of CRM (to CRM, or not – that is the question) following the Drilling Down method "pre-CRM" will allow you to uncover the potential benefits and ROI traps in your customer data **before installing CRM.** Learn how your customer base responds to database marketing and service techniques and use this experience to evaluate the features of analytical - marketing CRM packages and their potential ROI.

Drilling Down explains why Data-Driven marketing and service programs work, and shows you how to develop them step-by-step. You can learn at your own pace and implement simple techniques right away, then graduate to increasingly complex approaches as you experience the results. To top it all off, the book provides descriptions of advanced testing ideas discovered only through years of research in database marketing and customer behavior, with a special focus on interactive customers and their special quirks.

Introduction

I spend a lot of time in marketing and CRM-oriented discussion lists. If you do, you probably also sense the incredible frustration of people who keep asking about using their customer data to retain customers and increase profits. Everybody knows they should be doing it, but can't find out **how** to do it.

Consultants and agencies make this process sound like some kind of "black magic," something you can't possibly do yourself. I disagree. I think the average business owner can do a perfectly decent job analyzing customer data and use this knowledge to develop campaigns and programs that increase sales while reducing marketing costs. That is why I wrote the book.

This book is about the down-and-dirty, nitty-gritty art of taking data generated by your customers and making sense of it, getting it to speak to you; it's about creating insight into what types of marketing or general business actions you can take to make your business more profitable.

We'll be talking about "action-oriented" ideas you can generate on your own to drive sales and profits, ideas that will reveal themselves by analyzing your own customer data, using only a spreadsheet. Of course, you don't have to use a spreadsheet, and just by following the business rules, any average programmer can create all the analytics and reports you need in any standard database.

We have all heard how important it is to collect customer data, to "know" your customer. What I don't hear much about is what exactly you DO with all that data once you have collected it. How is it used? What exactly is Drilling Down into the data supposed to tell me, and what am I looking for when I get there? For that matter, what data should I be collecting and how will I use it when I have it? And can it be done without breaking the bank? The answer to the last question is yes, and the rest of the questions are answered in this book. The following outlines what you will learn and be able to do after reading the Drilling Down book:

What data is important to collect about a customer and what data is not

How to create action oriented customer profiles with an Excel spreadsheet and use these profiles to create marketing and service programs that retain and increase the value of customers.

How to use these profiles to define the future value of your customers and measure the general health of your business, now and in the future

How to use these profiles to encourage customers to do what you want them to

How to increase your profits while decreasing your marketing and service costs

How to design high ROI (Return on Investment) marketing / service programs

How to predict when a customer is about to defect and leave you

How to blow away investors with accurate predictions of the future profitability of your business

Before we get going, let me make some suggestions. Take it easy. Read the book slowly. Make sure you understand each section before you move on to the next, because each section builds on the concepts of the previous section. Important concepts are in **boldface** type. There are plenty of examples provided; please take the time to understand them.

Once you internalize these concepts, you won't believe how profitable your marketing and service programs will be when you do some Drilling Down. This book covers five decades worth of Data-Driven thinking, detailing valuable techniques from the beginnings of catalog marketing up through state-of-the-art techniques used in interactive CRM. It's a lot of serious material and no fluff; so take your time reading it. And if you like the book, tell your friends about it.

Jim Novo

P.S. The companion software application to the book is explained here:

http://www.jimnovo.com/software.htm

and can be downloaded here:

http://www.jimnovo.com/home/ddsoft.htm

About Jim Novo

Jim Novo is an interactive customer valuation, retention, loyalty, and defection expert with close to 20 years of experience generating exceptional returns on marketing program investments. His professional career has been focused on introducing Data-Driven marketing to new industries. In the 80's, cable television was the target and his groundbreaking programs were widely copied throughout the industry. In the 90's, Jim revolutionized the TV Shopping industry by focusing resources on the customer instead of the products. And for the 00's, the Internet lies squarely in Jim's sights.

At The Home Shopping Network, Jim Novo witnessed the entire business cycle of a hyper-growth interactive retailer. After the land-grab customer acquisition phase, he directed the critical transition to customer retention and credit marketing activities across the television, catalog, and Internet divisions. As Vice President of Programming & Marketing during the slowdown to the mature phase, Jim handled the integration of customer communications and marketing across all the distribution channels, creating a "cradle-to-grave" customer path from Television to Internet to Catalog.

These early interactive lessons are proving valuable to understanding visitor and customer behavior on the web. Jim is recognized for developing the "Friction Model" of behavioral targeting to explain how interactivity and increasing levels of customer control in a business relationship affect customer behavior tracking and measurement, the design of customer retention programs, and the management of "potential customer value" – the future stream of profits expected to flow from a customer.

Jim is an MBA Graduate of Babson College, a school known for a focus on entrepreneurial activity. He majored in Economics and Psychology as an undergraduate at Dartmouth College. Jim is currently working with software and marketing companies to improve their products and practices in database marketing and on the Internet.

You can schedule workshops, seminars, and speaking engagements based on the techniques and methodology described in this book. Jim will teach your marketing and / or IT staff the Drilling Down method using your own data - see **http://www.jimnovo.com/Customer-Consulting.htm** for more information.

Chapter 1
Jonesin' for Some ROI

It was a day just like any other day. The Customer Retention Clinic was open, yours truly at the helm. Both offline and online marketers trudged through, with the same old issues. One is drowning in data. The other has reports that provide no actionable information. Still others have fancy models and profiles, but don't know how to use them to increase the profitability of the company.

I became aware of a fresh-faced marketer, waiting eagerly in line. Something seemed different about this one. Untouched by CRM. Never been to a Business Intelligence demo. Ignores every e-mail plea to attend "educational" webcasts.

"Your question?" I ask.

"Jim, how can I tell if a customer is still a customer?" was the reply.

I stood there, floored by the question. I knew this marketer was special. How elegant, I thought: the summation of 20 years of my work in a single question. Nobody had ever asked it before. They always want to know about the money, you know - how can I make more money, show me the tricks. Addicted to ROI. They start off innocently enough, probably with a spreadsheet. Then maybe a simple model or two. Before you know it they're into data mining. But they don't make any money for the company. Devastating.

Then they show up at my Customer Retention Clinic, looking for the magic bullet, the secret to ROI. But not this one. No, this one was special.

"Why do you want to know?" I asked.

"Because I want to calculate our customer retention rate and track it over time" was the answer.

"You can't put a retention rate in the bank, you know" was my cynical answer. "What you really need is a formal, widely accepted definition of when a customer is no longer a customer in your company. Then you will be able to get at your precious retention rate."

Silence from the fresh-faced one. Then:

"In customer service, they say only 10% of customers complain and tell us they will stop doing business with the company. They say this means customer satisfaction is 90%. Does that mean customer retention is 90% too?"

Well, it's all well and good to be fresh-faced, but now we're getting into naive. Still, I think, maybe there is something here, something worth saving for the future of customer marketing.

"Are you saying the only defected customers are ones you have documented?" I sneer. "Ones who told you they will never do business with you again? Look, to me, a customer is a person or company you sell stuff to, who pays you for a product or service. You have identified 10% who are not going to buy from you anymore; they are definitely defected customers."

"But the word "customer" implies some kind of "future activity," doesn't it? I mean, if you know they will never buy from you again - as in the above complaint example - you don't call them customers, so the opposite must be true: to be a customer, there must be expectation they will buy again. If you know they will not buy again, they're former customers, correct?"

"So the definition of a customer would be someone who:

1. Purchased from you in the past, and
2. Is expected to purchase in the future."

"Just because somebody bought from you in the past and did not tell you they hate your guts now does not mean they are still a customer. A customer is somebody you expect to transact with you in the future; otherwise they are a former customer, by definition."

Not a bad sermon, I think.

"Wait a minute," says fresh-face, "what about customers who purchased in the past that we have no expectations for? We don't have any idea whether they are likely to buy or not, there is no "expectation." What about them?"

Oh, so fresh-face is going to play tough with me, I think. Probably an MBA. Wait a minute; I'm an MBA. Is it getting hot in here?!

"Listen, you know the answer to that question, don't you? Because you don't know crap about the people you sell to and their likelihood to buy, you simply call them all "customers." You have no more reason to call them customers than to call them former customers, but of course, you "default" to calling them all customers. They didn't call up and tell you they are not customers, so they are, right? Is that what you are saying?" It **is** hot in here...phew.

I go on. "What if they didn't tell you they hated your guts, but they told 10 other people they would never buy from you? Are they still a customer? Do you know how many there are? How many have had a bad product or service experience and never said anything? Is it 10%, 20%, 40% of your customers?"

No reply. Floor staring from the face-man. I have caused hurt feelings. But I have got to move on, there are all these people waiting for their magic bullet, people who need a customer marketing fix, they're jonesin' for some ROI...

"Look, I'm sorry" I say half-heartedly. "Let's come at this from a different direction that will perhaps be more helpful. Let's take all the customers who you think are customers, and ask just one question - when was the last time you had contact with these people?"

"For example, the last time you had any contact with a customer was 3 years ago. Are they still a customer? With no activity for 3 years?"

"Maybe" says fresh-face.

"OK, fine. What about if the last contact with the customer was 5 years ago? Is this person or business still a customer?"

"Maybe" is the reply.

"10 years ago?" I ask, sweating.

"Maybe."

That worked like gangbusters, I think. No wonder nobody knows how to sell more to current customers while reducing costs. All customers are customers for life - unless they tell you they aren't anymore. Sometimes it seems as if today's marketing people have no sense of reality. They are thinking every person or business that ever transacted with them is still a customer!

"All right, one more try," I say impatiently.

"Take two customers – the last contact with one was 10 years ago, the last contact with the other was 2 years ago. Would you be willing to go out on a limb and say the "customer" you last had contact with 2 years ago is more likely to still be a customer than the customer you last had contact with 10 years ago?"

"Yes," says the face.

"Finally," I gasp. "And if the customer you last had contact with 2 years ago is more likely to still be a customer than the customer you last had contact with 10 years ago, is the customer you last had contact with 2 years ago more likely to purchase good or services from you today than the customer you last had contact with 10 years ago?"

"Sure."

"More likely to purchase goods or services now, and in the future, from you?" I wheeze expectantly.

"Yes" is the reply.

"So, let me get this straight - when comparing two customers, the customer you have had contact with more recently is more likely to purchase, relative to the other customer?"

"I would think so" is the answer.

"What???" I gurgle, starting to lose my balance, eyes becoming glassy...

"I mean yes, Jim..."

"Then, if I was to define a customer as someone who:

1. Purchased from you in the past, and
2. Is expected to purchase in the future,

you would say the customer you last had contact with 2 years ago was more likely to still be a customer than the customer you last had contact with 10 years ago? Would you say that?" I ask breathlessly.

"Yes!" the face shouts triumphantly. "I get it!"

"So for any two "customers," the one you had contact with more recently, relative to the other, is more likely to still be a customer and keep purchasing goods or services from you, now and in the future?"

"Yes!!!" fresh-face screams.

"So as a marketing genius, you would then go out and treat these two customers exactly the same, spend the same amount of money marketing to them and servicing them, even though one is more likely to still be a customer and purchase than the other?" I scream back.

The trap was set.

"Yes!!" face blurts out. "That's what we do! We spend the same amount of money and resources on every "customer," regardless of their likelihood to still even be a customer!"

"I know, your company and most other companies out there. The question is **why do you do this**, when it is so darn easy to tell which customers are more likely to purchase goods or services relative to the others?"

And that, Dear Driller, is what this book is about. You are going to learn some very simple techniques for tracking which customers are more likely to purchase goods or services from you, and then you will learn precisely what to do with this information to increase your sales while cutting your marketing costs.

Because I don't want to see you down at the Clinic, the line is too long already.

First, we're going to talk a little bit about customer models – what they are and are not. Then we'll put a little background in place so you understand the basic objectives and strategy behind High ROI customer data-driven marketing. Next, we'll take a look at the simplest model of all – Latency – because it is the most intuitive model and often the easiest to implement for those just getting started with customer behavior models. Then it's on to the Recency and RFM models. Often used in tandem with the Latency model, Recency and RFM are "smarter" than the Latency model but a bit less intuitive.

And finally, we'll jump into the whole Customer LifeCycle marketing methodology and show you how to use what you will know about simple customer models to really drive the profitability of your customer marketing / retention / CRM programs. By understanding what the customer is likely to do even before they do it, you can use your modeling intelligence to craft the most profitable customer marketing programs you probably have ever been a witness to. The Customer LifeCycle is the key to the fabled "right message, to the right people, at the right time" marketing kingdom.

By the end of this book, you should be able to very clearly answer some basic marketing and service questions about your customer base. Questions you no doubt have asked many times yourself, such as the following:

- Who do I provide marketing or service programs to? When? How often?

- Should I contact some customers more often than others? (Yes, you definitely should.)

- How much and what kind of incentives should I provide to get a customer to do something I want them to? Can I predict which customers will be responsive to the program? (Yes, you can)

- How can I tell when I'm losing a customer or when service has failed?

- How can I put a value on my different customers and the business as a whole now, and project this value into the future?

- Is my business strong and healthy, or becoming weaker?

- What can I expect in future sales from my existing customers?

So what do you say, fellow Driller? Ready to cut that line at the Clinic?

Chapter 2
Customer Profile or Customer Model?

Many people think using your customer data for marketing efforts is about creating a customer "profile." It's a hot topic. Everybody wants to do it. But what is a customer profile? Here are 2 kinds of customer profiles:

- Customer is married, has children, lives in an upscale neighborhood, and reads Time magazine

- Customer visited the web site or business every day for 2 months, but has not visited at all in the past 2 weeks

The first profile is demographic, a set of characteristics. The second profile is behavior-based, involving what the customer is actually doing. **It's about customer activity.**

Which seems more important to you?

They're both important in their own ways. For someone selling advertising, or deciding on content for a website, the first profile could be important, because it defines the market for ad sales and provides clues to editorial direction. These are important considerations in attracting customers and generating revenue in the first stages of an online project.

The second profile is about action, behavior, and for anybody concerned about what his or her customers are **doing,** is more important than the first. Will they visit again? Will they buy again? These are the questions answered by looking at behavior. Customer behavior is a much stronger predictor of your future relationship with a customer than demographic information ever will be. You have to look at the data, the record of their behavior, and it will tell you things. It will tell you "I'm not satisfied." It will tell you "I want to buy more, give me a push." It will tell you "I think your service is awful."

I'd argue the second type of profile is more important longer term, because if the customer stops buying from or visiting the site, you're not going to have much of a chance to serve up the customized pages or ads based on any "profile" given to you. You could customize the heck out of the site based on demographics or self-reported survey data but customers would never see the results if they never come back. So for the long haul, if you had to choose the more important profile, the profile based on action and behavior would be more critical to you than a demographic one. **Customer behavior profiling is critical to a company interested in selling more to existing customers.**

Marketers who use data often talk about "customer modeling," instead of customer profiling. Modeling is kind of like profiling, but it is action oriented. Models are not about a static state, like "Customer is 50 years old." Models are about action over time, like "If this customer does not make a purchase in the next 30 days, they are unlikely to come back and make any further purchases."

It sounds so mystical, and it is. To see a mathematical model predict customer behavior is astonishing, to say the least. The model says, "Do this to these people and they will likely do this." The marketer or service provider goes out and does what the model says, and like magic, a good bunch of the customers do exactly what the model said they would. It works like a charm – usually.

Building heavy-duty models is expensive, because it requires an awesome amount of talent and experience. There are many mathematical techniques used to build models, each with their own pitfalls and gotchas. Success depends a lot on the type of business, the kinds of data available, and the experience of the modeler / analyst in building models for a particular business.

What is a model? Simply, it looks at customers who are engaging in a certain behavior and tries to find a commonality in them. The marketer might say to the modeler, "Here's a list of our very best customers, and here's a list of our former best customers. Is there any behavioral signal a best customer gives before they stop being a customer? What does the data say to you?"

So here's what's in it for you, what this book is about. You can do your own models, based on the decades of experience Data-Driven marketers and service providers have already invested. And while they won't be as good as the heavy-duty models done by Ph.D. analysts, they'll be pretty darn good. Plus, they will help you increase profits while cutting marketing and service costs. This book will show you how to do it, with just a spreadsheet. Ph.D. not required.

By the way, once you figure out your behavioral models, you can use them **in combination with demographics and characteristics** to produce an even richer picture of the customer. But the behavior comes first, because it is behavior you want to influence. Knowing the following about a customer is not very **actionable;** there is not much you can **do** with this information:

- Customer is married, has children, lives in an upscale neighborhood, and reads Time magazine

But if you add behavior to this demographic profile:

- Customers who are married, have children, live in upscale neighborhoods, and read Time magazine appear to be disappointed with our site, because a high proportion of them haven't visited the site in the last 30 days

you can start deciding what (if anything) you want to do about it, because you know these customers are engaging in a specific behavior.

The combination of behavior and demographics can be very powerful indeed. But without the behavior, demographic characteristics don't tell you much. You will learn how to use both in building your models. First we'll talk about customer behavior, and then add customer demographics later on.

Chapter 3
Data-Driven Marketing and Service Drivers

I came up with the phrase "Data-Driven" because I needed one name for the process happening in the background of all the marketing and business optimization approaches where customer data is used. As soon as you say "Relationship Marketing" or "Loyalty Marketing" or "1-to-1 Marketing" or "Permission Marketing" or "CRM," all kinds of extra ideas creep in, obscuring what's really going on in the background of all these concepts.

These approaches differ in how they are positioned to the customer, and how they are communicated. But back in the pits where the data analysts are, where customer profiling and modeling take place, they're much the same.

Data-Driven marketers and service providers generally have two objectives with customer value management, which is what the above approaches are all about:

1. Hold on to the most valuable customers

2. Try to make less valuable customers more valuable

So whether it's relationship marketing, a loyalty program, permission based, or 1-to-1, you still have to accomplish these goals, and to do it, you have to create marketing or service programs and execute them. This means you have to know the value of your customers and their likelihood to respond to a program, whether the program is customized based on books already purchased, uses loyalty points, or is service-oriented.

The marketing and service programs named above are all "wrappers" around what is really going on — you want the customer to do something, or perhaps not do something. This means you have to reach out to the customer and communicate your marketing and service programs. When you're going to execute the communication, you need answers to 3 questions — WHAT will you say, WHO will you say it to, and WHEN will you say it. It doesn't matter what you call your program, what "wrapper" you put it in for the customer — you always have to answer these 3 questions (and maybe a few more).

In addition, you probably care about how much you spend on these marketing and service programs. Ideally, instead of blasting out expensive stuff to every customer, you would want to spend money on the customers most likely to do whatever you want them to, and not waste money on those who are not.

You want customers to do something, to take action. You want them to visit your website, make a purchase, sign up for a newsletter, add new services. And once they do it for the first time, you usually want them to do it again, especially since you probably paid big money to get them to do this "something" the first time. You don't want to pay big money the second time. The data can tell you how to accomplish this, no matter what kind of front-end marketing or service program you are running or how you "wrap it up" and present it to the customer. As long as you have the data, you can interpret it for clues as to what steps to take next, and how to save precious marketing dollars in the process.

When you understand the fundamental ideas behind Data-Driven Marketing and Business Optimization, you will understand how to execute all of these customer retention-oriented programs, no matter what they are called. Here are the four primary ideas driving all of these programs:

1. **Past and Current customer behavior are the best predictors of Future customer behavior.** Think about it. Any entity you can define as a customer – external, internal, distributors, manufacturers, suppliers – they all pursue certain routines, and changes in these routines often indicate an opportunity or challenge is ahead in your relationship with them. When it comes to action-oriented activities like interacting with a web site, this concept really takes on a very important role. You can predict future behavior based on an understanding of past behavior, and use this knowledge to improve marketing or service programs.

    We are talking about actual behavior here, not implied behavior. Being a 35-year-old woman is not a behavior; it's a demographic characteristic. Take these two groups of potential buyers who surf around the 'Net:

    - People who are a perfect demographic match for your business, but have never made a purchase / subscribed to a service online

    - People who are outside the core demographics for your business, but have repeatedly purchased / subscribed to a service online

If you sent a 20% off promotion to each group, asking them to visit and make a first purchase, response would be higher from the buyers (second bullet above) than the demographically targeted group (first bullet above). This effect has been demonstrated for years with many different Data-Driven programs. **It works because actual behavior is better at predicting future behavior than demographic characteristics are.**

2. **Customers want to win at the customer game.** They like to feel they are in control and smart about choices they make, and they like to feel good about their behavior. Marketers and service providers take advantage of this attitude by offering programs and communications of various kinds to get customers to engage in a certain behavior and feel good about doing it. Customers like to "win" through these programs, whether they are consumer customers taking a discount, B2B customers getting enhanced attention or service, distributors receiving volume-based perks, or manufacturers partnering on supply chain issues. Communication programs encourage behavior. If you want your customers to do something, you have to do something for them, and if it's something that makes them feel good (like they are winning the customer game) then they're more likely to do it.

3. **Data-Driven programs are about allocating resources.** All businesses have limited resources, even the dot-coms (eventually). When you spend $1.00 on a program, you are looking to make back more than $1.00 in **PROFIT** (not sales). If you can't make back $1.00, the dollar is not worth spending. Given multiple places to spend the program dollar, if you can get back $2.00 in one place and only $.50 in another, wouldn't you rather spend it where you get $2.00 back? This approach is called **Return on Investment, or ROI, and is the reason why you want to do Data-Driven programs in the first place.** Data-Driven marketing and service programs are among the very few allowing you to accurately measure ROI.

It's about knowing you will make a $2.00 for every $1.00 you spend. If you know this for sure, wouldn't it be foolish not to spend every $1.00 you had in the budget to get $2.00 back? If you always migrate and reallocate program dollars towards higher ROI efforts, profits will grow even as the program budget stays flat. This idea is at the center of ROI thinking — reallocating capital with low return to higher return projects or programs, generating higher profits in the process.

ROI is often a difficult concept to understand because there are so many people using ROI in the wrong context and measuring it incorrectly. You will learn the correct way to calculate and use ROI later on in the book. If you have a financial background, you probably know that what people nowadays call ROI is really ROME (Return On Marketing Expense), but I'll use ROI to keep things from getting too confusing.

4. **Action – Reaction – Feedback – Repeat. Data-Driven marketing and service programs are driven by creating continuous communications and interactions between the business and the customer, and analyzing these interactions for challenges or opportunities.** Marketing and service programs are conversations, as the ClueTrain Manifesto (www.cluetrain.com) and Permission Marketing (www.permission.com) have pointed out (if you have not read these books, do so, they are not just dot-bomb fantasies). At a high level, service is just another form of marketing – and an extremely important one. Marketing and service provision using customer data is a highly evolved and valuable conversation, but it has to be back and forth between the program operator and the customer, and you have to L-I-S-T-E-N to what customers are saying through their actions and data these actions create.

That's why I will sometimes talk about the data "speaking to you." The data is, in effect, speaking for the customer, telling you by its very existence (or non-existence) that there has been an action (or not) that is waiting for a reaction. **An action or inaction is a raising of the hand by the customer, and the Data-Driven marketer or service provider not only sees the raised hand, but also reacts to it, then looks for the hand to be raised again by the customer.**

For example, if a customer visits your web site every day and then just stops, something has happened. They are unhappy with the content or service, or they have found an alternative source. Or perhaps they're just plain not interested in you anymore. This inaction on their part is the raising of the hand, the flag telling you something has happened to change the way this customer thinks about your site. You should react to this and then look for feedback from the customer. If you improve the content, e-mail them a notice, and the customer starts visiting again, the feedback has been given. The cycle is complete until the next time the data indicates a change in behavior, and you need to react to the change.

Let's say this same customer then makes a first purchase. This is an enormously important piece of data, because it indicates a very significant change in behavior. You have a new relationship now, a deeper one. You should react and look for feedback. You send a welcome message, thank the customer for the trust they have displayed in your site, and provide a 2nd purchase discount. Then you await feedback from the customer, in the form of a second purchase, or increased visits. Perhaps you get negative feedback, a return of the first purchase. React to this new feedback and repeat the process over again.

The Data-Driven model of marketing / service provision is 2-way, as opposed to the 1-way approach of media advertising or "data-blind" service. It is give and take, an exchange, a communication process. Using a lot of customer communications can be costly in the offline world. But communication costs are generally low on the Internet, so the Data-Driven model is ideally suited for use there. That's not to say this model doesn't work offline; the initial development and implementation of ideas has been happening in the offline world for decades.

How is this exchange accomplished? Can the data really "speak"? It can and does, but you need to know its language and learn how to listen. It's not very hard, and I'm going to teach you how to do it. But first we're going to run through an overview of how these four driving forces of data-driven marketing are turned into actionable campaigns and programs that will drive your sales higher while cutting marketing expenses.

Chapter 4
Customer Marketing Basics

No question about it, the constant drumbeat of the CRM machine over the past several years has confused the heck out of people. I've been doing this stuff for almost 20 years now, and I can tell you it is not as difficult as it is often portrayed. Sure, you can make it very, very complicated if you want to. But if you don't start with the basics, you're going to end up wasting a ton of money.

Let's start simple, shall we?

In this chapter I'm going to explain in a general sense how High ROI Customer Marketing campaigns and programs are developed and implemented, and in particular, address some of the misconceptions people have regarding customer value-based and relationship marketing techniques. Much of what is now called "CRM" from a marketing perspective is based on these fundamental ideas. Remember, CRM is an approach to managing a business, not a technology. You do not need to live on the bleeding edge of technology to take advantage of a customer-based management philosophy.

Generally, CRM / Relationship Marketing / Database Marketing attempts to define customer behavior and then looks for variances in behavior. When you hear people talk about "predictive modeling" or looking for "patterns" using data mining, they are essentially taking a behavioral approach using the latest tools. Once you know how "normal" customers behave, you can do two things with your business approach:

- Formally document "normal" customer behavior and internalize it systemically, leveraging what you know to improve business functionality and profitability.

- Set up early warning systems, triggering events, or "trip wires" to alert you to customer behavior outside the norm. This variance in behavior generally signals an opportunity to take action with the customer and increase their value - online or offline.

What is most important to measure in CRM is change. People spend way too much time worrying about "absolute" numbers, like LifeTime Value – the cumulative value of the customer now and in the future. What they should really be looking at is "relative" numbers - change over time. It's not nearly as important to know the absolute or exact value of a customer as it is to know whether this value is rising or falling over time. Customer behavior also changes over time, and these changes in behavior typically precede a change in customer value. That means if you track these changes in behavior, you can forecast a change in value, and if you can forecast a change in value, you can get your campaign or program out there and do something about it. This is the core idea behind Relationship Marketing, and these changes in customer behavior and value over time are called the Customer LifeCycle. Knowing and understanding the Customer LifeCycle is the most powerful marketing tool there is; you will learn how to track the customer LifeCycle and use it to increase the ROI of your customer marketing later in the book.

Segments of customers tend to follow similar behavioral patterns, and when any single customer deviates from the norm, this can be a sign of trouble (or opportunity) ahead. For example, if the average new cellular customer first calls customer service 60 days after they start, and an individual customer calls customer service 5 days after they start, this customer is exhibiting behavior far outside the norm. Is there a potential problem, or opportunity? Does the customer having difficulty understanding how to use advanced services on the phone? Or is the customer happily inquiring about adding on more services? In either case, there is an opportunity to increase the value of the customer, if you have the ability to recognize the opportunity and react to it in a timely way.

Understand, there is no "average customer," and a business will have many different customer groups, each exhibiting their own kind of "normal" behavior. The tools available to identify and differentiate customer segments using behavioral metrics are discussed at length in this book. For example, the type of media or offer used to attract the customer can have a dramatic effect on long-term behavior, and customers who come into the business on the same media and offer at the same time will tend to behave in similar ways over time.

In the cell phone case above, number of days from sign-up to the customer service call serves as the "trip wire," and detects a raising of the hand by the customer, which should say to the marketer, "I'm different. Pay attention to me." It is then up to the marketing behaviorist to determine the next course of action. Trip wire metrics like these provide the framework for setting up the capability to recognize the opportunity for increasing customer value.

This raising of the hand by customers, and the reaction by marketers, is the feedback loop at the center of Relationship or LifeCycle-based Marketing. It's a repeating Action - Reaction - Feedback cycle. The customer raises the hand, the marketer Reacts. The customer provides Feedback through Action — perhaps they cancel service, or perhaps they add service. The marketer reacts to this Action, perhaps with a win-back campaign, or with a thank you note. It's a constant (and mostly non-verbal) conversation, an ongoing relationship with the customer requiring interaction to sustain itself. It is not a relationship in the "buddy-buddy" sense. Customers don't want to be friends with a company, they want the company to be responsive to their needs — even if they never come out and state them openly to the company.

This relationship continues to cycle over and over as long as there is value in the relationship for both the customer and the marketer. If the customer takes an Action and there is no Reaction from the marketer, value begins to disappear for the customer, and they may defect. When value disappears for the marketer (the customer stops taking Action / providing Feedback), marketers should stop spending incremental money on the customer.

Notice I did not say "fire the customer" or any of the related drivel thrown around in some of the CRM venues. All customers deserve (and pay for) a certain level of support. The real question is this: for each **incremental**, or additional dollar spent on marketing to the customer, is there a Return On the Investment? If I have the ability to choose between spending $1 on a customer returning $.50, and $1.00 on another customer returning $2.00, I would be nuts not to choose the customer returning $2.00. I have not "fired" the customer returning only $.50; I have just **chosen not to spend incremental money** doing any special marketing or service programs with them.

Do you see the difference?

In fact, much of the profitability typical of High ROI Customer Marketing techniques comes from knowing who **not to spend on**. Most of the decreased profitability in any marketing program is a result of over-spending on unsuitable targets with lowered returns. But because marketers tend to look at results in the aggregate, or they are looking at demographically-based segments to measure a behaviorally-based outcome like purchases, they miss important details. For example, certain segments in the campaign or program may return $5.00 for each $1.00 spent while others may lose $5.00 for every $1.00 spent, even though the campaign as a whole may return $2.00 for each $1 spent.

When you are trying to encourage a customer to buy something, you are looking for a behavior to occur. To measure the results of such a marketing campaign using only demographic segmentation without any behavior-based metrics is misleading at best, and lazy otherwise. If you are trying to create behavior, use behavior as your measurement yardstick to define success.

Why is all of this important to understand?

Customers who are in the process of changing their behavior - either accelerating their relationship with you, or terminating their relationship with you - are the highest potential ROI customers from a marketing perspective. They represent the opportunity to use leverage, to make the highest possible impact with your marketing dollar. You may make some money marketing to customers who are just cruising along the LifeCycle, acting like an "average customer." But when you can predict the likelihood of an average customer to turn into a best customer, and you successfully encourage this behavior, or you can reverse a customer defection before it happens, then there are tremendously profitable longer-term implications for the bottom line. You will discover these opportunities by understanding behavior and setting up trip wires to alert you to deviations from normal behavior by a customer.

What about all the rest of the customers, those who are not either accelerating or terminating the relationship? Leave 'em alone. Whatever background marketing you are doing (advertising, branding, service campaigns, etc.) is serving them just fine. **High ROI Data-Driven marketing techniques are best used (and create the highest returns) when they are used to surgically strike at a trend in behavior, not when customers are comfortably plodding along.** However, there are not nearly as many comfortable plodders as you think; in fact, from 40% to 60% of your customer base is either in the process of accelerating or terminating their relationship with you right now. So the real question is this: how do you find out who these customers are, and how do you take advantage of the situation?

Latency, Recency, and all the other customer behavior metrics described in the Drilling Down book are simply tools for recognizing the opportunity to take an Action in Reaction to the customer raising their hand. If you don't have some kind of system to recognize customers in the process of changing their behavior, you will miss out on most of the highest ROI customer marketing opportunities you have. And don't count on the customer to e-mail or call you when they're thinking of changing their behavior - we both know that is not typically going to happen. A more likely scenario: they will just stop taking Action and providing Feedback. And by then, it's too late for you to do anything profitable about it. Set up your trip wires and predict the behavior, folks. It's the only way to sense when an average customer is ready to become a best customer. And reacting to a customer defection after the fact with a "win-back" campaign is a truly sub-optimal way to "manage" a relationship.

For example, a win-back program is triggered when the customer defects. Have you switched long distance or cellular providers lately? Did you get inundated with win-back calls begging you to reconsider? "Jim, we just wanted you to know we have lowered our rates." Yeah, well, thanks for telling me after over-charging me for the past six months! But could they have known I was about to switch by looking at my behavior?

Sure. If they had looked at the calling patterns of previously defected customers like me, they would have seen a common thread in the behavior. These patterns create the "trip wires" for initiating high ROI marketing campaigns before the defection. The proper profit maximizing approach is to wait until I **look like I'm going to defect**, and then call me and offer a lower rate **before** I defect. I would humbly submit marketing to the customer after they defect is a sub-optimal approach; the decision has already been made. If you can market to them when they appear likely to defect, you optimize your marketing resources by not applying them too soon or too late in the Customer LifeCycle.

Based on a national survey, 50% of marketing managers do not know their customer defection rate, and the other 50% underestimate the true defection rate. After reading this shocking statistic, I figured it was time write the book on using Customer LifeCycles to both track customer defection and define high ROI opportunities to retain customers before they defect. If you understand the Customer LifeCycle, you can predict the primary defection points and react to them before customers leave you. This is the highest ROI marketing you can possibly do; it's much cheaper than "win-back" (after the customer defects, response is much lower) and preserves the investment and profits you have in the customer already.

Chapter 5
Customer Marketing Strategy: The Friction Model

You have probably heard or read references to the "portfolio" approach to managing customers and their value. I think it's a sound idea and one I have used over the years because it's generally quite easy to understand in theory, though the actual implementation is always left for you to figure out on your own. So we're going to take a look at this portfolio approach for managing customers and I am going to supply you with the implementation tools you need to actually make it work. This is an important chapter, because understanding these concepts will provide you with the very foundation needed for developing all of your Data-Driven marketing campaigns and programs.

The general idea behind the portfolio approach to customer value management is this: your customer base is a business asset. Businesses can have lots of different assets, for example, real estate holdings, buildings, inventory, and common stock, along with other financial instruments. Each of these assets has a value to the business. This collection of assets is an "asset portfolio," just as you may hold your own personal portfolio of stocks.

The assets in a portfolio have a current value, which is what they can be sold for today. As we know, there can be changes in the current value of an asset portfolio over time, as what you can sell assets for changes almost daily. Assets also have an "expected" or future value, which can be rising or falling as well, depending on the market for an asset and the type of asset it is. For example, real estate generally appreciates in value over time, but machinery generally declines in value over time. This means at any point in time, an asset has a current as well as a potential or future value.

The customer base can be viewed as such an asset as well, and in fact, each customer has a current and a potential value. The current value is whatever the customer has created in value for the business as of today. Current value could be the cumulative profits for the customer since they became a customer, or the cumulative advertising value of all the visits made to a web site since the first one. Potential value is the future stream of profits expected from the customer as long as they continue to be a customer. If the customer terminates the business relationship, the potential value of the customer drops to near zero; this is the end of the customer LifeCycle, the defection by the customer. The sum of

Current Value and Potential Value is equal to the LifeTime Value of the customer; it's the Total Value contributed by the customer to your business.

If customers in your customer portfolio have both current and potential value, then you can set up a 2 X 2 chart describing the value of your customer base in terms of current plus potential value (LifeTime Value), shown below.

	Low Potential Value, High Current Value — Grow These Customers	High Potential Value, High Current Value — Keep These Customers
Current Value ↑	Low Potential Value, Low Current Value — Should You Spend Money Here?	High Potential Value, Low Current Value — Grow These Customers
	Potential Value ⏩	

Figure 1: The Customer Value Portfolio

Customers having both high current value and high potential value (upper right corner of chart) are the "rocket fuel" customers; these are the 10% - 20% of your customers generating 80% - 90% of your profits. You very much want to keep these customers and should be paying special attention to keeping them happy; these are your best buyers, heaviest visitors, and so forth.

In the lower left corner of the chart, you have the opposite situation; these customers have low current and low potential value. This group probably includes most of your 1X buyers, accidental visitors to the web site, and so on. For the most part, though it's nice to have these customers and they perhaps contribute to paying overhead costs, you probably should not go out of your way to spend a lot of resources trying to grow their potential. In fact, this group likely contains every customer you have **already** spent too much money marketing to – those that never respond. This is also the group customer "win back" programs often focus on.

The upper left and lower right corners of the chart hold customers with a mix of current and potential values. In the upper left, you have high current, low potential value customers. This area is populated mostly by defecting best customers – they were best customers at one time (by current value) but for whatever reason have slowed their profit-generating activity with you and are probably destined to fall into the lower left corner of the chart by defecting. If you're smart, you'll come up with programs that drag them back across to the upper right corner. Customer retention programs should be focused on this group, but more often than not, are not really focused on any group in particular, and that is why they have a high failure rate.

In the lower right corner, you have customers with high potential value and low current value. Who are these people? It's likely they are fairly new customers who have not had a chance to create a lot of value for you yet, but are **expected** to create value in the future. If they do, they will rise into the upper right hand corner of the chart and become "rocket fuel" customers. If they don't, they will fall back across the chart into the lower left corner and contribute very little. Customers in this corner should be the targets of programs designed to increase customer value, though as with the retention programs mentioned above, these "grow the customer" programs are often not focused on this specific group and tend to actually lose a lot more money than they make.

That's the portfolio approach to managing customers and their value, or at least my definition of it. There are others, which for the most part use lifestyle or demographic metrics to allocate the customers. But we're on to that charade, right? Demographics tell you nothing about the current or potential value of the customer, and if you're in a real business, what you care about is the money. For this reason, my approach uses actual spending or value-generating behavior to allocate customers into the quadrants of the customer portfolio.

You say, "Yea, but wait a minute Jim, you're pulling a fast one here. I get how current value is derived, I mean, it's the actual transactional value of the customer – sales, visits, whatever behavior is monetized by the business. But how do you do this "potential value" allocation, how do you measure potential value? I guess future behavior will create value in the future, but how do I measure behavior that has not happened yet? What kind of behavior indicates the potential value of the customer? I was with you until now, but ..."

Relax. Can you take the pebble from my hand, grasshopper? When you can take the pebble from my hand, it will be time for you to leave...

If you didn't get the reference above, you're not up on your 70's TV shows. Try a web search on "pebble grasshopper Kung Fu" if you really need to know.

You are right. This whole potential value measurement issue is, of course, the big problem embedded in the preaching you hear on LifeTime Value, CRM, and these portfolio models of customer value. How do you deal with this whole "potential value" question, how do you actually measure it and act on it?

Well, fellow Driller, would it surprise you to learn that the specific answers to those questions are what the rest of this book is about? I'm not going to give you a conference lecture about all these wonderful things you should be doing with customer value management and then not tell you how to actually do them. Oh no. You will find out exactly how to measure potential value, and as a bonus, you will be surprised how easy it is. In fact, there are specific metrics for potential value and you will learn what they are and exactly how to use them.

Recall this passage from the previous chapter:

It's not nearly as important to know the absolute or exact value of a customer as it is to know whether this value is rising or falling over time. Customer behavior also changes over time, and these changes in behavior typically precede a change in customer value. That means if you track these changes in behavior, you can forecast a change in value, and if you can forecast a change in value, you can get your campaign or program out there and do something about it. This is the core idea behind Relationship Marketing, and these changes in customer behavior and value over time are called the Customer LifeCycle.

So the following may not surprise you: there are LifeCycle Metrics you can use to forecast future changes in value **by tracking behavior in the present**. Pretty handy, huh? And just in time, it seemed like you were getting kind of unruly...

These LifeCycle metrics are where the idea of Friction comes into play. They measure Friction so that you can track and manage it. And if you can track and manage Friction, you can actually put the concept of the customer portfolio management from above into action.

Friction is really about the likelihood a customer will continue to do business with you. The actual causes of friction are created on the business side, and manifest themselves on the customer side as impatience, frustration, and lack of loyalty. Customers encounter varying degrees of this friction in their business relationships, and become more or less likely to do business with you as this friction changes. They already have low tolerance for poor customer service, processes that don't work as they should, pricing that changes unexpectedly or is confusing, interfaces that make it difficult to accomplish tasks, communications that are sloppy, not delivered in a timely way, or irrelevant. All of these friction points tend to create increasing levels of frustration and ill will, which over time mutate into dissatisfaction and defection. Friction accumulates to the point the customer simply decides to start seeking alternatives, and once alternatives are found, the customer terminates the prior business relationship.

Now, none of this may sound new to you, but here is something that is new. **The friction effect is especially true and is more pronounced as "customer control" of the business relationship increases.** Customers are demanding and taking more control of business relationships themselves, as is true with web retail, or have been forced to take control, as with the practice of pushing customers to serve themselves though the web or a telephone interface. **As the ability for the customer to exert control in the business relationship increases, customers become less and less tolerant of friction.**

And, as friction rises, the customer becomes less and less likely to do business with you in the future. If a customer is becoming less and less likely to do business with you, the value you could realize from the business relationship with the customer in the future has to be falling.

In other words:

Rising friction = falling potential value; falling friction = rising potential value

So, if you can measure friction, you can measure potential value. And measuring friction is exactly what LifeCycle Metrics do. By measuring friction, these metrics also measure the likelihood of a customer to do business with you in the future, and so also measure the potential value of the customer. Visitors and customers will "signal" their friction levels through their own behavior; LifeCycle Metrics organize and codify this behavioral data for you, and allow you to create reports and trip wires that flag increasing or decreasing friction.

And how do you reduce friction? By applying the **grease**, my fellow Driller – your innovative selling and service campaigns are the grease that will hopefully reduce friction and increase the potential value of the customer. Fortunately, you will have your LifeCycle Metrics to tell you precisely who needs the grease, when it should be applied, and even when it should be applied a second time. Your potential value metrics will also tell you when your relationship with the customer has already "seized up" and it's too late for the grease. You only have so much grease and the grease is expensive, so you want to apply it only when and where you think it is likely you can reduce friction and prevent the relationship from seizing up.

By the way, customers are not the only folks who experience friction, people **trying to become customers** experience it also. An easy way to measure this want-to-be-a-customer friction is to look at the visitor conversion rate on your web site. Navigational design and layout determine "physical" friction and copy elements determine "emotional" friction. Design and layout testing will reduce physical friction; persuasive copywriting will reduce emotional friction. Success at reducing want-to-be-a-customer friction is measured by an increased visitor conversion rate.

But back to customers. With our first LifeCycle Metrics, Latency and Recency, we're going to be looking at the tracking of **potential value** only, and how you can use changes in potential value to trigger High ROI Customer Marketing campaigns or programs. After the Latency and Recency metrics we will cover the RFM model, which uses both Current Value and Potential Value metrics to really juice up your results and drive even higher profits to the bottom line.

Chapter 6
Trip Wire Marketing

An easy to implement and proven powerful potential value LifeCycle Metric is called Latency. Latency refers to the average time between customer activity events, for example, making a purchase, calling the help desk, or visiting a web site. All you have to do is calculate the average time elapsed (Latency) between the two events, and use this metric as a guide for anti-defection campaigns. Many small business people naturally use Latency in an intuitive way, for example: "Gee, it has been a while since Mary Lou had her hair styled." What the stylist really means is this: Mary Lou is taking longer than the average customer to schedule a "refresh" on her hair. In database marketing terms, her Latency is exceeding the norm. So the stylist calls Mary Lou and finds either a customer who appreciates the reminder or a customer who has defected to another salon. The longer the stylist waits to contact Mary Lou after the average Latency trip wire has triggered, the more likely it is she has already defected, and the **lower her potential value** is to the salon.

In database marketing, we don't rely on "remembering" the habits of thousands of customers; we measure the behavior and react based on these measurements. When you see a particular customer's behavior diverge from the average customer behavior you have calculated above, you get a trip wire event. Since the calculation of Latency is very simple, and the diverging behavior is easy to spot, this type of anti-defection campaign is an ideal candidate for "lights-out" or automated rules-based customer retention campaigns.

As an example, let's take purchase behavior in a retail scenario. If you examine your customers and find the average time between the second and third purchase is 2 months, you have found "third purchase Latency." Any customer who goes more than 2 months after the second purchase without making a third purchase is diverging from the norm, and a likely defection candidate. It's simple logic. If the average customer makes a third purchase within 2 months of the second purchase, and a particular customer breaks this pattern, they are not acting like the average customer. Something about the relationship with this customer has changed; **friction is rising**. This particular customer's LifeCycle has become out of synch with the average customer LifeCycle, and this condition is a trip wire for a High ROI Customer Marketing event.

On average, if you divert marketing resources away from customers who have made a 3rd purchase within 2 months after the second purchase, and apply these resources to customers who are "crossing over" the 2 month LifeCycle trip wire without making a third purchase, you will end up spending less money and generating higher profits for any given marketing budget. You are applying your limited resources **(the grease)** right at the time in the LifeCycle when they create the most powerful impact – at the point of likely customer defection.

Now, will all these customers respond? No, of course not. But the ones that do generally become active, loyal customers again, and those that don't may not be good customers in the future. The behavior of the rest of your customers tells you so. These non-responding customers may not be worth spending money on to "win-back," and in fact, will have much lower response rates to a win-back campaign. They have already demonstrated their lack of interest with their behavior, and you could be better off financially by just letting them go and focusing on more responsive, more profitable customers.

The above example is a relatively crude approach to Latency. As you might expect, different customer segments will have different Latency characteristics, and the more you fine-tune a Latency campaign, the more profitable it will become. For example, let's say you execute the Latency campaign described above, and succeed in retaining 30% of the defecting customers, making a tidy profit. But you really have two major product lines, software and hardware, each 50% of sales. Could 3rd purchase Latency be different when comparing software with hardware customers? You betcha. On further analysis, you find 3rd purchase Latency for software is really one month, and for hardware it's three months. The average 3rd purchase Latency of all customers is 2 months, but the Latency by product line is specific to each line. So you bust the two groups apart, and run separate Latency-based campaigns, one for each product line.

In your original third purchase Latency campaign, you promoted to customers who did not make a third purchase within 2 months of the second purchase. This means you were "late" for software (because the average Latency is really 1 month) and early for hardware (because the average Latency is really 3 months). When you realign the timing based on the line of merchandise, you find instead of retaining 30% of customers, you retain 50% of the customers, because you have synched-up the marketing effort with the true customer LifeCycle.

And that, folks, is what LifeCycle-based marketing is all about - using your own customer's behavior to telegraph to you the most important (and profitable) time to market to them. The customer, through their behavior, raises a hand and asks you to take action. If you synch up your marketing efforts with the natural customer LifeCycle, you can't help but being more successful.

What if you were to look at an entire series of Latencies? The average number of days between the first and second purchases, the average number of days between the second and third purchases, third and fourth, fourth and fifth, etc. You don't have to use purchases; you could use contacts with customer service, visits to a web site, any behavior important to your business. What would that look like, and more importantly, what can it do for you?

It would look like a snapshot of the customer LifeCycle. And what it can do for you is start you on the path to predicting customer behavior and increasing the value of your customer base. Any type of event can be used – purchases, downloads, site visits – but the event must be one that repeats or be a series of events with an established "action sequence," like many B2B sales processes.

Let's say you look at average behavior across all customers, and end up with a "Latency Sequence" that looks something like following:

Time between 1st - 2nd event: 90 days
Time between 2nd - 3rd event: 60 days
Time between 3rd - 4th event: 30 days
Time between 4th - 5th event: 60 days
Time between 5th - 6th event: 90 days
Time between 6th - 7th event: 120 days
Time between 7th - 8th event: 150 days

What does this pattern say to you? Think about it.

I'll tell you what it says to me. First, as you probably realized, you are now starting to see something that looks like a "cycle," as in LifeCycle of the customer. It's a series of events you can graph with a line and make charts of. If you can measure it, you can try to affect it in a positive way, and determine the results of your efforts. Second, you now have a series of seven "trip wires" you can use as described above to more finely sift and screen behavior looking for deviations from the norm. If the average number of days between events for any single customer starts to exceed the average for all customers, a trip wire call for action is triggered on that customer. And third, somewhere around the 4th event, something significant happens to change customer behavior in a very noticeable way. The customer accelerates into the 4th event (the time between events gets shorter and shorter), and then begins to decelerate in terms of behavior (the time between events gets longer and longer). Depending on your business, this may be positive or negative.

How to use this information?

Regarding the Lifecycle and the trip wires, you could have a series of seven actions ready to take at any point in this LifeCycle where the customer deviates from average behavior. As long as the customer stays on track, save the money and take no action. But as soon as the customer misses or "rolls over" past one of these LifeCycle milestones, you know to pull the trigger on your action. If you follow this model, you will end up maximizing every cent of your budget and driving higher profits, because **you don't spend unless you have to, and when you spend, it creates maximum impact.** This is the recipe for High ROI customer management and marketing. Act only when you have to and always at the point of maximum impact.

Regarding the behavior change, if I was a retailer, this looks negative since the "ramp" in buying behavior reversed and went in the other direction. If I was running a pure service center, this may be a very desirable pattern; perhaps meaning the customer has "learned" the product and no longer needs as much service. It could be negative though, since opportunities to up-sell or cross-sell the customer are decreasing over time. It depends on your business. The important thing to recognize is this: there was a change in behavior, and you should try and determine how you might affect this change in a positive way. Reversals in the direction of a behavior like this are almost always significant turning points in the relationship with the customer.

Human behavior dynamics often take on seemingly "physical" properties. Inertia is one such property - an object in motion tends to remain in motion unless acted on by an outside force. This reversal in the direction of the customer "momentum" after the 4th event indicates there is something about your business - a process (or lack of a process), a product (or lack of a product), something - which causes the average customer to "slow down" and reverse their contact momentum. This reversal of momentum, fellow Driller, is evidence of **a change in friction**. Changes in friction can be positive or negative, depending on what activity you are measuring and the nature of your business and relationship with the customer.

In most business cases, more activity is better; you want more sales, more visits, more downloads, etc. In this business case, customers demonstrating a slowing in the rate of their activity means **friction is rising;** you need to find out why and do something about it. In some cases, primarily in service-oriented settings, less activity is better (think trouble calls). Under these circumstances, slowing activity can be viewed positively (through the eyes of the customer and business, fewer trouble calls is good) and this **means friction is falling**.

Let me say this another way to make sure you have the point: rising friction is always bad for the customer and the business because it indicates the likelihood to continue the relationship and potential value are both decreasing; falling friction is always good for the customer and the business because it indicates the likelihood to continue the relationship and potential value are both increasing. Whether a **particular behavior** is indicative of rising or falling friction depends on the business situation, as demonstrated with the Latency case above.

The slowdown in activity at the 4th event indicates rising friction if you are a retailer; it may indicate falling friction if you are Help Desk and you actually help your users. On the other hand, if you know your Help Desk users are generally a frustrated bunch, a slowing of activity at the 4th event perhaps means they are simply giving up and friction is rising. Frequently in a service center or Help Desk environment, the "reason codes" for contacts help you understand whether a certain behavior indicates rising or falling friction; you might want to run your Latency calculations not on all calls, but just for specific reason codes to gain more insight. And if you are not collecting reason codes for each call, what are you waiting for? That piece of data is important!

If I am profiling retail activity, this Latency sequence looks negative, a slowing rate of purchase indicates an increase in friction. If I had very limited resources, given the seven possible promotional opportunities listed above, but looking for the **absolutely highest ROI on a single promotional event**, I would send a promotion to the customer immediately after the 4th purchase - and no sooner. I don't want to spend money on a promotion or by reducing my margin if I don't have to, so as long as the customer is accelerating, there is no reason to spend any money. But I would really like the ramp to continue past the 4th purchase, and any way I can bring that 5th purchase in closer to the 4th is going to affect my bottom line, and perhaps lengthen the ramp into the 5th or 6th purchase and beyond. If I had more money to spend on promotions, I would test each of the seven trip wire opportunities, and pursue only those with the highest ROI, probably using a separate and unique discount approach for each of the seven trip wire opportunities.

If I am profiling contacts in a service center, this behavior might be a good or bad thing, depending on the circumstances. If this pattern of slowing contacts indicates frustration on the part of the customer, as in the retail example, friction is rising and I want to act on the problem. If I up-sell and cross-sell, I would look to weight more of this activity early in the process knowing I am not going to get as many chances as the customer becomes less likely to call.

However, on a help desk, slowing of contact behavior could mean the customer no longer needs as much help. If this is the case, what I am observing in the behavior is actually a reduction in friction. The fact it takes 4 calls to educate the customer in the first place might not be acceptable, and I would look for ways to decrease the length of time it takes, reducing friction earlier in the cycle.

Success in any of the cases above creates incremental value with very little expense; you're not necessarily changing what you do, just when you do it — to match more closely with the customer LifeCycle. The point of profiling the behavior is to discover the most profitable time is to act.

Of course, you can begin to subdivide the customer base, just as we did in the hardware / software example above. The Latency Sequence may look quite different for hardware buyers relative to software buyers, and it will certainly be different by the type of campaign you used to attract the customer in the first place. Once you are able to compare and contrast different customer LifeCycles by product, campaign, customer source, or by any other data point meaningful to your business, you will begin to paint a more complete picture of what parameters positively or negatively affect customer behavior. Once you understand the behavior, you can learn to profit from it.

Chapter 7
The Hair Salon Example

There are three main phases to a successful High ROI Customer Marketing program: **Measure, Manage, and Maximize**. We'll tackle each of these components one at a time in this example.

Two hair salons operate in the same town, Salon A and Salon B. Both are equally competent one-person operations and charge similar prices for similar services and products. And both salons practice CRM.

There is a difference though - Salon A does not use customer data to track and manage the CRM effort, but Salon B does. Salon B's CRM toolset consists of a paper appointment book and a PC with a spreadsheet program. Salon A has only a paper appointment book, and doesn't really track anything.

One day the owner of Salon A is thinking:

Where has Mary Lou been? She's a high value customer who comes in to get the whole job done - hair, nails, massage, the works. Seems to me she hasn't been in the Salon for a while. She's tardy in scheduling her session. I should call her and find out when she is coming in.

The owner of Salon A is practicing CRM. High value customers have been identified, and a change in the behavior of one of these customers has been detected. This situation has been evaluated, and an action to take has been decided on.

But the owner of Salon A is very busy that day, and forgets to call Mary Lou. What's more, the owner has no system for classifying the fact Mary Lou has not been in "for a while." How long is a while? Part of why the owner forgets to call Mary Lou is there is no real urgency; she's just "tardy." But how tardy is tardy? When should the call be made? If there were a rule about "tardy," perhaps there would be more urgency to make the call. But there isn't, so it may seem like a waste of time. The owner thinks later on:

She'll come in sometime soon. I'm too tired to make the call tonight.

As we sit here gazing into Salon A, some other thoughts probably come to mind. How many Mary Lou customers are there? And how "tardy" will they get before the owner calls them? When you are making money cutting hair all day, it's probably hard to face calling Mary Lou customers, right? Time spent on the phone calling customers or sending them postcards is time not spent cutting hair, and the owner of Salon A can't afford to not cut hair. If the owner had only the time or energy to call just three Mary Lou customers, which three would it be?

If the owner has to give up time cutting hair to make calls, these calls better result in more business than was lost by not cutting hair to make calls. This potentially negative outcome is called "opportunity cost." If resources are allocated away from an income producing activity towards another activity, you better make sure these resources create more value than they did before re-allocation. If they do not, an opportunity cost has been created. The two fundamental rules of High ROI Customer Marketing are designed to avoid these opportunity costs:

1. Don't spend until you have to, and
2. When you spend, spend at the point of maximum impact

Over at Salon B, the owner has been thinking along the same lines as the owner of Salon A, about a High Value, tardy customer named Angela. The owner is cleaning up for the night, and thinks:

How many Angela customers do I have? If I keep forgetting to call my Angela customers, I may eventually lose them. But they always come back. Or do they? I'm going to start **Measuring** Angela customers. I'm going to start tracking "tardy" customers and find out exactly what this issue is about. If it's a real issue, I'll worry about it then. If it's not an issue, I can forget about it once and for all, and spend my time cutting hair.

So the owner of Salon B sits down with the paper appointment book, looks through the customer names, and enters all the "High Value" customer names into the spreadsheet, one to a line. The owner reasons the choice to track high value customers in this way:

If there is anything to this "tardy Angela" customer thing, I get hurt the most financially by losing High Value customers. If it's ever going to be worth spending time on this instead of cutting hair, then it will be most worth it to spend the time marketing to high value customers. If it's not worth it for them, it won't be worth it for any customers and I can forget all about the whole thing.

Once the high value customers are entered into a spreadsheet (about 50% of the customers are considered high value), the owner of Salon B then enters all the appointment dates for each high value customer into the columns of the spreadsheet, next to each name. To keep this project manageable, the owner decides to enter only appointments for High Value customers for the past 6 months. The owner also creates columns to subtract the dates from each other for each customer and find the average number of days between visits for each customer. The spreadsheet (nothing special, off the shelf software) is smart enough to know these entries are dates and is able to easily subtract them and convert the result into days, so all these calculations are easy and take less than an hour to create.

The owner of Salon B is then astonished to discover these facts about customers: About 30% of high value customers have not had an appointment in 6 months. Since 50% of all customers are high value, this means 30% of 50% = 15% of all customers are already defected best customers. The average number of days between appointments is very similar across all the high value customers. It is, however, not the 30 days the owner expected, but 40 days.

The owner then assumes a high value, supposedly loyal customer who has not been to the salon in over 6 months is a lost customer - at least for the near future. The owner then calculates the value of the lost business for the 6-month period by multiplying the number of customers lost by the average sale of $150 per trip at 40 days between trips. Needless to say, the resulting number is a very large, representing many days of total sales for Salon B:

Total Customers	200
Defected Best Customers @ 15 % of Total	30
Number Trips in 6 months @ 40 days between trips	4.5
Revenue per Trip	$150
Lost Revenue: Defected Best Customers	$20,250
(4.5 x 30 x $150)	

Figure 2: Lost Revenue from Defecting Customers

The owner of Salon B then thinks:

I must be crazy for not looking at this before. I would make more money by not cutting hair for a couple of hours a week if I could get back even one of these high value customers. I'm going to do something about this right away - before I lose even more high value customers. Now that I have **Measured** this effect and know how much money it is costing me to not address the tardy Angela customers, I need to **Manage** the process somehow. How can I set up some kind of "system" that will help me figure out what to do with this data I have discovered? How can I turn the data into an action plan?

Over at Salon A, the owner knows the names of best customers who "have not been in for a while." But this owner has no system, no way to measure what the dynamics of the situation are. How long is "a while"? But at Salon B, the owner knows the average time between best customer visits is 40 days, and there are customers in this group who have not had an appointment in over 6 months. How can the owner get this business back? The owner thinks:

I'll just mail all these best customers who have not had an appointment in over 6 months a postcard offering them a discount. The postcards will say, "Since you are a best customer, you are entitled to a 15% discount if you come in for a visit within the next two weeks." They will come in and I will start a new relationship with them, and find out why they have not been in. The owner of Salon B prepares the targeted postcards, mails them out, and awaits appointments from these customers

The appointments never come.

A bunch of the postcards come back as "undeliverable," and the owner gets several phone calls from customers saying "I now go to Salon A, take me off your mailing list." Undaunted, the owner of Salon B reasons:

Clearly there is something wrong with this approach. Best customers who have not had an appointment for 6 months must already be "defected" customers. They obviously do not want to come back to me, and feel the relationship is broken already. They have moved on and established new relationships. I will try a new approach with the postcards, and will use the same offer. But this time, I will mail the postcards out as soon as the best customer has not been in for over 40 days. Since the average best customer comes in every 40 days, a best customer who fails to do so is not acting like a best customer. So each week I will use my spreadsheet to identify best customers who have not been in for 40 days, mail the discount postcard out to them, and track the results.

After a month of mailing the postcards to best customers who had not had not had an appointment in over 40 days, the owner of Salon B sat down to analyze the program. Of all the best customers mailed to, 1/3 had made new appointments, and 2/3 had not. But even with the discount, the additional profits from these customers paid for the postcard mailing many times over. High value Customer defection was being **Managed** by the program.

Despite this success, two things bothered the owner of Salon B. The first was what customers who responded said when making their discounted appointments. The second was the 2/3 of best customers who did not respond.

The owner thinks:

Half the customers who responded said to me, "I'm so glad you mailed me a discount, I was planning on making an appointment in the next week and would have made one anyway, so it was great to get the discount." So I gave up margin and profits I did not need to give up. And how is it possible that so many of my best customers never responded to my offer? I wonder if there is a way to address these two issues? If I could reduce the number of "would have come in anyway" customers who got a discount, and get more customers to respond overall, I would be really making a ton of money on my best customer retention postcard program. I have **Measured** my best customer defection, and am **Managing** it with this program. I wonder if there is a way to **Maximize**, to make it even more profitable?

Well, fellow Driller, have you got an idea? You know Customer Retention is all about this process: Action - Reaction - Feedback - Repeat. The owner of Salon B has taken an action, and there has been a Reaction. How should the owner go about analyzing the Feedback? The owner of Salon B then has an idea:

What about this group of customers who said "they would have scheduled anyway without the postcard." Are they similar in any way? If there is a common reaction to the postcard among these customers, perhaps there is a commonality in the behavior or backgrounds of the customers. If I can find the key linking these customers together, perhaps I can understand why this is happening with them.

The owner of salon B goes back to the CRM software (a paper appointment book and the customer spreadsheet). The owner has entered "response date" in a spreadsheet column for each customer who responded to the postcard and any comments. The owner sorts the customers by the responders and looks at those customers who said, "would have scheduled anyway without a postcard." For each customer who responded and said this, the owner looks the customer up in the appointment book to find more details.

"Long hair cuts!!!!" the owner exclaims. "They all have long hair cuts!" which the owner immediately realizes is the problem with the discount postcard mailing program. The owner thinks:

Best customers with long hair styles can come in much less often than every 40 days, even through the average of all best customers is a cut every 40 days. So customers with long cuts are getting the postcard too early - they're not really "defected," and schedule a planned appointment with a discount I did not have to offer. They should get a postcard possibly at 60 days, or even 90 days or longer after their last appointment. Since I have a lot of customers with long cuts, most are getting the postcard too early for the cut. This explains the low overall response rate. Best customers with short cuts however, are probably getting the postcard too late. By the time I get them in the mail and they reach the customers with short cuts, it could be too late, they may have already gone elsewhere for their short hair cut.

The owner of Salon B resolves to recalculate the average days between appointments separately for best customers with long cuts and best customers with short cuts. The owner divides the customer base in two - by length of cut, and finds the average time between trips of long cut customers is actually 75 days, and for short cut customers is actually 20 days. Rethinking the retention campaign, the owner resolves to track each group individually, and to do two types of mailings each week - one to long cut customers over 75 days since last visit, and one to short cut customers over 20 days since the last visit.

Using the advanced CRM system (a spreadsheet program with one customer per row), the owner creates a column for acceptable number of days since last visit - 75 days for long cut customers and 20 days for or short cut customers. Using the date of last appointment, the owner creates a simple equation that uses today's date and last appointment date to calculate days since last visit, and to subtract this number from the number in the "acceptable" column.

The salon owner thinks:

I have created a "trip wire" system for the best customer retention postcard program. When the number in this column approaches zero or goes negative for a customer, it is time to mail the discount "where have you been" postcard. Since each customer has an acceptable number of days since last visit based on hair cut length, the timing of the mailings should more closely reflect whether or not the customer has actually defected.

The salon owner tests the new campaign - and it works. Not only does the owner get many fewer customers saying "thanks for the discount, would have been in anyway," the response rate among targeted best customers increases by 30%. The program now is maximized for this level of detail - it makes even more money than it did before, and retains more customers while decreasing the cost of discounts given away. A beautiful thing, the owner thinks. But then another Eureka moment comes to the owner of Salon B:

If I use this system there is another benefit - I should be able to actually forecast what my volume should be months in advance based on customers likely to schedule an appointment. If I see a week coming up where visit volume looks to be low, I can promote to some customers and fill up empty slots, maybe give them a discount for scheduling on a specific day when my traffic is light. That way the customer is happy because they get a special one-time discount, and I am happy because I am maximizing my revenue per day by filling up light traffic days with happy customers!

Just then, the owner of Salon B hears someone walk in the door. A voice calls out, "Can we schedule appointments?" The owner recognizes the voice - it belongs to lost best customer Angela, the one who started this whole project by being tardy in scheduling an appointment. Angela is the reason the owner of Salon B first asked the question, "How many tardy best customers do I have?" But what does she mean "we"?

As the owner of Salon B comes around the corner, Angela smiles and says, "This is my friend Mary Lou. She was going to Salon A, but is dissatisfied with the results she is getting. She would like to try Salon B. And I need a cut too! I tried growing my hair out long, but I decided I like it better short."

The owner of Salon B thinks: I can't predict everything, but my new system is sure better than not predicting anything at all!

Chapter 8
The B2B Software Example

A B2B software company has an appealing pitch to business - their software makes a company more efficient and saves more money for the company than the software costs. The software is modular, with a base application and additional add-ons that are specific to certain business challenges. The selling strategy is to under-price the base application to get market penetration and then make a higher margin on the add-ons. The add-ons drive the profitability of the business, as does the installation and customization of these add-ons.

The company has been quite successful with this selling strategy. But lately the CFO has noticed sales of the base application have risen, but revenue from add-ons has not risen in the same proportion. In other words, the company is further penetrating the market and gaining new customers but getting less revenue from each customer. The CFO thinks:

I can't understand this. Sales of the base application are rising according to plan but overall company revenue is not growing at the same rate. The only thing I can think of that would create this particular situation is fewer basic application customers are buying add-ons. How can I figure out why this is happening?

The CFO calls the heads of business development and marketing to ask about the situation. They both report they are aware of slowing add-on unit sales per customer, but cannot attribute it this to anything specific. The company is simply penetrating the overall market more deeply they say, and as we penetrate further and further, add-on sales seem to have slowed.

The CFO is not particularly satisfied with this answer, and thinks:

If it shows up in my financial statements, it has to be measurable. I'm just seeing this from too high a view. All the sales of the different base applications and add-ons roll up to total sales, so the data I need to better understand this must exist somewhere. The CFO picks up the phone to call the CIO, and then hesitates. The IT people are going to want to know specifically what I am looking for, the CFO thinks. Do I really know?

What is needed here, fellow Drillers, is quantification, some framework for analyzing the situation. What is the real question to be answered here? The CFO knows IT has limited resources to apply to this kind of ad hoc work - if the request just generates information that leads to another question, then time and resources are wasted.

The CFO could ask for monthly product sales percentage by type over the past year. In a lot of ways, this information would simply confirm what the CFO already knows - sales of add-ons have gone soft. But does it answer the core question of **why** they have gone soft? It does not, and that is the real question at hand. Since customers have different LifeCycles, any monthly sales data will contain customers in various stages of being likely to buy an add-on. So raw monthly financial data - the kind the CFO is used to working with - is not going to answer the "real" question. The CFO thinks:

Customers buy the base package and once they get it integrated and tuned up they start to buy the add-ons. During any one-month period, we have customers who just bought the base package, customers who are in different stages of integration, and customers who are buying add-ons. What I really need to know then is this: what is the average number of weeks between the purchase of add-ons, this year versus last year? If this number of weeks is rising, that is where the softness in add-on sales is coming from - customers are simply taking longer to make the purchase decision. If this number of weeks is constant or falling, then something else must be going on.

With a definition of the question at hand, the CFO picks up the phone and calls the CIO. The CFO gets the report on the average number of weeks between the purchases of add-ons. The information looks like this:

Last Year	This Year
8.6 weeks	8.9 weeks

Figure 3: Average Weeks between Add-on Purchases

So it **is** taking longer for them to purchase, the CFO thinks, and darn it, now I have another question. The IT people are going to have me for breakfast for not thinking this all the way through the first time! I got the information I asked for, but this information is not actionable, I can't **do** anything with it. There is not enough detail in the information to act.

Fellow Drillers, when you are plumbing the depths of your data, try to think of what you will do with the information you are asking for. Imagine getting back your results, and taking an action based on those results. **If you can't imagine the action you would take knowing the information, you are not asking the right question yet.** The CFO thinks:

Our add-on modules have different prices and different levels of difficulty involved in their integration. And they are usually installed in a particular sequence. So what I really should have asked for is the average number of weeks between the purchase of add-ons **by add-on** - the time between base purchase and the first add-on, the time between the first add-on and the second, and so forth. Maybe there are problems with installing one of the add-ons due to changes in the next generation of operating systems, for example, and this is slowing the installation of a particular add-on down. If I can get the average number of weeks between add-on purchases by add-on, I can act on it, because I will know which particular add-on is causing the slowdown.

The CFO reluctantly picks up the phone to call the CIO. At least this time, the CFO thinks, I have thought the question out all the way through, and I know what action I can take with the information once I get it. Shortly after a slightly heated exchange involving resource allocation, budgets, and a hiring freeze in IT with the CIO, the CFO gets this report:

	Last Year	This Year
Base app to 1st add-on	12.3 weeks	12.1 weeks
1st add-on to 2nd add-on	10.5 weeks	10.2 weeks
2nd add-on to 3rd add-on	8.7 weeks	8.9 weeks
3rd add-on to 4th add-on	6.1 weeks	6.7 weeks
4th add-on to 5th add-on	5.2 weeks	6.5 weeks
Average Time Between Add-Ons	8.6 weeks	8.9 weeks

Figure 4: Average Weeks between Add-On Purchases by Add-On

Fellow Drillers, it would be nice if the pattern were a bit more clear, yes? It appears customers are ordering their first and second add-ons more rapidly than last year, but as they get to the third, forth, and fifth add-ons, they are ordering more slowly than last year. What could this possibly mean? The CFO thinks:

Well, I answered my question, but I've got another. The reason why add-on sales appear soft is a longer purchase cycle for the average add-on, and the reason this is happening is the later add-ons are taking much longer to be purchased than they were last year, even though the first add-ons seem to be cycling much more quickly. What does that mean? I promised the CIO I would be able to act on this information, and I simply do not know how.

Fearing another phone call right away to the CIO, the CFO thinks:

What I have here is change. There has been a significant change in the way this business works for some reason. Change doesn't happen in a vacuum though; something must have caused these changes to happen, a significant event now being reflected by these average weeks between add-on purchase numbers.

What could it be?

The CFO remembers the heads of business development and marketing saying the company was "penetrating the overall market more deeply, and as we penetrate further and further, add-on sales seem to have slowed." Was this the change the CFO was looking for? What did it really mean, in terms of how the business may have changed?

Getting the heads of business development and marketing on the phone again, the CFO asks if this market penetration situation had created any changes in the way the company does business. The CFO hears for the first time about a new trade campaign and a new sales person hired to address a particular market segment. This is most assuredly the change the CFO has been looking for!

Gingerly, most humbly, the CFO calls the CIO once again. This time, the CFO wants to see average number of weeks between add-on installs by add-on **by salesperson**. After a promise to review the hiring freeze is extracted from the CFO, the CIO delivers the following report:

	Last Year	This Year	Sales 1	Sales 2	Sales 3	Sales 4
Base app to 1st add-on	12.3	12.1	12.3	12.3	12.3	11.6
1st add-on to 2nd add-on	10.5	10.2	10.5	10.5	10.5	9.4
2nd add-on to 3rd add-on	8.7	8.9	8.7	8.7	8.7	9.3
3rd add-on to 4th add-on	6.1	6.7	6.1	6.1	6.1	8.3
4th add-on to 5th add-on	5.2	6.5	5.2	5.2	5.2	10.2
Avg. Time Between Add-Ons	8.6	8.9	8.6	8.6	8.6	9.8

**Figure 5: Average Weeks between
Add-On Purchases by Add-On by Salesperson**

And there it is.

Clients of Salesperson # 1, # 2, and # 3 are purchasing add-ons at the same rate they did last year. The clients of the new salesperson # 4 are purchasing in a dramatically different pattern, with much shorter purchase cycles in the beginning and much longer cycle purchases later on. Literally, the LifeCycle of the customers in this market segment are different from the LifeCycles of the average customer from previous years, and dramatically so.

It takes these customers on average 14% longer to purchase any add-on - 9.8 weeks versus 8.6, or 1.2 weeks. Over the entire purchase LifeCycle of the add-ons, this increases the purchase cycle by 4.8 weeks (1.2 x 4). If this new segment is doing a lot of dollar volume compared with the old segments, this could significantly affect sales and make add-on purchases look soft - even though they are in fact getting purchased!

At this moment, the head of business development appears in the door with another person who turns out to be new Salesperson 4. The CFO looks up and the head of biz dev, somewhat sheepishly, introduces the new salesperson.

"Glad to meet you," the CFO says. "By the way, can you tell me something? Do the customers in your new segment purchase and install our add-ons in the order we suggest in our operations manuals?"

"No, they don't" said Salesperson # 4. They install them in a different order, because they are having some difficulty installing a couple of the add-ons, and usually delay those to the end of the purchase cycle when they have more experience with the applications. Is there something we can do about that?"

The CFO just smiles, and thinks:

Looks like I just found the money to pay for unfreezing some hiring in IT.

"I think so," the CFO tells new Salesperson #4, calculating the improvement in cash flow on the fly if these add-ons were installed faster. "I really do think so."

Chapter 9
Turning Latency Data into Profits

Customer LifeCycles are a reality: there is going to be a LifeCycle and you will not be able to stop it. You probably don't know about LifeCycles because you have not measured them. You don't even hear many pundits talking about them. This is most amusing given all the jaw flapping and tongue wagging about LifeTime Value; if you don't understand the customer LifeCycle, how would you ever know when the "LifeTime" was over to measure value? The plain fact is people have it backwards; LifeTime Value is the last thing you want to try to wrestle with when just starting out with customer relationship and value management. You start with the LifeCycle, and only after fully playing out that card, do you move on to the idea of LifeTime Value. You do not have to mess around with calculating absolute customer LifeTime Value to be successful using data-driven marketing. Only after you have nailed down the basics of data-driven marketing do you need to go there; you will learn all about Lifetime Value later on in this book. What you need to understand first is the customer LifeCycle, and how to use knowledge of it to your advantage.

Customers are not just customers one day and then not the next day; there is a process to customer defection, and the smart data-driven marketer creates High ROI Customer Marketing programs by taking advantage of understanding the complete customer defection process.

There are two ways you can increase the value of customers:

- Extend the customer LifeCycle, leaving more time for the customer to increase in value, by increasing the time the customer takes to defect.

- Increase the value of the customer within the existing LifeCycle. The customer still defects pretty much on schedule, but you have done everything you can to increase their value before the defection.

The first approach usually requires some pretty sophisticated tools and can be expensive; loyalty programs are a classic example of extending the LifeCycle. Not for the faint of heart financially and organizationally, loyalty programs also do not work well for every type of business. But they do work and can be extremely profitable if they are designed and executed correctly. If you are interested in how this type of loyalty program is constructed, visit my website at http://www.jimnovo.com/download.htm and download the loyalty case study.

The second approach to increasing customer value above is easier to execute, and for many companies, is the right way to go. It involves what I would call a customer retention or anti-defection program as opposed to a loyalty program, and this is how you go about setting it up.

Recall this table from the Latency Toolkit chapter titled "Trip Wire Marketing":

Time between 1st - 2nd event: 90 days
Time between 2nd - 3rd event: 60 days
Time between 3rd - 4th event: 30 days
Time between 4th - 5th event: 60 days
Time between 5th - 6th event: 90 days
Time between 6th - 7th event: 120 days
Time between 7th - 8th event: 150 days

The first place I would look to address the above customer LifeCycle is the fourth event. Why? This event looks to be the one that is "low hanging fruit," since the average customer is accelerating into it, meaning the response rates should be quite high. In other words, we are taking advantage of the natural behavior customers have demonstrated, rather than trying to force them to do something out of the ordinary.

For the average customer, this fourth event happens at 180 days after the first event. How do I know? Just sum the first 3 lines of the table above: 90 days + 60 days + 30 days = 180 days. Any customer who is 180 days old and has not yet made a 4th purchase, a 4th visit to the web site - whatever the event is you are tracking - is acting outside the behavior of the average customer and is a prime candidate for an earlier than normal defection. This is where you focus your efforts. You set up this fourth event as the "trip wire" - if the customer doesn't trip the wire by engaging in the 4th event by day 180, you take action and try to affect this behavior. If you can save just a small percentage of defecting customers, the ROI can be very high, because these customers represent "found profits" which would not have existed without your efforts. And yes, you can measure these found profits - I am going to show you how to do this below.

This may not be the highest short-term ROI promotion we can do, but in terms of reducing customer defection and extending the LifeCycle, it is probably the highest long-term ROI promotion we can do, because we are helping "slow customers" accelerate into that 4th purchase. We have a reasonable expectation, based on looking at average customer behavior, that a certain percentage of customers will do this and continue on into the 5th and 6th events. We are choosing a specific group of customers at a specific time in their LifeCycle to promote to, a group with the highest likelihood of success.

Why concentrate on these defecting customers? The **two fundamental rules of High ROI Customer Marketing:**

1. Don't spend until you have to, and
2. When you spend, spend at the point of maximum impact

You don't have to spend on customers who make the fourth purchase or visit within 180 days, because they are acting like "average" customers. Why spend on them if everything there is OK and they are behaving normally? You want to concentrate your spending where it will have maximum impact - on the customers who "roll over" the 180-day barrier without engaging in "average" behavior. These customers are the most likely candidates for a complete defection, and by focusing your resources laser-like on these people, you can spend more per customer and really have some impact.

Put another way, let's say you have a customer retention budget of $20,000 and you have 20,000 customers. You currently spend $1 per customer each year sending all your customers the same lame retention stuff - statement stuffers that say you care and so forth. But if you could tell which 5,000 customers were the most likely to defect, and only spent on them at the point of maximum impact - when the defection was taking place - you could spend $4 per customer trying to stop or slow the defection with the same budget, have a much higher success rate, and actually realize the "found profits" I spoke of earlier. Make sense?

How To Execute a Latency-based Promotion

We'll use a retail example because the numbers are easiest to understand and convey. But the same thought process is valid for any kind of business.

1. Determine the timing of your promotion. You normally want to take action as close to the "trip wire" event as is reasonable and practical,

taking into consideration the cost. If you have a ton of customers, there may be enough customers rolling over the "180-day with no 4th purchase" barrier to execute your promotion every week; if not, then gather up enough customers to execute efficiently. Some may be anywhere from 180 - 210 days old with no 4th purchase. That's fine; but don't let them get more than 30 days past the trip wire without taking action.

2. Create the offer. In a retailing business, this could be as simple as a discount of some kind. You could sub-divide the 180 day old / no 4th purchase customers into "best" and "other," creating a VIP service offer to best customers and a discount offer to other customers.

3. Prepare the list. Select all your 180 day / no 4th purchase customers, and then randomly select 10% of them to not contact. This is called your control group. People will tell you to only use 2% or 3% as control, and statistically they **could** be right about this. But the first time out of the box, I like to go with 10%, for two reasons:

   a. It's a "no argument" control group size. If your effort works and you can prove it, there won't be chattering from the sidelines about the possibility of a "defective" control group.

   b. Why spend more than you have to the first time? By taking a large control, you reduce the number of people you are spending on to execute your promotion.

      If you created the two groups "best" and "other," you need to take a 10% random sample of each. The other 90% of a group is called the test group; they are the ones who will receive the promotion by direct mail, e-mail, or other means. The creation of proper control groups is absolutely essential to measuring the "found profits" referred to above. If this step has you puzzled, you will read more details on creating control groups and random samples later on in the Advanced Toolkit chapter titled "Predicting Campaign ROI: Set Up" or see **http://www.jimnovo.com/Random-Sample.htm** for more.

4. Now you have two lists of people, control and test. Set up your tracking capability, which at minimum is the ability to run a report

every 30 days that reveals the sales of each group starting from the beginning of the promotion, which is when you execute the e-mail, snail mail, or other communication of your offer to the test group. The metric you are interested in here is revenue per customer, so you would take the total sales of each group from the time the promotion is delivered and divide by the number of customers in the group, for both control and test groups.

5. Deliver your promotion to the test group.

6. Monitor the revenue activity of test and control groups. Run a sales report weekly or every 30 days, and look for divergence in the revenue per customer. The customers in the test group should be registering a higher sales per customer level (you hope). Keep running the report until the increase in revenue between test and control remains stable or begins to fall. When this happens, the LifeCycle of the promotion is over (promotions have LifeCycles too!). Let's say this takes 90 days, so 90 days after the event, you have a revenue per customer number for activity during the promotion, for both the control and test groups.

7. Calculate ROI. I'll use some plug numbers as an example. The idea here is to compare the revenue behavior of the test group with the control group, and determine how much additional revenue occurred because of your promotion. Since the control group experienced no promotion, any difference in revenue between test and control can logically be attributed to the promotion. We then take out costs, and see if we added value to the customer LifeCycle - in more mercenary terms, did we make money or not?

	Control	Test
90 day Revenue per Customer	$100	$110
Gross Margin @ 30%	$30	$33
Additional Margin Due to Promo		$3
Per Customer Cost of Promo		$.50
Additional Gross Margin per Customer		$2.50

Figure 6: 180 Day / No 4th Purchase Promotion

Here's the key to the above. The people in control generated $30 in Gross Margin per customer over 90 days; the people in test generated $33 per customer. So $3 in additional Gross margin per customer was created because of your promotion, since the two groups are the same in all other ways (if control was truly a random sample).

This $3 nets down to $2.50 because the cost of doing the promotion was $.50 per customer. Note: Nowhere in here are we talking about response rates. Response Rate doesn't matter in the measurement of profitability (it matters a lot in other cases); what matters is actual buying behavior. When you use control groups, you pick up buying behavior you never could have measured by just looking at response rates.

Now, the Per Customer Cost of Event is usually where you get into some arguments. If the event included a discount, the per customer cost of this discount must be included in the calculation:

Discount	$5
Number Used	500
Total Discount	$2,500
Number of Customers	5,000
Per Customer Discount	$.50
Gross Margin / Customer from Above	$2.50
Gross Margin / Customer - Discount	$2.00

Figure 7: Calculating the Promotional Discount

Also, in the strictest sense, there is probably additional overhead attributable to the additional revenue: the cost to take a call and ship the box, the cost of additional salespeople needed to cover the promotion, and so on.

Cost of sales people for Promo	$2,000
Number of Customers in Promo	5,000
Per Customer Cost of Salespeople	$.40
Gross Profit per Customer from Above	$2.00
Net per Customer Value - Sales Cost	$1.60

Figure 8: Calculating the Promotional Overhead

These costs would not exist if you had not executed your promotion, so they should be included in the calculation to the extent you can calculate these additional overhead costs. In Figure 8 on previous page, we calculate the overhead costs of the additional salespeople to get the cost per customer after Discounts and Overhead.

This $1.60 is profit after all expenses have been paid back. You have added $1.60 in value to the LifeCycle (and LifeTime Value) of the average customer in the promotion. To get to ROI, we need to look at what the promo cost, and compare this to the value we generated; this is the definition of ROI. How much did we invest, and how much did we get back? We know what we got back $1.60 per customer Net of all costs, so we need to calculate total costs:

(Data from tables above)

Per Customer Cost of Promotion	$.50
Per Customer Discount	$.50
Per Customer Cost of Salespeople	$.40
Per Customer Total Cost	$1.40
"All Expenses In" 90-Day ROI	114%

Figure 9: Calculating the Total Costs and ROI

Note: $1.60 / $1.40 = 114%

You spent $1.40 and you generated $1.60 after all costs. It's a 90-Day ROI because the additional revenue generated was measured over a 90-Day period. A 114% return is not something the CFO is going to be against, trust me. In fact, you could make the argument that since ROI in financial circles is usually measured on an annual basis, and this is a 90-day ROI, the real ROI here is 4x the 90-day ROI, or 456% on an "annualized basis."

These are the found profits you have generated from your effort. By comparing the test group with the control group, you have proven these profits would not exist without your 180-day trip wire promotion. A smaller percentage of customers in the test group defected when compared with the control group; at least some portion of test made a purchase, and some kept right on buying for at least 90 days. These are found profits that would not have existed without your effort. You have proven the 180 day / no 4th purchase trip wire promotion added value to the customer LifeCycle, a total of $1.60 per customer x 5000 customers = $8000 to be specific, and you did this without costing the company a single dime, since you paid back all your costs with profit from the promotion, and still had $8000 left over to put in the bank.

I can hear you now. C'mon Jim, looks good on paper, but 485% annualized ROI? An $8000 profit on a promotion that with every cost imaginable thrown in costs $7000? How is that remotely possible?

Folks, it's not just "possible," this kind of return is **normal** in LifeCycle-based promotions. Remember the two rules of High ROI Customer Marketing:

1. Don't spend until you have to, and
2. When you spend, spend at the point of maximum impact

By focusing your resources squarely on the problem, each dollar you spend works much harder. By waiting for the trip wire you narrowed the population you were promoting to, weeding out people you would normally waste money on. And by acting when the wire was tripped, you spent at the point of maximum impact.

Here is why this type of promotion makes so much money. It's anti-defection. You literally kept customers from leaving the company, and the control group proves this. The people you did not promote to in the control continued to slip away, while some portion of folks in the test group were stopped and their behavior reversed. This is where the huge returns come from - it's the relative spending disparity between the groups that creates the "found profits," which would have slipped away had you not done the promotion. It's a "tipping point" kind of idea - if you can be in the right place at the right time with the right catalyst, it doesn't take much change to create a big impact on the scene.

This promotion was not designed to extend the customer LifeCycle, but to add value to the LifeCycle. Did it in fact actually extend the LifeCycle, and how would you measure this effect? All the customers in both the test (received promotion) and control (did not receive promotion) groups were 3x buyers who failed to make a 4th purchase by 180 days after their first purchase. This was the Latency "trip wire" selected to trigger the promotion.

So let's look at tracking these two groups for another 90 days, and look at continuing purchase activity using what I call the Hurdle Rate method.

A Hurdle Rate is simply the percentage of customers in a group who have "at least" a certain amount of activity. You define the behavior hurdle they have to reach, and measure the percentage of customers who have achieved this "threshold" (rate). If you track these percentages over time, you can use them to compare the actual and potential value of customer groups as a whole.

At the point of the promotion, 0% of both groups had made a 4th purchase. Recall we measured the profitability of the promotion over a 90-day period after we sent it to the test and control customer groups.

To track the Hurdle Rates for each group, we ask, "What percent had made at least 1 more purchase at 30 days, at 60 days, and at 90 days after the 90-day promotion was over, in both the test and control groups?" We know some percentage of both groups made a purchase during the promotion, because there were revenues generated in both groups. We made a profit in the first 90 days because the revenues were much higher for the test than control group. So at the beginning of this "post promotion" tracking, we see 1% of control and 3% of test have made 4 or more purchases. For the following 90 days after the promotion was over, data might look like this:

% 4 or more purchases	Control	Test
End of 90-day Promotion	1%	3%
30 Days After Promotion End	1%	5%
60 Days After Promotion End	2%	8%
90 Days After Promotion End	2%	10%

Figure 10: Percent Purchasing After Promotion End

Realize this: we have already made money on this promotion, a 114% ROI. We have already added value to the LifeCycle, increasing LifeTime Value - no matter how long a "LifeTime" is (does it really matter, as long as you are making increased profits?)

But as you can see from the chart above, we also extended the LifeCycle itself, because the percentage of customers exceeding the "4 or greater Hurdle" in the test group is far higher than the percentage of customers over the same Hurdle in control, and it appears to be growing over time.

There is a group of customers in the test group who just keep on keeping on - and this percentage (10% at 90 days after Promotion End) is much higher than both the initial group who responded to the promotion and made a 4th purchase (3%) and the test group. What's going on with that?

It's called the Halo Effect. It represents customer activity stimulated by the promotion not occurring within the promotional period. Now, we don't know exactly where it's coming from, and we can't show any measure of profit from it (we defined our promotion period as 90 days), but it is clearly there, plain as the nose on your face. Recall when describing the original promotion, I stated, "Response Rate doesn't matter in the measurement of profitability (it matters a lot in other cases). When you use control groups, you pick up buying behavior you never could have measured by just looking at response."

This "buying behavior you never could have measured" is the Halo Effect, working its magic during the promotion. People you have no way to track will respond to the promotion. They want to make a purchase but forget the coupon, for example. So they go ahead and make the purchase anyway - because the promotion "woke them up" to a need for something you sell.

After the promotion is over, the same thing continues. It's the Halo Effect again, working after the promotion. For example, people think about participating in the promotion but wait too long. They've missed it. But they're now in a new state of awareness about your company because of the promotion, and as a result, are more likely to make a purchase given any random positive stimulus. Perhaps some product appears on a TV show. Maybe a competitor promoted a product to them, the customer remembers you sell it also, and prefers your store. It doesn't really matter. Fact is fact, and because of your promotion, you extended the customer LifeCycle. You created a situation where people became more likely to purchase from your company in the future.

Not bad for a beginner. In the first 90 days, your promotion created present value - real bottom line, measurable ROI - adding Value to the customer LifeCycle (LifeTime Value). In the 2nd 90 days, your promotion created future value - accelerated repeat purchase rates - by extending the LifeCycle. CFO sings your praises! At last, somebody who can prove they are making more money than they are spending with marketing!

There is an important lesson here: you will never know how much money promotions really make without using control groups.

Chapter 10
Predictive Marketing

The concept of Recency as a human behavioral metric goes back to the early 1900's. A whole body of research was conducted, building on the work done by Pavlov and his famous dogs. Just before feeding time, Pavlov would ring a bell, then feed the dogs. By repeating this over and over, the dogs began to associate the ringing of the bell with being fed, to the point of salivating when the bell rang - even if there was no food present. Stimulus and response; the bell rings and the dog salivates. Edward Lee Thorndike took this idea a step further with humans and proposed the Law of Effect - the response to any particular situation, if followed by a rewarding experience, will become the likely response to the situation. Now, you may think to yourself, "Wow, how brilliant - duh" but he was the first guy to say it, so there.

J.B. Watson, building on the work of Pavlov and Thorndike, was the first to formalize the idea of Recency. He noted a man was more likely to get up from his chair when a woman entered the room if he had done so Recently; the more Recently he had done this, the more likely it was he would do it again. Apparently, he was able to get a hold of some bums who didn't stand up when a lady walked into the room for comparison. The point is, these "behaviorists," as they were called, studied human behavior and watched for patterns. They then used these patterns to make predictions about human behavior.

Recency found its way into the psychological literature in many ways, because it simply kept popping up on the radar screen. When studying the ability of a subject to remember a list of words, two effects were found: Primacy and Recency. When a list of words was spoken, subjects had far better luck remembering the first and last words spoken than ones in the middle. Primacy refers to words at the beginning of the list - those spoken first. Recency refers to words at the end of the list - those spoken most Recently, or last.

Why is there a Recency effect? One theory: there is simply something about human behavior and decision-making that draws us to the familiar - that which has happened to us Recently. These events are fresh in our minds; we understand all the details and implications of them, and they tend to strongly influence our behavior going forward - positively or negatively. A Recent bad experience can be just as powerful as a Recent good experience - right?

Here is the way I look at Recency in the context of marketing: Recency simply reflects the power of the Customer LifeCycle. As customers pass through different stages of their relationship with you their needs change, and keep changing until they don't need you any more. At this point, the LifeCycle ends and customer value accrual (either positive or negative) stops.

Note: A LifeCycle does not cover a human lifetime, and LifeTime Value is based on the LifeCycle, not a human lifetime. Until you know the LifeCycle of a customer, you cannot compute LifeTime Value, because you don't know where the "LifeTime" ends. So please stop worrying about LifeTime Value, and concentrate on first things first - understanding the customer LifeCycle.

But I digress; where was I? Yes... Recency.

Think of it this way. If I have just engaged in a transaction with your business, something has changed or occurred in my life that caused me to need your products or services and to reach out for them. Some event has taken place that changed my outlook or need for your business. Perhaps something I own needed to be replaced. Perhaps I got a new job and can buy more stuff. Perhaps I moved and now need a different set of services than before.

The point is, there was a triggering event and it changed my behavior. Going forward, there is no reason to believe this change is not permanent until through my behavior I tell you things have changed again. If this event caused me to need your products or services, it is likely I will need them again and again, unless something changes. And the point where this need is greatest is the point closest to the triggering event. Right after this event, I need your products or services the most. As time goes on, I need your products or services less and less, because I either have what I need or I find substitutes - better quality for the price, a higher level of service for the price, and so on.

If the above scenario is true, then the more Recently I have engaged in a transaction with you, the more likely I am to engage in another transaction with you - relative to those who have not engaged in a transaction as Recently as I have. People who have not transacted with you for a long time are simply less likely to transact with you again, relative to those who have transacted with you

Recently. Please note the use of the word "relative." We are not talking about absolutes here; we are talking about comparisons of one customer to another. A customer who has transacted with you Recently is more likely to transact with you again **relative** to a customer who has not transacted with you in some time. In fact, customers can be ranked by their Recency (number of days or weeks since the last transaction); this ranking in effect sorts all your customers by their likelihood to transact with you. Those in the top 20% of the Recency ranking are far more likely to transact with you than those in the bottom 20% of the Recency ranking.

If Recent customers are more likely to transact, then two other ideas follow:

1. The more Recent they are, the more likely they are to respond to promotions
2. The more Recent they are, the higher their potential value to the business

The first idea is just common sense. If a customer is are more likely to transact they are more likely to respond when contacted about a transaction - you are in effect pushing customers who are already predisposed to transact right off the fence. Like shootin' fish in a barrel, so to speak. If you are more likely to go rock climbing than somebody else, if somebody asks both of you if you want to go rock climbing, you are a lot more likely to say yes than the other person. No science to that, just logic. This assumes, of course, you can actually tell who is more likely to go rock climbing. Oh, but you can, remember? The person who has gone rock climbing more Recently is the one more likely to go rock climbing again. This does not mean the person will go, just that they are more likely to go rock climbing relative to the other person.

The second idea is just as logical, but perhaps a bit mysterious at first. Customer transactions normally increase customer value. A customer who is more likely to transact and more likely to respond has the potential to contribute more value to your company by transacting than a customer who is less likely to transact and respond. So it follows that the more Recent the customer relative to others, the higher potential value they have, because their likelihood to transact and contribute value is higher than others less Recent.

Over the past five decades, a lot of research and testing has been done concerning the profiling of customer behavior based on transactional data. The appearance of computers and "data-mining" created the ability to carry on even more extensive studies across a wide range of industries.

The end result? If you had to pick one variable to most universally predict the likelihood of a customer to repeat an action, Recency, or the number of days / weeks that have gone by since a customer completed an action (purchase, log-in, etc.) is the most powerful predictor of the customer repeating this action.

As each day goes by after the customer completed the action, the customer gets less and less likely to repeat it. Plain and simple. You can run all the fancy data-mining scenarios on "likelihood to buy" or "likelihood to visit" you want to - Recency almost always comes up as one of the most important variables in predicting the likelihood of a customer to repeat an action.

Recency is the number one most powerful predictor of future behavior. The more recently a customer has done something, the more likely they are to do it again. Recency can predict the likelihood of purchases, log-ins, game plays, just about any "action-oriented" customer behavior. Recency is why you receive another catalog from the same company shortly after you make your first purchase from them. They know you are most likely to order again immediately after your first order. Recency is the most powerful predictor of future behavior.

Please note: I am going to use the term "visit" when describing the activity created when someone views pages on a web site. It makes more sense to look at visits than individual page views. If you are tracking page views back to the visitor but are not tracking visits, you don't have to create visits out of these page views to do any of the work we talk about in the book. The most recent visit would be represented by the page view with the most recent date. Just substitute "page view" for the word "visit" in your mind for the rest of the book.

The chart on the next page is visitor Recency based on last visit date. The number of unique visitors is on the left (y-axis) scale; the number of days since last visit on the bottom (x-axis) scale. This site has about 5 million unique visitors a month. "Yesterday" is at the far right of the chart – 1 day ago. The left side of the chart is 90 days ago. Customers are plotted by the number of days since their last visit. Look at it for a minute.

What does this data below speak to you?

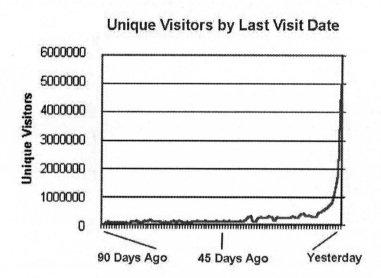

Figure 11: Visitors by Recency # 1

If your answer is these guys have a great business, you're right. I mean, they have millions of uniques and **most of them** have visited in the past few days. Not only that, but virtually **all** of them have visited in the last 10 days! This is a smokin' business. But you wouldn't know that without looking at Recency, would you? You **have** to know this stuff. It means something very important, not only to marketing, but also to the potential value of your business.

Now, the graph above is a "snapshot" of visitor Recency on a single day; almost all visitors who visited in the past 90 days visited again very Recently. Maybe you don't see the implications; this data is not speaking to you. You're having trouble projecting what this behavior means. I can understand that. You're thinking, "Hey, just because all those folks who last visited over 45 days ago have not come back Recently, that doesn't mean they won't come back in the future. And for that matter, just because a huge group of folks last visited yesterday, that doesn't mean they will come back in the future." Wanna bet?

90-Day Revisit Index by Days Since Last Visit

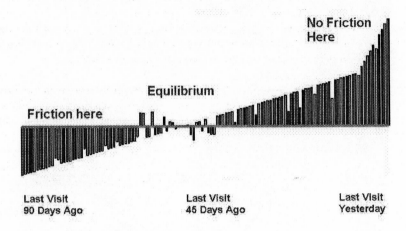

Figure 12: 90-Day Revisit Index

Let's take a look at the graph above. I took the same visitors from the first graph and tracked them over the next 90 days, identifying who visited again and who did not by their original Last Visit Date from the first graph. For **each of these Last Visit Dates**, I created a ratio of those that visited again in the next 90 days to those that did not and created the graph above. If the visit / did not visit ratio was 1 (equal numbers visited and did not visit again), then you don't see a bar on the cart. This occurs mostly in the area labeled "Equilibrium," where folks are just as likely to visit again as not visit again – roughly the area between a Recency of 50 – 60 days in the original graph. A bar above the line means more visitors came back than did not, and the height of the bar indicates how high the ratio of visited again to didn't visit again is. For bars below the line, fewer visitors visited again than didn't visit again.

Look at the overall pattern. Scary how consistent it is, right? If you had to make a bet on who would come back or not, is it pretty clear to you where the odds are in your favor? How about with the visitors on the far right, who are about 438 times more likely to visit again than the visitors on the far left?

You were right with your doubts about Recency above – in an absolute sense. Single out any one visitor and you just might be right – the visitor's Recency does not predict **absolutely** whether they will come back or not. But you're wrong in a **relative** sense, as in the likelihood of them to visit again, the odds they will visit again **versus other visitors**. If you are going to put your money down, make a marketing bet on a visitor or on a customer, you want the odds with you, don't you? You want to put your money down where and when it is more likely you are going to win the marketing bet, don't you?

Further, recall from the first graph that most of the visitor **volume** is in the more Recent visitor segments. The Revisit Index data above graphs the ratio of people visiting to people not visiting for each daily segment of Recency. But the most Recent segments have **millions** of visitors; the segments in the Equilibrium area and further to the left have **thousands** of visitors. So if you are looking for financial impact, both the odds of success and the volume are with you in the more Recent segments. For fun, take a look at this third graph:

Figure 14: Visitors by Recency # 2

Once again, a graph of customer Recency, based on last visit date. Unique visitors are on the left (y-axis), and days since last visit on the bottom. Yesterday (1 day ago) on the far right, 90 days ago on the far left. This is a smaller site, with a paid subscription business model. They launched with about 60,000 uniques 90 days ago, but only about 3,000 a day come back now. What's the future of this business? What's the data say to you, does it speak?

Just to make sure you didn't forget, what do we know about visitors who are more Recent?

1. The more Recent they are, the more likely they are to respond to promotions
2. The more Recent they are, the higher their potential value to the business

This site is toast, man. Absolutely moribund. They'll be lucky to keep the visitors they have. They need to make major content changes get people to come back to the site. If they don't, there's not much hope. I'd show you the Revisit Index graph for this site, if I had it. They went out of business before I could collect the data to create it. My guess is it would look like this: the most Recent visitors would be about as equally likely to come back as not come back, and it would go straight downhill from there.

These two businesses didn't just magically get to where they were overnight; there was a process, where customer behavior changed over time. If the owners of this site had started tracking visit Recency from the beginning, they would have known they were in trouble before it was too late. And just to be clear, this Recency effect doesn't only apply to visitors to a web site, it applies to any actions customers engage in that create value – purchases, service usage, visits to a office, whatever actions your customers engage in.

By the way, think about that Equilibrium area in the second graph above (Revisit Index, Figure 12). This area is where the ratio of people who visited again to people who did not visit again is dead even. Does this metric remind you of anything, perhaps the Latency metric? I mean, if you were going to set a trip wire somewhere, setting it where the average visitor is as equally likely to visit again as not can't be a bad choice. This is how Recency and Latency are related; Recency works on a "scale," a **relative** comparison of behavior. Latency is an **absolute** cut-off, looking to find the average or break-even behavior and use this point as a trigger for action.

As a matter of fact, you can use Latency and Recency together to track rising or falling Friction. Think about this scenario. The average Latency of visitors to a web site is 2.5 days, meaning on average, there are 2.5 days between visits. Sounds pretty good, right? Now, what if I tell you that these same visitors have an average Recency of 8.5 days – the last visit was 8.5 days ago. Think about it.

If on average they come back every 2.5 days, but the last visit date averages 8.5 days ago, what do you have? Well, fellow Driller, you have increasing Friction, of course. The Latency pattern has been broken, the wire tripped. These visitors are simply not (on average) visiting as often as they used to, and in fact are falling back on at a fairly alarming rate. They are having trouble, not finding what they need for info, not moving towards conversion. Likewise, if visitors had an average Latency of 7.0 days, but these same visitors also had an average Recency of 3.4 days, what would that mean? Of course. Friction is falling, the visit rate is increasing, these visitors are indicating an acceleration of the relationship, they are finding what they need, increasing their engagement. Now, what if you could see this data broken out by campaign, or search phrase?

Retention by Initial Search Engine (Organic)

Initial Search Engine	Initial Search Engine Phrase	Frequency	Days Since First Visit	Avg. Recency	Avg. Latency
1. kvasir	friction increasing	10.5	29.0	8.5	2.5
2. compuserve		22.7	65.2	12.4	12.8
	friction increasing	18.6	63.2	10.8	6.6
	friction decreasing	8.5	74.7	4.7	7.0
		3.5	35.4	3.4	7.0
	friction increasing	3.0	85.0	68.0	42.0
3. mamma		9.0	31.2	3.5	4.4
4. cnet search.com	friction decreasing	6.5	33.0	1.0	5.5
5. yahoo	friction stable	43.8	73.0	2.1	2.1
		17.4	41.5	6.2	6.3
		14.0	39.0	3.0	3.0
	friction decreasing	9.5	42.5	0.5	4.5

Figure 14: Visitor Friction by Search Phrase

Glad to oblige, my fellow Driller. This is a WebTrends report looking at visitors by Organic (not pay-per-click) Search Engine source with Average Recency and Average Latency data by Search Phrase. The report is tracking visitors by the **first (Initial) search engine** they used to reach the web site. The search phrases are hidden by a light blue color to protect the identity of the client:

What can you do with this piece of intelligence? Now you are talking about the Friction of visitors rising and falling by campaign source, and now you are into **predicting the likelihood of a campaign conversion.** Not just conversion today, but likelihood to convert tomorrow. Given any two ad campaigns, e-mail drops, search phrases, etc. with the same initial conversion rate, and faced with where to put the money on the next round, you would bet more money on the campaign generating visitors with falling Friction, because they are the most likely to convert in the future, and they have higher potential value. In the case of Organic Search in the example above, you would want to take a look at the pages these visitors are initially landing on and figure out why certain pages tend to increase Friction and certain pages tend to decrease Friction.

Capiche?

Think about this. Latency, or Trip Wire metrics tell you when something bad or good has already happened. Using Recency, you can **predict the likelihood of something bad or good to happen.** There is a huge difference between these two metrics, my fellow Driller. Customers who are more Recent have higher potential value than customers who are less Recent, for any given activity. Customers who made a purchase 15 days ago have higher potential value than customers who made a purchase 60 days ago. Customers who logged in last week are much more likely to visit than customers who logged in 30 days ago, and have higher potential value.

"Now hold on just a minute, Jim," you say. "Recency is a very cool concept, but I can think of some specific instances where it can't possibly work. A person who just filed a tax return 30 days ago is not more likely to file one than a person who filed one 60 days ago, and the same thing is true for people who bought a new car. Explain yourself!"

There are two issues to consider when using Recency – external forces and time frame. If there are powerful external forces shaping behavior – like the April 15th tax deadline – these forces may overcome the Recency effect. An accountant trying to manage customer relationships would probably look more to Latency and set a trip wire: I will call best customers who don't schedule an appointment by March 15, for example. The tax deadline is simply too powerful a force and overcomes normal human behavior.

One also needs to consider Recency in light of the cycle of normal behavior. It is unrealistic to think of Recency in new car buying in terms of 30 and 60-day periods, when the normal purchase cycle may be 3 or 4 years long. It's not a rational use of the Recency metric. However, for the dealer selling the original car to the customer, as this purchase gets to be 3 or 4 years old, the longer it has been since the purchase, the less likely the customer is to make the car purchase from this same dealer.

Recency is a very powerful metric, but there are times when it simply is not appropriate to use without some adjustments. If there are powerful cycles acting on behavior, Recency often takes a back seat to Latency. Often the two concepts can be used together – there is first a Latency trip wire and then Recency kicks in. For example, up until the April 15th deadline, the accountant is really operating in the world of Latency. If customers don't call by a certain day, they are unlikely to be using the accountant for their tax return. Once the April 15 deadline passes though, the accountant is in the Land of Recency – the longer it has been since the last tax filling, the less likely it is the customer will be using the same accountant next year. The accountant needs to get on the phone with these high value customers and find out what happened right away if the customer is to be recaptured.

The new car dealer is in a similar situation. Let's say the average customer trades in every four years. Up to four years after the new car purchase, the dealer is in the Latency world – there is a trip wire at 4 years, and any customer who has not purchased again at the 4-year point is in danger of being lost. After the 4-year point passes, the more time passing, the less likely it is the customer will come back – the Recency effect. As time goes by after the trip wire triggers, it becomes more and more urgent the customer be contacted and made an offer. And, the more time that passes, the higher the offer will have to be to get the customer to come back. This phenomenon is called the Discount Ladder and we'll go through a detailed example in later on in the book.

Make sense so far? Good. But how is Recency implemented, how do you actually do anything with this information? Glad you asked.

Chapter 11
The Ad Spending Example

Let's use Recency to compare the potential value of customers coming from two different ads (Ad #1 and Ad # 2) that ran at the same time, for the same duration. The following example uses a spreadsheet, but if you know your way around databases and can query your customer records, have at it your way.

1. Identify the groups you want to compare for potential value. In this example, it's the customers who clicked on either of two ads, Ad #1 or Ad #2 (two groups). If you are not keeping the source of customers in your database, start doing it right now – it is one of the most important variables you can analyze.

2. Decide which activity is most important to you for these groups. If you're a publisher, probably log-ins or page views are most important. If you were selling merchandise, you would use purchases. For this example, we will use purchases. An example using visits (or log-ins, if you don't track visits) is below.

3. Import all the purchase records of people who clicked on Ad #1 or Ad #2 into separate spreadsheets. These transactions need to have a date; most interactive activities are date-stamped so this should not be a problem. If an activity you want to profile for potential value has no date stamp, start collecting the dates of activity.

4. Pick a time frame to look at Recency. For page views, it might be 1 week; for purchases, maybe 30 days. The exact length is not very critical, because you are interested in comparing the activity between the Ad #1 and Ad #2 groups - you want to know which is "better." As long as you use the same time frame for both groups, you are fine. Pick something reasonable based on what you know about your customers. Anywhere from 30 to 90 days would be reasonable for purchases; let's use 30 days.

5. Sort the purchase records for Ad #1 from most Recent to least Recent and find out what percentage of the people who clicked on Ad #1 and made a purchase have made at least one more purchase in the past 30

days. Count back 30 days using the transaction dates, total the number of customers making a purchase, and divide by the total people in the spreadsheet. Perhaps it is 20%. Note: The software that comes with the book will automatically aggregate multiple transactions by customer and sort customers by their most Recent transaction for you.

6. Run the same analysis for people who clicked on Ad #2 and made a purchase. Let's say only 15% of these people have made at least one purchase in the past 30 days.

7. You're done, and you know the answer. A higher percentage of people who clicked on Ad #1 are Recent - active and purchasing - when compared with Ad #2. This means Ad #1 generates customers with higher potential value. You need to take this into account when analyzing the success of the ads.

Do you understand how powerful this idea is?

If you go through this process for customers grouped by product they bought first, you can determine which products generate new customers with highest potential value. Go through this process for customers grouped by which area of the site they visit most, and you will find which areas generate highest potential value customers. If you go through this process for customers grouped by the demographics or the survey data they provide, you can determine which data points define customers with the highest potential value. All you have to do is create your groups and compare their Recency. The group with the highest percentage engaging in the activity you are measuring over some time period is the group with the highest future value to the company.

This is a simple example of how companies with experience in managing remote shopping customers find ways to maximize sales and minimize expense. The customers, through their actions, tell them which route is the most profitable to take. The most Recent customers for any particular activity are always the ones most likely to repeat that activity, and so have a higher potential value.

You can track multiple activities for the same customer groups. In the first example, you found customers who clicked on Ad #1 and made a purchase are more Recent on purchases, so they have a higher potential value on the activity "purchases." But what about the Recency of people who clicked on the ads for visits? If they keep coming back, they could be of some future value. Let's see how this Recency study might look.

Visits / log-ins example:

1. Import all the visits (or log-ins if you don't track visits) into two separate spreadsheets of people who clicked on Ad #1 or Ad #2 (transactions need a date stamp).

2. Pick a Recency cut-off. Again, we are interested in a comparison, so the number isn't critical. Let's use 1 week.

3. Sort each spreadsheet from most Recent to least Recent and find out what percentage of the people who clicked on Ad #1 have visited (logged-in) at least once in the past week, as was done above for purchases. You might come up with 10%.

4. Run the same analysis for people who clicked on Ad #2. Sort most Recent to least Recent, and do your percentage. You might come up with 30% who have visited / logged-in at least once in the past week.

5. You're done, and now you have an interesting situation. It appears the customers who clicked on Ad #1 have a higher potential value on purchases, but people in general who clicked on Ad #2 have a higher potential value on visits. Maybe they're just tire kickers, or maybe they're doing research. We'll take a closer look at finding answers to this situation in a minute.

Note that this method is based on the actual facts of customer behavior - not speculation or "best guess" theories. The behavior of the customer is the most accurate yardstick you will find for assessing potential value. Once you complete studies like these, you can begin to organize all your business practices around the potential value of the customers they generate. If you allocate money away from activities generating low potential value customers, and allocate this money to activities generating higher potential value customers, you will become more profitable over time. It's really as simple as that.

At the beginning of the previous example I specified the ads you were comparing should have "run at the same time, for the same duration." Do you know why? Customer LifeCycles. It's not fair to compare the customer

Recency percentage of an ad that ran 90 days ago with an ad that ran 30 days ago, because customers tend to leave you over time. You learned this in the previous Latency model. If one ad has more time to "lose customers," then comparing them would be unfair or biased by the element of time.

This tendency of customers to leave over time has different names depending on the business model - some call it attrition (credit cards), it is an element in churn (cable, long distance, wireless), and in retailing and database marketing it is often called defection. You can compare ads having different start points, as long as they're not so far apart that seasonality comes into play (comparing ads that ran in July with those that ran during November, for example). Simply synch up the LifeCycles and do a Recency analysis at the same point in the customer LifeCycle. This is usually defined as "days from an event," for example, the day they became a new buyer or visitor.

If you want to compare the potential value of an ad running 30 days ago with one running 90 days ago, you have to look at the Recency of the 90 day ago ad 30 days after it ran to take out the LifeCycle effects. Using the previous example, if Ad #2 ran 90 days ago, you would want to find out what percentage of people who clicked on Ad #2 took action 30 days after it first ran. If you always run your analysis referencing the start date of an ad (or any other variable you are measuring), and measure for equal time periods after the start date, you will eliminate most of the LifeCycle effect and can compare the results on an equal basis.

So what about these LifeCycles? Is there a way this information can be tracked and used? Sure; using LifeCycles can solve the little problem we left at the end of the previous example. Thinking about the Ad #1 and #2 example, what if you repeated the Recency query for each ad (made at least one purchase in the past 30 days) every 30 days for 6 months? What would you get? You would have a series of measurements looking at the potential value of the customers generated by the ads over time. You would be able to chart the defection patterns of Ad #1 and Ad #2 customers.

Why is this important? Because if you want to get at the true value of the customers generated by the ads, you have to measure their value over the LifeCycle. You might be surprised. Take a look at the chart below from our previous example:

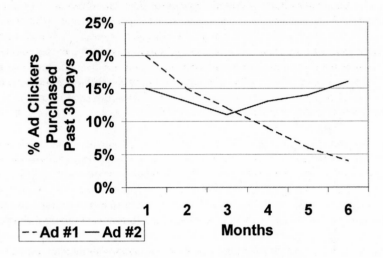

Customer LifeCycles: Ad #1 and Ad #2

Ad #1 Customers Start with Higher Recency, but have a Shorter Lifecycle than Ad #2 Customers

Figure 15: Recency Percentage over Time

Top to bottom on the left side of the chart is the percentage of customers making a purchase in the past 30 days; left to right at the bottom of the chart are the months each Recency analysis was performed since the start date of the ad campaigns. Both the Ad #1 (dotted line) and Ad #2 (solid line) start at the percentages we came up with in the Recency of purchases analysis above.

If you look at the chart above, you can see that Ad #1 (dotted line) starts at 20% of customers having purchased in the past 30 days, and after 6 months, the percentage drops to less than 5%. Ad #1 also seems to be headed even lower in Recency; these customers are losing even more potential value as time goes on. Ad #2 (solid line) starts at 15% of customers having purchased in the past 30 days and falls into month 3, but then starts rising in later months, ending up higher than it started, and is still rising. Customers from Ad #2 might end up having greater potential value than customers from Ad #1 over the longer term.

So it could be that, after looking at the LifeCycle of customers from Ads #1 and #2, you may find even though Ad #1 looks best based on Recency at a point in time, Ad #2 creates higher potential value customers when Recency is looked at over time. In looking at the LifeCycles, we have perhaps come up with a clue to the behavior we saw in the Recency of visits analysis on the previous page. It would appear that the customers from Ad #2 might take a little longer to make a purchasing decision, but become more valuable customers over the long run. This is a very common occurrence in customer behavior mapping and if you are not tracking it, you won't know it is happening, leading to poor decisions about the profitability of your ad campaigns.

This is a picture of the customer LifeCycle at work, and you can conduct this type of study with customer segments based on ads, products, areas of the site, survey data, demographics – any type of customer information you can get Recency data for. If these two customer ad segments were stocks, which would you want to own? For more on the similarity between managing "customer portfolios" and managing "stock portfolios", see Segmentation in Financial Services / The Mutual Fund Scoring Model under the "Customer Segmentation and LifeTime Value" section in the chapter titled "Fellow Drillers at Work."

Let's talk about one of the most confusing and misunderstood parts of customer marketing, LifeTime Value. The LifeTime Value of a customer is the net profit the customer generates over their LifeCycle. People tell you not to spend more to get a customer than their LifeTime Value, or you will lose money. This is true on the face of it, but actually figuring out what the LifeTime Value of a customer is can be a difficult task, especially if you don't have the right tools. Besides, what if you are a new company, or have never tracked the data you need to calculate LifeTime Value? Is the concept useless to you?

Not at all. LifeTime value is used to make decisions about allocating marketing or service efforts to ideas that generate high potential value customers, and away from ideas generating low potential value customers. And to do this, all you need to know is the **relative** LifeTime Value of the customers generated by each idea. Recall LifeTime Value is the net profit the customer generates over their LifeCycle. So if you know what the LifeCycles look like, you should be able to do a pretty good job of determining who the highest LifeTime Value customers are, relative to each other. If you do your Recency tracking on ads, PPC keywords, newsletter links, and so on, you should be able to compare the relative potential value of the customers generated by each approach and easily decide where your ad budget is most profitably spent.

Let's say you have run 20 campaigns and you know your cost per new customer from each of them. You want to run the top 10 (lowest cost per new customer) but you only have the money for 5 campaigns. With Recency and LifeCycle tracking on the 10 campaigns, all you have to do is choose the top 5 campaigns generating customers with the highest potential value based on Recency. If you allocate your budget to those and away from the bottom five, you are maximizing your budget ROI, regardless of the actual LifeTime Value in dollars of the customers generated. What else could anybody ask for?

Continuing with our Ad #1 and Ad #2 example, based on the LifeCycle chart you just saw, can you make a judgment about which ad generates customers with higher potential value? Looks like Ad #2 to me. Ad #2 appears to generate customers with a longer LifeCycle, so their relative LifeTime Value is higher when compared with Ad #1 customers, given the costs of acquiring and maintaining customers from both ads is roughly the same. Period.

And by the way, with the LifeCycle information in hand, is cost per new customer really the issue? Probably not, because you have to weigh the cost per new customer against the length of the LifeCycle. Customers who are the cheapest to acquire may have the shortest LifeCycles, and customers who are expensive to acquire might have very long LifeCycles. So you really need the potential value and LifeCycle tracking to get the whole picture.

The problem people run into with LifeTime Value is the whole question of determining a LifeTime. There's no easy way to do it, and so the whole idea gets tossed. People get frustrated because there's nothing to grab on to, and no easy way to make comparisons. But when you track the LifeCycle, you know for a fact one group has a longer LifeCycle than the other. Who needs the absolute LifeTime Value number in dollars and cents? As long as you allocate money towards higher potential value customers and away from lower potential value customers, you are maximizing your resources in everything you do. And that is the reason people want to look at LifeTime Value in the first place.

If you really need a hard number, don't be afraid to call an end to the customer LifeTime. They are much shorter than you think. When you are tracking your LifeCycles and they start to approach 0% of customers making a purchase in the past 30 days (or whatever standard you're using), the LifeTime generated by these particular ads is over. Don't hope customers will magically come back; it usually doesn't work like that. Once you call the end to the LifeTime, subtract your costs (cost of products sold, ad costs, an allocation for service costs) from the revenues for both Ad #1 and Ad #2 customers, and you'll have your LifeTime Value. We'll talk more about Lifetime Value calculations later on.

Chapter 12
Turning Recency Data into Profits

So what do the financials look like on the ad campaign from the previous chapter? ROI, or Return on Investment, is a concept from the financial world frequently applied to database or customer marketing. What people seem to forget is ROI implies the concept of time, because "Return" happens over time. So an ROI calculation really asks, "What was my return over time?" And without looking at time, you can't calculate the "real ROI" of a campaign.

Think about a bank account. The bank says if you put money in, they will pay 2% interest. This is an annual number; if you put in $100 and don't do anything else, you will have $102 in your account at the end of a year. Your annual ROI is 2%. At the end of 6 months, it's close to 1%. So ROI depends on what time frame you are using for the calculation. Let's go back to our example of Ad #1 and Ad #2, and look at some ROI numbers.

Ad campaigns #1 and #2 were pretty similar. The ad units were the same and the Cost Per Thousand ads (CPM's) were the same, but they ran on different sites and had different creative. As a result, the response rates (click-throughs resulting in purchase) were different. Here's what they look like at the end of their campaign runs:

Parameter	Ad #1	Ad #2
a. Cost of Campaign	$5,000	$5,000
b. People Clicking	2,000	1,000
c. Number of Buyers	185	230
d. Average Price	$90	$70
e. Product Sales	$16,650	$16,100
f. Product Margin	30%	30%
g. Net Margin (f x e)	$4,995	$4,830
h. Campaign profit (g - a)	-$5	-$170
i. Campaign ROI (h / a)	0%	-3%

Figure 16: Financial Analysis of Campaigns: Short Term ROI

This is short-term ROI, right at the end of the campaign. It's based on what customers first bought during and immediately after the campaign. Ad #1 looks to be the clear winner, even though it only broke even; Ad #2 has a negative ROI (lost money). You might just leave it at that. But you're smarter now. You know about Recency and customer LifeCycles. Your first Recency tracking is 30 days later, and you find that 20% of the buyers from Ad #1 have made another purchase and 15% of the buyers from Ad #2 have made a purchase (these numbers are from our original example). The rest of the numbers from the LifeCycle charts are included below. Now what does the campaign ROI for Ad #1 and Ad #2 look like?

Parameter	Ad #1	Ad #2
1 month Repeat Buyer %	20%	15%
2 month Repeat Buyer %	15%	13%
3 month Repeat Buyer %	12%	11%
4 month Repeat Buyer %	9%	13%
5 month Repeat Buyer %	6%	14%
6 month Repeat Buyer %	4%	16%
j. Total Repeat Buyer %	66%	82%
k. Original # of Buyers	185	230
l. New Purchases (j x k)	122	189
m. Average Price (d above)	$90	$70
n. Product Sales (m x l)	$10,989	$13,202
o. Product Margin	30%	30%
p. New Net Margin (o x n)	$3,297	$3,961
q. Initial Margin (g above)	$4,995	$4,830
r. 6 Month Margin (q + p)	$8,292	$8,791
s. 6 Month Profit (r - a)	$3,292	$3,791
t. 6 Month ROI (s / a)	66%	76%

Figure 17: Financial Analysis of Campaigns: Long Term ROI

Surprised? These ad campaigns at 6 months have ROI numbers many times higher than they did at 30 days. And, Ad #2 has emerged as the winner because at 6 months, it has passed Ad #1 in profits and ROI. If you recall the LifeCycle chart, at the 6-month point, Ad #1 is going downhill fast while Ad #2 is still climbing. Looks like the spread in profits and ROI is going to get even wider still over time.

Now, is this the best and most accurate way to determine the true ROI? No, it's a "down and dirty" approximation of campaign ROI you can make on the spot, a "back of the napkin" kind of idea. You're looking for trends and comparisons in order to get a feel for what's working. But it is a heck of a lot better than just looking at conversion to first purchase.

For this example, we don't know how many of the repeat customers may have made multiple purchases in a month - we only know they made "at least one." And we're using "average price" from the original campaign; this has probably changed. The point of this example is making comparisons between the potential values of customers generated by different ad campaigns, and using these comparisons to make more money with your advertising. Once you see important trends emerging, you can decide whether it's worth spending the time and resources to take ROI down to the last penny.

Could the customer LifeCycle for Ad #2 suddenly turn down and undercut the customer LifeCycle for Ad #1? Sure, it's possible, but not likely. This late in the LifeCycle, when a group of customers is moving in a certain direction, they tend to keep moving in the same direction. Good customers tend to remain that way (until they leave you) and poor quality customers tend to remain as they are. That's one reason there is so much money wasted in customer marketing; marketers are not targeting using the LifeCycle, and as a result they're making untargeted offers at the wrong times to most customers. Early in the LifeCycle, it can be difficult to tell if a customer will become profitable or not. That's why it is so critical to track trends like this from the beginning; later on, it becomes less important as the customers tend to remain either profitable or unprofitable. There's no reason to guess though, is there? You'll be tracking these LifeCycles, because that is what smart marketers do.

Recency in Promotions

You will generally see response rates to a promotion asking for a specific action (purchase, visit, click a link) fall as the number of weeks or months since the customer last engaged in the activity you are trying to encourage rises – in other words, as the customer becomes "less Recent." This relationship is a smooth curve and quite predictable once you establish the "slope" of it for your business. Response rate by Recency might look like this:

Customer inactive for 31-60 days, Response rate = 20%
Customer inactive for 61-90 days, Response rate = 10%
Customer inactive for 91-120 days, Response rate = 4%
Customer inactive for 120+ days, Response rate = 1%

The absolute response rates will be different depending on the business, media used, and offer, but the relative response rates will follow a decelerating curve as shown above, that is, the less Recent the customer, the more dramatic a drop in response rate you will get to your request for an action. In terms of using this information for promotions, you will find some point along the curve where you will hit "breakeven," meaning the cost of the campaign will equal the profits or benefit generated. For example, let's say you offer a discount, gift, or other incentive in your retention / lapsed customer campaign and need a response rate of at least 4% to pay back the campaign cost. This is your breakeven point. The implication for this 4% breakeven campaign contained in the Recency information above is this: don't bother to promote to any customer who hasn't engaged in the activity you are trying to encourage for over 3 months, because you're wasting your money. Response will be too low to pay back the cost of the campaign with any customer who has been inactive for over 3 months.

This Recency effect is very stable over time, allowing you to predict in advance what response to a campaign will be, once you do an "establishing" campaign to see what your response rate is for any particular offer. Recency will predict average response rate for any specific combination of offer and media used. You can save a tremendous amount of money by forecasting your response by using Recency, and not promoting to customers unlikely to be profitable.

Let's set up and execute a Recency test. Classify customers in 30-day Recency segments by the last date of the activity you want to profile for Recency. If you want to profile purchases, customers could be segmented by date of last purchase, for example:

31 – 60 days ago
61 – 90 days ago
91 – 120 days ago
120+ days ago

Take a 10% random sample of customers from each segment (every 10th person in the segment), and send all of them a promotion with the same offer, say 20% off any purchase in the next 30 days. Look at the response rate by these 30-day segments. You will find response falls off significantly as you look at Recency segments further back in time. If you repeat the test using the same offer to a different sample of each 30-day segment, the response rate by segment will be very close to the response rate by segment in the first test. This kind of stability allows accurate predictions of marketing ROI before promotions are even sent out to customers.

The response rate in any one of the 30-day segments above will be influenced by the value of your offer, and both response rate and cost of the offer have significant impact on the profitability of your campaign to any segment. As offer value increases, so does response rate, and so do costs. Ideally, you want to find the ideal mix of response rate and offer value creating the highest profitability for each segment you promote to.

You can use Recency to "ladder" the promotional discount, gift, or incentive value offered in a promotion, boosting overall response while cutting expenses by minimizing discount or other incentive costs.

Let's use purchases as an example, and say you usually e-mail all your customers a 10% discount when you do a promotion. If you were using a Recency ladder approach for this purchase incentive, you might apply your discount strategy this way:

Customer inactive for 31-60 days, Response rate = 20%, discount = 5%
Customer inactive for 61-90 days, Response rate = 10%, discount = 10%
Customer inactive for 91-120 days, Response rate = 4%, discount = 15%
Customer inactive for 120+ days, Response rate = 1%, discount = 20%

Using this approach, you are allocating the most "bang for the buck" discount-wise where you need it most - the least Recent, lowest response customers, and pulling back on some discounting where you don't need it as much - the most Recent, highest response customers. Since your most Recent customers are most likely to respond, you can back off on their discount and you reduce the cost of giving discounts to customers who "may have bought anyway without a discount." You then reallocate this discount money to where it is needed most – boosting the response rates of those much less likely to respond - the less Recent customers. Your response rates will vary depending on the offer, media used, and your business. You have to test these ladders with different combinations of offer and media to find the optimum profitability for each Recency segment.

The interesting and quite useful benefit of this approach is the "automatic" overall customer retention effect discount ladders have.

Using a ladder of this type means your promotional discount budget is automatically working harder and harder to keep a customer active with you as they drift further and further away from you. The less Recent a customer is, the less likely they are to buy or visit again, and by using a discount ladder you are counteracting the customer LifeCycle (the tendency of customers to leave you over time) with stronger discounts as the defecting customer behavior plays out. If a most Recent customer does not respond to the 5% offer, as they get less Recent, they automatically get offers rising in value, and at some point, many will take advantage of an offer. The customers who run through this system without taking any offers were likely lost to you as a customer already, and not worth the extra expense to try and keep promoting to them. Let's set up and execute a discount ladder test.

Pick any one of the segments from your Recency test above and now test discount level for the segment. Let's say you used a 20% discount in the first test. Pick a segment (say 91 – 120 days), and create a 20% random sample of the segment (every 5th customer) divided into 4 equal test groups. Send each test group a different discount - say 5%, 10%, 15% and 20%. Look at your response rates and calculate the profitability for the 91 – 120 day segment at each discount level. You will find your result looks similar to the following:

Customer Sample	1000	1000	**1000**	1000
Discount Offer	5%	10%	**15%**	20%
Response Rate	2%	4%	**6%**	8%
Responders	20	40	**60**	80
Average Price	$80	$80	**$80**	$80
Totals Sales	$1,600	$3,200	**$4,800**	$6,400
Gross Margin	30%	30%	**30%**	30%
Gross Profit	$480	$960	**$1,440**	$1,920
Discount Cost	$80	$320	**$720**	$1,280
Net Profit before Media Expense	$400	$640	**$720**	$640

Figure 18: Discount Ladder Test Segment Performance

As you can see, the most profitable offer to the 91 – 120 day Recency segment is 15% off. If you offer 20%, you get a higher response rate but lower profits; any offer under 15% significantly diminishes response rate. Repeat this test for each Recency segment, and you will find the most profitable discount rising as the customer becomes less Recent, creating your discount "ladder."

When you implement your promotions based on a Recency / Discount ladder, as customers become less Recent and therefore less likely to respond to a promotion, they will be automatically offered a higher discount – one that maximizes profit for each Recency segment the customer passes through. Discount ladders create in effect a "lights-out" customer retention program suitable for automation.

There is a subtle but important side benefit to using a Recency / Discount ladder approach to manage e-mail efforts. Instead of blasting out indiscriminate offers to the whole customer base, taking a ladder approach more closely matches the offer value to the "attitude" or point in the LifeCycle a customer has reached. Following the mantra of Permission Marketing, this is called being "relevant," and will tend to increase open rate and response as customers begin to put a higher value on your e-mail relative to other offers they may get.

In addition, as e-mail clutter and execution expense increase, response will fall and profits will decrease, as customers get tired of receiving multiple promotions. Over time, you will find it is simply more profitable to e-mail customers less often, because you know for a fact the most profitable offer to make and when to make it, based on the Recency / Discount Ladder. Using this approach will generally help you rise above the clutter by sending fewer, higher impact promotions. The Recency / Discount ladder approach to creating a customer retention program is clean, simple, and easy to implement. And if you don't have any formal customer retention program in place, much better than what you're using now!

Chapter 13
The Online Retail Example

"Yes, things are sweet," thinks the owner of IMissAsia.com (not the real name of the site), ending a phone conversation with a supplier. Who would have thought! In just one short year, with the remains of the dot-com bust scattered all about, IMissAsia.com was running at sales of $25,000 a month. With an operating margin of 40%, "The Miss," as the owner liked to call the site, was going to generate about $120,000 this year pre-tax - certainly enough to keep the spouse warm, fed, and reasonably happy.

Who knows what next year would bring? Could the business double in size? The owner figured The Miss could do about $2 million in annual sales with the current infrastructure set up - a web site / shopping cart that cost about $40 a month and assorted software / hardware purchased for a total of about $1,000. The owner put up the very simple web site and ships every box - the order management system is highly integrated with both the shopping cart and UPS WorldShip, so order processing and customer service are a breeze. All other costs of the operation were basically variable to sales. Sweet, indeed. Of course, the owner / only employee has done a lot of things right in the first place to get to this place.

IMissAsia.com is a site for people who used to live in Asia and now don't, and are scattered all over the world. The core business idea takes natural advantage of what the web is very good at - aggregating niche vertical demand.

A person who used to live in Asia but now doesn't is cut off from a lot of things they liked and now "miss" - food, clothing, beauty items, culture. IMissAsia.com aggregates all those things into one web site, and then offers it as a "one stop shop" to a very geographically dispersed group of people all over the world. IMissAsia.com is "patient zero" in all this, the intersection of diverse needs with a fragmented customer base - a perfect application for the web.

The site is set up smartly, using mostly free resources to attract and hold on to traffic - news feeds, free newsletters, and discussion boards. The store is tightly integrated into all the content, so there are many opportunities to get visitors to take a peek at the merchandise. The Miss gets pretty high natural search rankings for important search terms because it's a plain HTML site without a lot of script and database-driven components, and has been written carefully with search engine optimization in mind.

In other words, the site is a little cash machine that requires almost no maintenance. Shipping packages, customer service related to those shipments, and the newsletter are about all the day-to-day work done on the business. However, storm clouds are on the horizon.

Response to the weekly newsletter is falling, and the owner is thinking of going bi-weekly or even monthly. In addition, to try and keep response up, the owner has been discounting more aggressively in the newsletter, and this practice is starting to depress margin. This situation is of deep concern to the owner, because the newsletter generates a big chunk of sales volume.

Niche markets are a double-edged sword. While they fit perfectly into the natural search-driven model of the web, by definition, niches are small. This kind of business has a tendency to ramp up very quickly, but then plateau as the entire niche is discovered and filled out. You can quickly capture 80% of the market, but then there is nowhere to go.

And as soon as you are successful, you will attract copycats, who chip away at your share, often undercutting your prices in start-up mode. The copycats have now started to appear. How will the owner grow the business when it already dominates the niche, and defend against the copycats? Not to mention address the worrisome situation with the newsletter.

IMissAsia.com offers an e-mail newsletter on every page of the site. The owner tries to create a broadly appealing piece, mixing some new content with links back to areas of the site experiencing high activity - specific discussion boards, products, news clips, etc.

The owner has always felt the visitor / customer should drive the direction of the site; if certain topic areas were getting the most traffic, then those must be the most interesting or attractive topics, and likely the ones with appeal to the most people. This "swim with the tide, not against it" approach had always worked well in the past as a driver for newsletter content.

Within this content, the owner carefully mixed contextual sales opportunities directly related to the content, along with one or two more aggressive product pitches. This formula had worked well and the newsletter drove a good chunk of sales. But the owner of IMissAsia.com was getting worried about response to the newsletter, which has been falling. Perhaps swimming with the tide was not a good idea, and the content should explore "not popular" issues and products? Perhaps the product pitches were too frequent and aggressive? Perhaps this market was just slowing down because of the economy? Or worse, perhaps the owner had already "creamed" this market and the best days were over?

One thing the owner knew for sure - the percentage of total sales from new customers was falling. Now, this could be a good thing, the owner thought, because it means more sales are coming from repeat buyers. But it could be a bad thing, if what it means is the market is saturated and the best days are over. How to resolve this question? And how is the newsletter affecting this issue?

The owner thought a lot about new customers, repeat customers, and the newsletter. What is a "new" customer, anyway? Are they new only the day they make a first purchase? Are they still new if they haven't made a purchase 30 days later? 60 days later? 6 months later? Do they have to make a second purchase to not be "new"? When do they stop being new?

For that matter, when is a customer not a customer any more? If they purchased twice or more and have not purchased again for 6 months, are they still a customer? What about no purchase in 2 years? 5 years? When do customers cease to be customers? What does the customer base of IMissAsia.com really look like?

The owner realized the only way to answer these questions was to actually look at the customer data, and to make decisions on what these ideas meant for this business. Customer types for IMissAsia.com probably would not be defined the same way as customer types for Boeing, Wal-Mart, Oracle, or Ford. No, these customer definitions needed to be based on the facts of this particular business model. The owner also realized something else - if there are no definitions, there can be no measurement. And without measurement, there is no way to understand the dynamics of what is happening to the business, for example, why the response rate to the newsletter is falling. All the owner knows is one thing, the "what" - response is falling. The owner wants to understand "why." And there is no way to get to "why" without understanding the "who" first.

Response to the newsletter is falling because not as many customers are responding. Who is not responding to the newsletter? Is it new customers? Is it repeat customers? Is it "best customers"? The owner realizes there is no definition of best customers either. If these things were defined, the owner might be able to measure and understand what is happening. Then another realization - not just defined, but tracked over time. It does no good to define customers and count how many there is of each type; what the owner needs to know is how these counts are changing over time.

And since the specific topic at hand is the newsletter, what the owner needs to do is not only define the customers, but also to define them relative to the newsletter. What percent of new customers respond now, and over time? What percent of "old customers" respond, now, and over time? What percent of "best customers" respond, now, and over time? Knowing these numbers would almost certainly help the owner understand why response to the newsletter is falling overall. The owner resolves to address this situation immediately by digging into the data. Yes folks, the inevitable Drilling Down...

If different types of customers were defined, the owner might be able to understand what is happening. What the owner needs to do is not only define the customers, but also to define them relative to the newsletter. What percent of new customers respond? What percent of "old customers" respond? What percent of "best customers" respond?

When thinking about defining new customers, customers, best customers and so on, one concept keeps coming up, and that is "how long." How long has it been since the customer last made a purchase? Surely this concept must have a direct bearing on defining customers; at some point a customer who has not purchased in a long time is no longer really a customer, the owner thinks.

Also, at some point a customer who made a first purchase is no longer a "new customer" – they are just a "customer." A "best customer" would also need some kind of definition involving last purchase date.

For example, customer #1 who purchased $500 in the past month must be more valuable than customer #2 who purchased $500 2 years ago and has not purchased since. It seems to the owner customer #1 is much more likely to buy again than customer #2; if this is true, customer #1 has a higher value to the business, because customer #1 has a higher likelihood to buy even more. This "potential value" makes customer #1 more valuable than customer #2.

The owner's brain was starting to hurt thinking about all these possibilities, and it seemed like time to quit thinking and "do something" about it. Since last purchase date seemed like the most critical element, the owner decided to classify the IMissAsia.com customers by last purchase date, and then take it from there. Perhaps the data would spark some ideas on how to think about and define customers.

The owner decided the easiest way to do this would be to put customers in monthly "buckets" of 30 days each - last purchase date 0 - 30 days ago, last purchase 31 - 60 days ago, last purchase 61 - 90 days ago, and so forth. By creating a standard classification like this, the owner could compare the number and percentage of customers in each bucket month to month, and see what was happening to the customer base. The owner was not quite sure what to do with this information yet, but knew one thing - if the percentage of customers purchasing Recently was low and the percentage not purchasing in a while was high, that could not be a good thing.

The owner completed the calculations and found the following percentages of customers in each "Last Purchase Date" bucket:

What Percentage of Customers Last Purchased How Many Days Ago?

Days Ago	Percentage
0-30	3%
31-60	6%
61-90	10%
91-120	14%
121-150	16%
151-180	20%
181+	31%
	100%

Figure 19: Purchase Recency

The owner of IMissAsia.com was devastated.

Things looked bad, the owner thought, but what did this information really mean, and what could be done with it? It appeared as if the customer base was "sliding downhill" or aging; the largest group are customers who have not purchased for a very long time, almost like people would buy, then give up, and fall down to the bottom of the "purchased recently" barrel.

The owner used to think of all customers as pretty much equal, they were just "customers," and all equally likely to buy at any time. But to see this, the customer base kind of looks like a pyramid in time, with very few people at the top and a huge number at the bottom. What did it mean?

Fellow Drillers, I encourage YOU to do a "30-60-90," as I call it, on your own customer base. You will find it looks very similar in form to the one from IMissAsia.com. Pick any activity - purchases, visits, board postings, game plays - and rank all your customers, not just a group you choose, by how long it has been since they engaged in that activity.

You will find your very own activity "pyramid" in your customer database. Compared with IMissAsia.com, it may be "flatter" or it may be "taller," but you will generally see a much smaller percentage of customers in the most Recent group than you will see in the least Recent group, very often by a factor of 10.

Of course, the real question is, what can you do with this information, how can you change this state of affairs, and how much money can you make doing it?

Pondering this question, the owner went about the usual business tasks for the day. Scanning the new newsletter subscriptions, the owner notes the different sources producing the majority of new subscribers, and then moves on to process orders for the day. Folks, recall that response to the newsletter has been falling, and the owner was pleased to see the latest newsletter generated decent order activity.

As usual, some orders stood out from the rest; the owner recognized repeat buyers and people who had just placed an order Recently. "What makes them do that, I wonder?" thinks the owner. They buy something then they buy something else only a week later. Why don't they buy both at the same time? They could save money on shipping, the owner thinks...

As the owner processed orders, thoughts returned to the 30-60-90 bucket analysis. I have all these orders, day after day, the owner thinks, yet most customers have not bought from me in quite some time. How is this possible? It doesn't make any sense.

Then the owner has a brainstorm: What would the 30-60-90 Last Purchase Date information look like just on people who responded and purchased from the recent newsletter? I could match people who bought from the newsletter with their Last Purchase Date before I sent the newsletter, and then could find out how effective the newsletter is at getting my "lost customers" - those who have not purchased in months - to buy again.

In other words, what percentage of people in each 30-day bucket purchased through the last newsletter I sent out? Perhaps this would provide the clarity needed to demonstrate what this Recency data means, and provide some insight into the kind of action that needs to be taken to keep people buying for a longer time. The owner sorted responders to the newsletter according to the Last Purchase Date before the newsletter was mailed out, with the following results:

Days Ago	All Customers	All Newsletter Responders
0-30	3%	31%
31-60	6%	18%
61-90	10%	18%
91-120	14%	14%
121-150	16%	10%
151-180	20%	6%
181+	31%	3%
	100%	100%

Figure 20: Last Purchase Date Before Newsletter Drop

The owner was slack-jawed. How could this be? Is it possible that (top row) almost 1/3 of the responses came from 3% of customers? That (top two rows together) nearly 50% of the responses came from 9% of customers? The owner's head was swimming! What was the implication here? Is it possible - and just this simple - that the response rate of a customer to the newsletter could be predicted based on how many days ago they last made a purchase? The implications were stunning. One simple calculation; incredible ability to predict purchase behavior.

But what to do with this information?

As the owner of IMissAsia went about the favorite task of the day - reviewing and packing orders - thoughts were on this topic of "doing something" with this Recency info. The owner then noticed orders coming in from the "CRM program" started last month for best customers. Finally, some good news.

It was a very simple idea really - the owner took the time to identify best customers who had not shopped in 180 days and sent them a special discount. This idea came from a friend in town who had a hair salon. It was a really big discount though, and the owner disliked seeing so much margin go out the window - but was happy to have the orders. If the only way to get them to respond was to be aggressive, so be it. After all, it was very targeted, and generated large orders.

All of a sudden, clarity hit the owner like a ton of bricks.

The less Recent a customer is, the less likely they are to respond. So you should be able to "rank" customers by likelihood to respond. But what if customers go through "stages" of being likely to respond, a predictable "cycle"? As the customer drops through 30 day, 60 day, and 90 day Recency, they become less and less likely to respond. With best customers, when they get to 180 days, it takes a huge discount to get them back, and not many even come back. What if I got involved in this "cycle" earlier? Why should I wait for them to get to 180 days before acting?

Right now, the owner thinks, I send the same 10% discount to everybody who gets the newsletter and the response varies by Recency - the more Recent the last purchase, the higher the response rate. So what if I altered the discount by Recency, giving a bigger discount to folks who were less likely to respond - the ones who are less Recent. In other words, vary the discount by the stage of the "cycle" the customer is currently in.

I could probably cut discount costs while increasing response rate, because I would not be giving away as much margin to those most likely to respond, and would be making more aggressive offers to those least likely to respond. Lower discount costs, higher response rates across the entire mailing.

But what is the right discount to offer for each Recency bucket? The more aggressive the discount offer, the higher the response, but higher response means more margin going out the window. Surely there is a "tradeoff" of low discount cost with high response for each Recency bucket, and it is probably different for each bucket - since "normal" response is so different in each Recency bucket. So all I have to do is test each bucket across a range of discounts to find out what discount is most profitable for each of the buckets!

Looking at the buckets, the owner chooses the 91 - 120 bucket to test first because that is where customer response seems to really start trailing off; customers in this part of the "cycle" appear to be the most at risk to never respond again. So the owner divides customers in the 91-120 bucket into 4 equally sized groups, and each group is sent a different discount.

Discount Test: 91 – 120 Day Recency

Discount Offer	5%	10%	15%	20%
Customer Sample	1,000	1,000	1,000	1,000
Response Rate	2%	4%	6%	8%
Responders	20	40	60	80
Average Price	$80	$80	$80	$80
Totals Sales	$1,600	$3,200	$4,800	$6,400
Gross Margin	30%	30%	30%	30%
Gross Profit	$480	$960	$1,440	$1,920
Discount Cost	$80	$320	$720	$1,280
Net Profit Before Media Expense	$400	$640	$720	$640

Figure 21: Discount Ladder Test Segment Performance

The most profitable offer for the 91-120 day Recency bucket, the one that generates the highest response while giving up the least margin dollars, is 15% off - not the 10% off these people were used to seeing. And what is more, in subsequent repeats of this test, 15% off is always the most profitable offer to use with the 91-120 Recency bucket - the outcome of the promotion is consistent.

Well fellow Drillers, you can imagine how excited the owner of IMissAsia was to lower net costs while increasing response rate. And if this approach works for the 91-120 day Recency bucket, it probably works for all the other buckets as well, don't you think?

(Jim's hint - it does).

But all the owner of IMissAsia.com has right now is a more profitable newsletter promotion. The biggest discovery - the one with the most potential to increase profits for IMissAsia.com - still lies right around the bend.

The owner had learned a lot in the past few months, from understanding how to define an "active" customer to predicting the likelihood of a customer to respond to a promotion; from improving the profitability of newsletter promotions to actually being able to predict the profitability in advance based on the Recency buckets. Despite all this, the owner of IMissAsia.com still had not answered the original question that started it all: why was the response rate to newsletter promotions falling while sales remain flat month-to-month?

The owner started packing boxes, thinking about how Recency had proved to be so significant a factor in customer behavior. While packing, the owned recognized the names of best customers, and also the names of some of the new buyers. Why were these new buyer names familiar?

While pondering this question, the owner realized where the names had appeared before - on the daily new subscriber list to the newsletter. Then an idea struck the owner like a bolt of lighting: since Recency of purchase predicted the likelihood to purchase again, is it possible that Recency of subscription could predict the likelihood to make the first purchase? Again with this Recency thing?

The owner's head was now spinning; this was too much, too fast. It was a struggle just to go into the subscription records. Figuring out when Newsletter Responders had joined the newsletter seemed like an insurmountable obstacle. The owner was sweating, looking out at the spreadsheet with barely one eye open, murmuring "too much, too fast." The owner's hand trembled on the keyboard, as the last table join came into view.

And there it was.

Looking Only at **Buyers who are Subscribers**, they subscribed to the
Newsletter How Many Days Before they made a First Purchase?

Days Between Subscribe and First Purchase	Percentage of Buyer - Subscribers
0-30	31%
31-60	18%
61-90	18%
91-120	14%
121-150	10%
151-180	6%
181+	3%
	100%

Figure 22: Newsletter Responders by Sign-up Recency

The owner gasped aloud. How long ago someone subscribed to the newsletter
predicted whether they would respond to the newsletter with a purchase! And
how long ago someone responded to the newsletter and made a purchase
predicted if they would respond to the newsletter and make a purchase again! It
was like a chain of events, a sequence, with the likelihood of a customer to
move to the next step in the sequence at any point in time ruled by the Recency
of the customer for the prior step.

It's that whole "cycle" thing showing up again - customers seem to pass through
"stages" and these stages are predictable based on the previous behavior of the
customer - as long as you know how to measure and track the behavior. If you
are using the wrong metrics, the owner thinks, you simply can't see or take
advantage of these cycles.

Well, fellow Drillers, we know what the owner of IMissAsia.com is talking
about, don't we? It's the Customer LifeCycle, the most powerful tool you could
possibly have to increase the ROI of a marketing campaign and increase the
profitability of a customer. If you understand what a customer is likely to do

before they do it, then you can plan for and customize offerings and campaigns to maximize profitability – a powerful "secret weapon."

Marketing based on the Customer LifeCycle is "event-driven" marketing. You use LifeCycle metrics like Recency to mark or define customer events, and then spend only when you have to, and always at the point of maximum impact. This creates extremely high ROI marketing and service programs, because the targeting mirrors customer behavior.

Most of the buying activity was coming from people who Recently joined the newsletter. Since the number of new people per month joining the newsletter was flat, sales are flat month to month. But as the newsletter list keeps growing each month, this "new blood" - new subscribers who are likely to respond and buy - becomes a smaller and smaller percentage of the total newsletter list. So sales remain flat as response rate is falling.

Newsletter response riddle solved.

But how can you increase profits knowing this? Well, if you offer discounts to people who have just signed up for the newsletter - the people already most likely to purchase - then you probably are giving away margin you don't have to give away. Save your discount budget for those less likely to purchase, customers who are deeper into the LifeCycle, the ones who are "less Recent."

The owner continues to ponder these cycles, with the likelihood of a customer to move to the next step in the sequence at any point in time ruled by the Recency of the customer for the prior step. The owner had read some stuff about CRM and wondered if this "sequence" was what all that CRM noise was about. Maybe the owner should see if the rep who called yesterday "stands in awe" of IMissAssia.com. Perhaps, the owner thinks, I could learn "how to keep customers front and center" without hearing "Five Hundred It Is" from this rep.

No, "CRM" would have to wait. It now appears increasing new subscribers to the newsletter is the most important thing that can be done to increase sales, because Recent newsletter subscribers are the most likely to buy. And after all these discoveries about Recency, the owner wondered if Recency could have something to offer on the newsletter subscription challenge. What do you think?

The owner always tried to follow hot topics or trends talked about in the online community at the site, both in the newsletter and merchandising of the site. The owner felt it was more logical to "put products in front of the traffic" than try to force or bend the traffic to come to the products. Find a group of people and give them products they are already looking for - it's same reason why search marketing works so well for the site. The owner was not sure if this was the right thing to do on the **content** side, but there was really no way to prove anything in this area one way or another. For example, some parts of the site get very high traffic, others lower traffic. Would more newsletter subs be generated if the high traffic areas had more content? If the low traffic areas were downplayed in the navigation? Who knows, and implementing would be a lot of work, so just guessing was not a good idea.

The owner had done some content analysis along these lines. There were 10 major content areas on the site; all the pages in a single area are set up as "Content Groups" in the visitor analysis tool the owner is using. This means the owner can track stats at a macro level for content areas as a whole very easily, instead of having to deal with tracking down individual page views and aggregating them into a report.

The owner used these Content Group reports to detect "hot spots" on the IMissAsia.com site. By looking at the trend in total visits and page views over time, the owner got a good idea of where the interests of the audience were flowing, and used this information to "stand in front of" this topical traffic with articles and products. But was following the traffic really the right idea? Certainly not all traffic is created equal; quantity is not equal to quality. But what else would you look at?

Wouldn't you know it, the owner had just upgraded the visitor analysis tool, and found out that it now supports visitor Recency as a native reporting metric right out of the box. Just in the nick of time, eh?

So, the owner excitedly turns Visitor History on in the analysis tool, and it starts building a record of last visit date for each visitor. Then, looking at the 10 different Content Groups, the owner ran a report on the average Recency (average days since last visit) of visitors to each of the Content Groups. What do you think the owner found? You guessed it. There are dramatic differences in average Recency by Content Group.

In fact, the Content Groups with highest overall traffic generally had the worst average Recency (longest time since last visit), and the low traffic groups had the best average Recency (shortest time since last visit). The owner has just discovered another truism of data-based marketing: if "quality" is defined as likelihood to become a "best customer" over time, often the highest volume / response rate comes from the lowest quality visitors / customers, and the lowest volume / response rate from the highest quality visitors / customers:

Content Group Traffic Rank	Content Group Average Recency
1	36 days
2	32 days
3	24 days
4	29 days
5	27 days
6	23 days
7	14 days
8	17 days
9	7 days
10	4 days

Figure 23: Content Groups, Ranked by Total Traffic and Recency

Well, there's a shocker, thinks the owner, who was getting used to this kind of "slap upside the head" from the Recency metric by now. But it made sense.

The areas with specific, targeted content had the lowest traffic but this traffic was on average more Recent - visitors to these areas didn't just "repeat," they were Recent Repeaters. The high traffic areas had relatively untargeted content so they drew a lot of activity but not a lot of loyalty; after a few visits that was it.

"How interesting" thinks the owner of IMissAsisa.com. Perhaps the high traffic / low loyalty areas are frequented mostly by new visitors and potential customers, where the low traffic / high loyalty areas are frequented primarily by current customers. Clearly there was an actionable idea in this chart, though it would take some more crunching with the visitor analysis tool to draw it out.

"Wait a minute," the owner thinks.   "I have been tracking newsletter subscriptions by Content Group. You don't suppose..."

Well, fellow Driller, can you guess what the owner of IMissAsia.com is on to here? What will the data say? You guessed it. The more Recent visitors are in the Content Group, the higher the conversion of visits into newsletter subscriptions. Here it is, presented as Figure 24:

Content Group Traffic Rank	Content Group Average Recency	Content Group % Visits Subscribing
1	36 days	.2%
2	32 days	.6%
3	24 days	1.1%
4	29 days	.9%
5	27 days	1.4%
6	23 days	1.7%
7	14 days	3.8%
8	17 days	2.1%
9	7 days	5.6%
10	4 days	7.2%

**Figure 24: Content Groups,
by Traffic, Recency, and Newsletter Conversion Rate**

The owner, once again slack-jawed by the power of the Recency metric, sums it all up for us:

"On average, the more Recent the visitor is, the more likely they are to subscribe to the newsletter, relative to other visitors.

The more Recent the newsletter subscriber is, the more likely they are to make a purchase, relative to other newsletter subscribers.

The more Recent the last purchase is, the more likely the buyer is to make another purchase, relative to other buyers."

The owner continues on, a bit breathless with the rush of all this stuff coming together at one time with such fury:

"What I am seeing is that becoming a "best customer" on IMissAsia.com can be seen as a process, one that starts with a visit, moves on to a subscription, then a purchase, and hopefully multiple purchases. I always sort of knew that; now I see it in action. But what's really powerful is I can rank each member of a group

– content visitors, subscribers, buyers - against all the other members of their group for likelihood to move forward in the process using the Recency metric.

Knowing this provides me with three benefits:

1. Having the source of the visitor, subscriber, or buyer, I can "track backwards" and find out what sources (media type / offers) generate visitors most likely to become subscribers, buyers, and multi-buyers - and using Recency, predict which of those are most likely to complete any step in the LifeCycle process on the web site.

2. I can customize communications to the members of each group based on their likelihood to move forward in this LifeCycle using Recency. By addressing specific people with the right message at the right time (like I did with the discount ladder), I will generally get higher response and conversion of the visitor to multi-buyer while lowering my marketing and discount costs.

3. I can track retention and failure to progress in the LifeCycle with Recency, and be proactive about trying to "save" customers who are in the process of defecting. At any point in the visitor - subscriber - buyer - multi-buyer LifeCycle, I can track decreasing likelihood to progress and take special action with those who have high potential or current value based on their source or past buying behavior."

It was late, and the owner was exhausted. No point in trying to map out all the implications of these discoveries now, the owner thinks; this Recency thing was obviously quite powerful and it would take some time and testing a few ideas to fully develop the potential of it. For example, rather than determining "what's hot" just by visit volume, if I look at the Recency of visitors I can make a better guess on whether the issue is important to core customers or casual visitors, and adjust the message and offers appropriately. To think all of this came out of trying to answer one simple question on newsletter response.

Having now discovered the secret of the Recency Chain, the owner was absolutely sure IMissAsia.com could be taken to the next level of profitability. Things are sweet, the owner thinks, as she turns off the light and "heads home" - down the stairs to her living room.

Jim's Note: The capability to track visitor Recency (or Latency) has up until 2003 been addressed with either a home-built system (all you need is a way to recognize users and store last visit date) or a data warehouse solution like WebTrends Intelligence Suite, CoreMetrics, Quadstone, or one of several others. In 2003, WebTrends introduced Visitor History in the Enterprise Version of their Reporting Center product. However, as we go to press in mid 2004, the availability of Visitor History tracking without building it yourself or getting into a solution that has too much horsepower in other areas for what you need has been mitigated. In other words, it just got a lot cheaper and easier to track visitor history - and also to have these critical metrics integrated into the rest of your web site reporting, along with critical visitor source data.

WebTrends 7 provides Visitor History (they call it Segmentation Analysis) capabilities across all 3 editions (Small Business, Professional, Enterprise) of the product line, storing Recency and Latency data, plus many more "source" variables such as First or Most Recent Search Engine & Phrase, Campaign, Referrer, etc. Intellitracker and ICEtracks out of the UK also provide reporting on visitor Recency. Of course, if you warehouse your web traffic data, you can create your own Latency and Recency metadata as you see fit.

Bottom line: You've got no excuse now... get out there and start Drillin'.

Chapter 14
Cash Flow Marketing

Where Did RFM Come From?

Have you ever heard somebody refer to his or her customer list as a "file"? If you have, you were probably listening to someone who has been around the Data-Driven block a few times. Before computers (huh?), catalog companies used to keep all their customer information on 3 x 5 cards.

They'd rifle through this deck of cards to select customers for each mailing, and when a customer placed an order, they would write it on the customer's card. These file cards as a group became known as "the customer file," and even after everything became computerized, the name stuck around.

Who cares? It happens that while going through these cards by hand, and writing down orders, the catalog folks began to see patterns emerge. There was an exchange taking place, and the data was speaking. What the data said to them, and what they heard, were 3 things about customer behavior:

1. Customers who purchased **recently** were more likely to buy again versus customers who had not purchased in a while (you get Recency now, right?)

2. Customers who purchased **frequently** were more likely to buy again versus customers who had made just one or two purchases

3. Customers who **spent the most money** in total were more likely to buy again. The most valuable customers tended to continue to become even more valuable.

So the catalog folks tested this concept, the idea past behavior could predict future results. They tracked how the group of people who qualified for the 3 categories above responded to their mailings, and compared this response to the group of people who didn't qualify. It always worked. The group who qualified for the 3 categories above always had higher response rates than the group who didn't qualify. It worked so well they cut back on mailing to people who didn't qualify, **and spent the money saved on mailing more often to the group who did qualify.** And their sales exploded, while their costs remained the same or went down. They were increasing their marketing efficiency and effectiveness by targeting to the most responsive customers.

That's ROI thinking, folks. Costs shrinking while revenues rise. You may have guessed by now what this data-speaking language is called today: RFM, or **Recency** (# 1 above), **Frequency** (# 2 above), **Monetary Value** (# 3 above). It's one of the most basic of all the behavioral models ever developed, and yet one of the most powerful.

The more **Recently** someone has engaged in an activity, the more likely they are to do it again. The more **Frequently** someone has engaged in an activity, the more likely they are to do it again. And the more **Monetary Value** someone has created by purchasing, the more likely they are to continue to purchase. These concepts are the beating heart of Data-Driven marketing. They are the foundation on which the entire Drilling Down marketing process is built.

Remember our old friend, the portfolio approach for managing customers?

	Low Potential Value, High Current Value Grow These Customers	High Potential Value, High Current Value Keep These Customers
Current Value ↑	Low Potential Value, Low Current Value Should You Spend Money Here?	High Potential Value, Low Current Value Grow These Customers
	Potential Value ➡	

Figure 25: The Customer Value Portfolio

When you are working only with Latency or Recency (or both), you are looking exclusively at the Potential Value part of the equation. When you add

Frequency and Monetary, you are now also addressing the Current Value part of the equation. RFM integrates both the Current Value and Potential Value concepts into a single, standardized method of ranking the value of customers to the business – now, and in the future. For this reason, the RFM model can be used as a predictor of the LifeTime Value of the customer.

RFM works everywhere, in virtually every business. **And it works for just about any kind of "action-oriented" behavior you are trying to get a customer to repeat or not repeat**, whether it's purchases, visits, sign-ups, surveys, games, calls to a service center, complaint management, error detection – just about anything where a human decision has to be made and an action (or non-action) taken. I'm going to use purchases and visits as examples for the rest of the book. If you need help understanding how RFM can apply to your business, e-mail me: RFMhelp@jimnovo.com just as hundreds of others have. Or check the web site, http://www.jimnovo.com where there are dozens of industry-specific examples.

Just as Latency and Recency can be used to evaluate a single customer or segments of customers, so can RFM. One application of RFM is Hurdle Rate Analysis, where "hurdles" are selected for R, F, and M, and the entire customer base is evaluated against these hurdles as a group. A **Hurdle Rate** is simply **the percentage of your customers who have at least a certain activity level for R, F, and M**. It's the percentage of customers who have visited since a certain date, have bought or visited a certain number of times, or have purchased a certain amount. Understanding this Hurdle Rate application will help you understand the overall concept of RFM, so next up is a quick example of using Hurdle Rates; a more detailed example is provided later in the book.

Let's say you know some things about your good customers from looking at their sales records. From comparing a few good customers, you see the following patterns in behavior:

> Good customers who haven't visited or purchased in the past 30 days seem to start slipping away. They tend to stop buying or visiting. You decide to use 30 days as the Recency Hurdle.

> Good customers have purchased 10 times; you decide to use 10 orders as the Frequency Hurdle.

Good customers have spent around $500; you decide to use $500 as the Monetary Value Hurdle.

You then check to see what percentage of the customer base is "over the Hurdle" for each of the variables R, F, and M. What percent have purchased or visited in the last 30 days? What percent have purchased over 10 times or visited over 10 times? What percent have spent over $500 in total?

Once you establish these baseline Hurdle Rates (% of customers over the Hurdle) you simply re-check the customer base each week or month, and determine the percentage over each Hurdle. Over 8 weeks a healthy business would look like the following Figure 26:

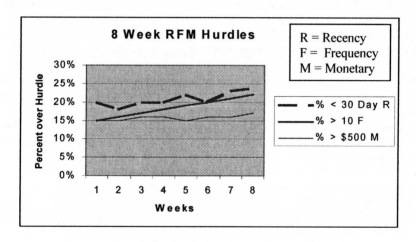

**Figure 26: Percent of the Customer Base
Over each Hurdle by Week is Growing!**

The lines in the chart show the percentage of customers over each Hurdle tends to be rising over time. The percent of customers who have purchased or visited in the last 30 days (Recency, broken heavy line) is rising. The percent of customers who have purchased over 10 times or visited over 10 times (Frequency, heavy solid line) is rising. The percent of customers who have spent over $500 in total (Monetary Value, light solid line) is also rising. Business is looking good!

If the percentage of customers over each hurdle is growing, your business is healthy and thriving. This is great news. You're adding customers who have a high Potential Value, and converting low Current Value customers to higher Current Value customers. If the opposite is true, and the lines are sloping down over time, well, you better get going and do something about it, while you still have a business. We talk a lot about how to do this later in the book. Better yet, you will learn how to prevent it from happening.

RFM in Action: Individual Customer Scores

How is RFM scoring at the individual customer level implemented? Customers are scored, they receive a ranking based on each of the attributes of RFM. Simplistically, you need a customer's last purchase or visit date (Recency), total units of activity (orders or visits) you want to measure, (Frequency), and the total dollars sold to them (Monetary Value). Let's just call them R, F, and M going forward, OK? **R = Recency, F = Frequency, M= Monetary Value.**

You then sort customers from highest to lowest on each of R, F, and M, then assign a numeric rank to them. These rankings are combined in some way to produce an overall "score" for the customer.

Let's say you have 100 customers. For R, you would sort all your customers by last purchase (visit) date, most recent to least recent in descending order; then you would label the top customer "100," the next customer "99," the next customer "98," and so on to the bottom customer labeled "1."

For F, you would sort all your customers by total instances of action (visits, orders, downloads, log-ins), most frequent to least frequent in descending order; then you would label the top customer "100," the next customer "99," the next customer "98," and so on to the bottom customer labeled "1."

For M, you would sort all your customers by total dollars spent, highest to lowest; then you would label the top customer "100," the next customer "99," the next customer "98," and so on to the bottom customer labeled "1."

Using this rather ugly process, (I'll show you a much easier version later) each customer ends up with 3 numbers identifying how they ranked compared to all the other customers on R, F, and M. The customer with a rank of 100 in Recency (the most recent buyer), 100 in Frequency (the most actions taken), and 100 in Monetary Value (the most dollars bought) would be your best customer.

This customer would have a **score of 100-100-100**. A 50-50-50 customer is the "average" customer in terms of R, F, and M out of these 100 customers.

If you don't have an "M" (Monetary Value) for your customer action because you're not a commerce site or are focused on service issues, don't worry; you can use just R and F very effectively by themselves, as you will see later. The important thing for you to understand at this point is how customer RFM scores are created — it's a ranking of **each customer** on R, F, and M **compared to all your other customers**. These separate rankings are then combined to produce an overall RFM **score** for each customer in the database.

Once scored, it's easy to look at the customer base (and your business) in terms of the scores. These scores, or changes in scores, become the trigger points for your highest ROI marketing activities. High scoring customers tend to repeat the action being profiled; low scoring customers tend not to. A customer with a rising score is (usually) becoming a better customer and you want to encourage them, let them "win" at the customer game. A customer with a falling score is beginning to lose interest, and if it's a valuable customer, you should hit them hard with a marketing or service program before they stop purchasing / visiting.

Have you heard of the 80 / 20 rule? In many businesses, 20% of the customers generate 80% of the sales or service activity. Well, guess what? The 20% of your customers that represent 80% of your sales or activity are likely among the most recent (R), most frequent (F), and highest Monetary Value (M) customers you have. If you can identify your high RFM customers, you will know who is most likely to respond to your request for an action, to order, visit, or sign-up for something at the site.

But here's the big secret and where much of the money is made: Think about a high RFM customer who all of a sudden stops buying or visiting. This customer's R (Recency) would begin to drop, relative to other customers who continued to buy or visit. What does this mean? You guessed it; they are getting ready to boogie on you (or already have). So RFM can be used not only to target customers most likely to repeat, but also, and more importantly, to target people **likely to stop an activity completely.**

This means RFM scores can be used to assess the potential value of your business. The best 20% of your customers all have high RFM scores, and your weakest customers have low RFM scores. Just looking at the scores, and how the scores change over time, can tell you whether your business is moving in a positive or negative direction.

Hurdle Rates, RFM Scores, and Lifetime Value

Why are Hurdle Rates and RFM scores important? Because RFM is closely related to another Data-Driven Marketing concept: LifeTime Value (LTV). **LTV is the expected net profit a customer will contribute to your business as long as the customer remains a customer** – the sum of Current and Potential Value.

If a customer has a high RFM score, they are already a "best customer" **and** are likely to continue contributing to your revenues and / or visits; they're a satisfied customer, and visit and/or purchase often. For this reason, **consistently high RFM score customers will tend to have high LifeTime Values; consistently low RFM score customers will tend to have low LTV.**

RFM techniques can be used as a proxy for the future profitability of your business. If the percentage of customers as a group over the RFM hurdles is shrinking, the current and potential value of your sales and visits is shrinking. If the percentage of customers over the RFM Hurdles as a group is rising, the current and potential value of your sales and / or visits is growing. If a customer with a high RFM score begins to drop in score, the potential value of their sales and / or visits is shrinking. If a customer with a low RFM score begins to rise in score, the potential value is of their sales and/ or / visits is growing as well.

This makes sense because high RFM score customers are already valuable, are most likely to continue to purchase and visit, AND they are most likely to respond to your marketing or service promotions; **these customers likely have the highest LifeTime Value.** The opposite is true for low RFM score customers; they currently have low value, are the least likely to purchase or visit again, AND the least likely to respond to marketing promotions, **so these customers tend to have low LifeTime Values (LTV).**

High scores represent future business potential, because the customers are willing and interested in doing business with you, and have high LTV. Low scores represent dwindling business opportunity, low LTV, and are a flag something needs to be done with those customers to increase their value.

And let's not forget our other old friend, Friction. I bet I don't even have to tell you about the relationship between RFM scores and Friction, but just in case, I will. As with the Recency metric, falling RFM scores indicate rising friction, and rising RFM scores indicate falling friction. What is the implication when you see a high RFM score customer drop in score like a stone? Rising Friction, and a red flag for defection. It's a trip wire for taking action with a customer retention program, you are about to lose a best customer. What is the implication when you see a low RFM score customer rise in score like a rocket? Falling Friction, and a green flag for "future best customer." It's a trip wire for taking action with value creation and enhancement programs like up-sell / cross-sell, VIP Service, and introduction into a higher loyalty program "tier."

One point left on RFM for you to know: is it possible that a high RFM score customer will not have high LTV? Yes. RFM is all about activity and the **revenue** implications of that activity, whereas LifeTime Value goes a step further and nets out all the **costs** of the revenue generating activity. If the cost to acquire and maintain a customer is higher than the revenue generated, the customer has a negative LTV. Examples of these types of customers would include customers with a high return rate, customers who were very costly to acquire, and customers who are "high maintenance" and require a lot of after-the-sale service and hand-holding.

OK, you've had a major dose of Data-Driven lingo. Let's move on to some issues pertaining to interactive behavior and RFM. But first, here is a summary of the terms just discussed:

RFM (Recency, Frequency, Monetary Value) is a customer scoring model used to assign a score to **each customer** representing his or her current value and likelihood to continue any particular type of behavior (potential value) – orders, visits, etc. – **compared to all your other customers.** The higher the RFM score, the more likely it is the customer will repeat a behavior and respond to promotions or encouragement to continue the behavior. RFM is about "top line" activity and doesn't take into account any costs of doing business, like how much it cost to acquire the customer.

LTV (LifeTime Value) is the sum of current and potential net value of a customer to your business, and takes into account both revenue and expense considerations. High RFM customers tend to have high LTV's, but this is not always true; it depends on the cost of selling to the customer and maintaining the customer relationship.

The nirvana customer is one who has a high RFM score (current and potential value are high) and has a high LTV (expenses to acquire and service the customer are average or lower than average). These customers are already "best customers," have a high propensity for revenue generating activity in the future, and are inexpensive to acquire and maintain.

Because of the link between a high RFM score and high LTV for a customer, **Hurdle Rate percentages on a group of customers, or RFM scores on individual customers**, can be used as a measure of the future profitability of a business. When the percentage of customers over the Hurdle for R, F, and M is increasing, future revenues will also increase, and marketing or service programs will have higher response rates. When it's dropping, future business will decrease, and response rates to marketing or service programs will be lower.

Please note: In some service programs, the relationship of RFM score to LTV could be reversed, and high RFM scores will mean low LTV (recall the Help Desk examples from the Latency Toolkit chapter titled "Trip Wire Marketing"). For example, if you are scoring trouble call activity, high scoring customers may be both already costly to the company (low current value) and highly likely to repeat expensive service requests (low potential value). These customers could end up with very low LifeTime Values. As with the other earlier service examples, the interpretation of when "high score" = "good" depends on the activity being scored; if you are scoring activity that is costly to the company, "high score" probably equals "bad," as in the customer is already very costly and likely to get even more costly.

Chapter 15
A Tweak for Interactive Customers

When computers came on the scene, people could literally study hundreds of variables that go into predicting action-oriented decisions. This "modeling" of customer data was not possible until computers, and it's very expensive. Today they call it "data-mining". Here's a simplistic explanation of the process: Modelers take every piece of data you have on the customer and rank the data for ability to predict behavior. They would look at payment types, visit time of day, product category, price paid, survey results, and so forth, and try to determine which of these variables was best at predicting a future activity.

Know what the modelers found? In every "likely to respond" model I have seen, Recency, Frequency, or both ranked near the top, if not at the top, of the list of all data analyzed for ability to predict behavior. In fact, Recency and Frequency in some form often supply 80% or more of the predictive power of a "likely to repeat an action" (visit again, order again, etc.) model.

Look, modeling is a good thing, and I've used many of them, when there's a budget for it and when you have done the underlying work — when you're already using Recency and Frequency to the best of your ability. In fact, most good modelers will want to see the results of marketing you have done using Recency and Frequency to help them build their models – Recency and Frequency are indeed fundamental to the modeling concept.

But you can do your own "modeling" using just Recency and Frequency and increase your sales, visits, or any action item tremendously while cutting your marketing costs – and without spending a ton of money on models.

But hey, what happened to M, Monetary Value? What's this Recency-Frequency business, where is RFM? Why doesn't M make it to the top of the modeler's models for ability to predict behavior, like R and F? Glad you asked the question. You must be paying attention.

It turns out that F, or Frequency, represents the power of M, in most cases. The modelers found this little gem. If you have R and F, M doesn't usually make it to the top of the list. Let's think about it. The more Frequent a customer is, the larger their M will be. M acts as a "check" on F, and can provide additional insight into F, but in many cases, the power of M to predict behavior is at least partially represented by F.

This idea of F representing M happens to be even more powerful in interactive businesses, where the customers are "in control" and have the ability to take action whenever they want to very easily. You can only take action on a catalog if you receive it, or take action in a store if you get in the car and go there.

But on the web, you can take action whenever you want to. This ability to take action immediately whenever you want to results in more "fickle" consumers, able to change their minds more rapidly and more often. When M is used with R and F to create a customer rank or score, it has the effect of smoothing out changes in R and F, changes that can happen very rapidly. But you probably don't want these changes smoothed out; you want to know when they happen — fast. So Recency and Frequency alone end up being more powerful predictors of interactive behavior without using M in the mix **if you want to be able to uncover and react more quickly to potential customer defections**.

Another problem with M is it can confuse the ranking of customers over short time periods, causing customers to be "mislabeled." For example, a **new customer** who is taking action Recently and Frequently but has a **low Monetary Value** could be a future best customer. If you used the low M with the high R and high F to create the customer score, this customer would get a **lower score** for a while and look less valuable, until the M got larger. On the Internet, you don't want to wait for this to happen, you want to recognize the potential of this customer as quickly as you can.

The flip side of this example is a long-time customer, with a **high Monetary Value**, but without any Recent activity. This is usually a customer who has likely already defected; if you used the high M with R and F in the ranking, this customer would have a **higher score** for a while, and you might not notice the defection until it was too late to do anything.

The following is a dirty little secret of interactive behavior:

The customer lifecycle for interactive businesses is more exaggerated than for traditional Data-Driven businesses. The behavior ramps up faster at the beginning of the cycle, but then falls off faster into the end of the cycle.

Why does this happen? It's human nature. People experiencing interactivity have short attention spans and wide access to alternatives. They tend to "gorge" themselves on a new thing **when they control access to it**, overdoing the behavior in an accelerated way. This borrows activity from what would normally be future behavior, and when they finish gorging themselves, they drop off a cliff (behavior-wise, that is).

So instead of a slow smooth ramp up and a slow smooth taper down over time, interactive behavior ramps up steeply and falls off quickly. You can see why in this environment, it is imperative to keep an eye on Recency and Frequency of visits, purchases, or whatever behavior you are looking at. Once customers start to slide in activity, it may be very difficult to start them up again. To get the most you can from the customer / prospect before they disappear completely, you have to take action quickly with a promotion, service offering, or other contact strategy – or give up on the customer. If you wait too long, the customer will have already defected and it will be too late.

For these reasons, you don't want the data, or customer scores, smoothed out. You want to see change when it happens. By dropping M from RFM, and just using R and F, **(let's call it RF from now on)** you hype up the sensitivity of the original RFM model. You need it to react faster to change in interactive environments where behavior can change rapidly.

And finally, for many types of behavior, there is no "M," no financial component to the transactions being profiled. This is particularly true in service environments and many online applications.

So we're going to focus on Recency and Frequency, for these reasons:

1. R and F are the most powerful variables for predicting behavior; M is the weakest, and is typically represented in F anyway. Also, M doesn't apply to non-purchase related activities like visits, so it has limited usefulness on the 'Net for many web site managers.

2. R and F are even more important when looking at interactive behavior because of the exaggerated changes interactivity creates

3. It's easier to work with 2 variables than with 3 when you're just starting out with this stuff, and if you knew all about how to use behavioral modeling, you wouldn't have bought this darn book!

Trust me, dropping M will make our lives a lot easier, and it will take a lot less of your time to produce sales generating and money saving action plans. If you have the programming chops or raw desire to include M, be my guest. My suggestion is to become familiar with the power of RF first, then graduate to RFM. The extra lift you get by using M may not be worth the effort until you understand what RF can do for you and how to take action on the data.

A couple more things about Frequency (F) and Monetary Value (M), before we say goodbye to M and move on to putting these ideas into action with your data:

If a customer is buying only your very cheapest stuff frequently, they could have a high F with a lower than average M. And it sometimes happens, resulting in an RF ranking for the customer higher than it should be – any customer who buys only real cheap items probably has low LTV. This is the way M acts as a "check" on F. But this is not the normal case, so on average, F is a good proxy for M. If it occurs, it's usually in a very small percentage of the customer base, so it's not really an issue, particularly in an interactive business.

Frequency or F can be defined in a number of different ways, and the best way to define it for your business can depend on the kind of data you collect and how you believe customers / prospects behave. In most cases, you will want to use the core or basic transaction "unit" that your company measures success with to count Frequency – orders, visits, calls, etc. Since frequency is used to determine Current Value, units should be directly tied to revenues or costs (negative value). The most common way Frequency (and Monetary) are tracked is "Life to Date" – units since the date the customer became a customer. However, this is not required, and you can use "past 12 months" or whatever makes sense for your business, as long as you **are consistent in applying your definition**. Be aware: if you use a time period like "past 12 months" you are screening your data by Recency **prior to scoring;** make sure you understand what this could mean to the outcome of the scoring. Generally, this approach will raise the importance of Potential Value and decrease the importance of Current Value.

If everybody talks about how many "orders" or "visits" you had last week, these are probably the units you want to use for F. If people are focused on "items sold" or "page views," then these sub-units are the ones to use. This decision on which unit to use for F has to do with what you might call "granularity," and what the focus or intent of the scoring effort is.

If your business has a lot of simple transactions, you probably want to use these transactions as "F." If your business has fewer but more complex transactions, you might want to use the individual line items of these transactions for F. In most retail situations and in traditional RFM analysis, "orders" would be used for F, since "more orders" are what we want from the customer and your scoring should be focused on "orders." If you choose "items" for F, the lowest level you want to use is a SKU (e.g. ordering a box of 1,000 paper clips is not 1,000 Frequency units, it is 1 Frequency unit). In certain B2B and service situations, "orders" are expected (or contractual), routine, and infrequent, but each order is complex and has many items or issues within it. In these cases, and especially if the real business focus and leverage is in increasing or decreasing the number of line items in an order, then these item units should be used for F.

If the transaction unit is so Frequent it is overwhelming to analyze (typically when the transaction value is small, as with page views) you might consolidate these transactions to a larger unit (such as a visit). In a service center, you may expect a number of calls to be made for **each** service incident but the issue of focus is really "incident," not the number of calls received. Since you want to focus on decreasing (or perhaps increasing) "incidents," you should use "incidents" as the unit for F, not calls. Think about the focus of the scoring effort and the business issues involved, and use the most appropriate unit for F.

If you only have sales for a customer (M) and not the number of orders or total units sold (F), then M will do. Just substitute the total sales for a customer (M) for units (F) wherever you see me use F in the rest of the book. Using RM instead of RF is a valid approach and will work tons better than anything you're using now, though probably not quite as well as RF, depending on your business and your goals. So don't feel left out, go for it!

You say,

"Great! Very cool. Ready to go. Finally, we get to DO something! But, um, database? Customer database? Ah, I have a bunch of sales records, single transactions, but I don't have a database of them. I mean, I save them, but they're not all together, you know? And wait, I get the concept of RF-M, but how do I use it for anything? You said you would show me how! I want my money back!"

Cool your jets man, that's next.

Chapter 16
No Customer Database? How to Set Up
a Spreadsheet to Score Customers

Quick Start – For those of you familiar with spreadsheet import operations and pivot tables, all we're doing here is importing the customer transactions, and aggregating multiple transactions for the same customer together. For each customer, the most recent date of activity is chosen, and the units of activity (orders or items, visits) are summed, so that each customer has one consolidated record of their transactions, with most recent activity date and a sum of the Frequency units). The final product would look something like Figure 27:

Customer ID	Date of Most Recent Activity	Total Units of Activity
30	9/1/00	3
5	8/6/00	12
3	5/6/00	20
22	5/6/00	5
45	5/5/00	12
8	3/19/00	9
26	2/10/00	4
6	2/3/00	4
18	4/6/99	2
54	4/5/99	32
177	3/11/99	11
7	2/4/99	3

Figure 27: Sample of Aggregated Customer Records

If you understand what you just read, and can generate a file with customer ID, most recent order (visit) date, and total Frequency units in some other way, you don't have to read the rest of this chapter. After you create the file, if you wish to score the customers in a spreadsheet, export the file to a spreadsheet. Then skip to the next chapter "How to Score Your Customers" for the RF scoring instructions. **End Quick Start**

You now have a basic background in the theory of using customer data to increase profits. You're excited about Drilling Down, like they say in all the conferences and newsletters, about Profiling, no, Modeling your customers. You want to know HOW it's done. The first thing you have to do is build the Scoring Database.

Building the Scoring Database

There are many different approaches to creating customer databases, depending on the resources available, format of the data stored, operating system in use, etc., so I won't try to get into all the specific methods. There are far too many possible combinations.

The following is an outline of the general process and where you need to be when it's finished. We'll tackle it at the most basic resource level – a Microsoft Excel spreadsheet, very minimal formulas and functions, and an hour of the CEO/CIO/CMO/only employee's time. If you understand it at this level, it should be easy to build a more sophisticated (read: less manual labor involved) process yourself or by hiring an Excel / Access programmer to do it for you.

Or, for a basic version of the database creation and customer scoring we discuss in this chapter and the next, download the Drilling Down software at http://www.jimnovo.com/home/ddsoft.htm and follow the ReadMe instructions. If scoring your customers as fast as possible is your primary concern use the software; if you can give up some speed for more flexibility, follow the book method. It's probably a good idea to read the next 2 chapters even if you use the software; you will want to know the basics of how it processes and scores the customer data.

First, we walk through an overview of the process. If you survive that, a step-by-step explanation follows.

Process Overview

In order to do customer modeling, you have to consolidate all the transactions pertaining to one customer to a **Customer Scoring Record**, or single line of data containing all the customer information, usually rolled up and imported from different sources. You can't compare or rank customers based on a list of transactions, the transactions have to be consolidated, or summarized, in some standard way so they can be compared with each other. This is generally done by using the customer ID as a key to pull summaries of activity from different databases into the Customer Scoring Record. These summaries would then be updated at some interval, depending on how much data you generate and what your time frame is for measuring activity. All of these Customer Scoring Records taken together are the **Customer Scoring Spreadsheet (Database)**.

You want to "roll-up" all your transactions from the same source to the single customer level. By "from the same source," I mean all the transactions having the same format and fields, usually generated by a single system. It's likely you may have data in different databases you would like to analyze; you may roll-up data by source first before combining the data sources. Orders / items might be in one database and visits (page views) in another, for example. You would summarize each at the customer ID level then import the result into the Customer Scoring Record.

Assuming you have a customer ID, system ID, or cookie ID unique to each customer, you would run a simple mathematical process to look at all the transactions for each customer (orders, entries in the log file, etc.) in a data source, and produce a single value for the chosen fields for each customer.

The process could be a selection of one piece of data, as in "most recent date" (R), the method used to create the **Recency score**. A simple sum of all orders or visits (page views) made (F), as in "total units," is used to create the **Frequency Score**. Some fields in the transaction, such as internal codes, name of customer and so forth, you would not deal with at all – they're not relevant to RF analysis. The idea is to create a single record for each customer representing his or her activity over a period of time.

The Real Deal

Sound like a mouthful? OK, let's break it down and go through some specific examples of how to do this.

First, a word about importing data into your spreadsheet. There are many different data formats, and many ways to approach the import, depending on your equipment and software. Spreadsheets generally have excellent import capabilities, and extensive help functionality. Before you proceed, make sure you understand what kind of format your files are in (the file ending is usually the key to this, like .csv, .txt, .dbf, .htm, .dif, and so forth) and how to import this format into the spreadsheet you are using.

You may have to convert or export your files from the system where they reside into a format the spreadsheet can import. There are tons of utilities for this and much information on the Internet if you need help beyond the spreadsheet help.

Let's move on. We will use sales records as an example, but the following would work with any type of activity records. You have a bunch of individual sales transactions, or maybe a file of them, or maybe a database of them.

These transactions may include date of order, number of units sold, and revenue per order, among other things, such as name and address. Let's use these transactions to create a database for RF analysis. Please note that if you have more than 65,000 transactions, you will have to break them up into more than one spreadsheet and unify them after they are processed. If you do have this many, you really should be using MS Access, Oracle, SQL Server, or some other method anyway (get real, will you? This is a business!)

Import these transaction records, or files, or the database, into a spreadsheet so that each customer transaction is on a different row. If the import is successful, you should see each transaction as a row in the spreadsheet, with each piece of information in the transaction (Customer ID, Date of Activity, Units of Activity, Address, and so on) in it's own column. If you have several months or weeks of these files, import the others as well into the same spreadsheet.

You can delete any columns with data you don't need for RF analysis or keep them if you wish, depending on how you will generate a promotion. If you can just export customer ID's and pick up their email address or any other data from another database, you don't really need to keep the address in your RF analysis table. If it's easier to keep the address with the customer, fine.

If you have any characteristics like survey data or demographics you'd like to use later on and it will be difficult to match it up later using the Customer ID, keep that data. The minimum you need is customer ID, date of activity (R), and orders / visits or units sold / page views (F), and that's the example I will show you (the Drilling Down software also uses only this minimum required data). For the 3-D guys out there, you'd also include sales (M) in the spreadsheet.

After you do the import, it will probably look like Figure 28 on the next page:

Customer ID	Activity Date	Units
3	1/5/00	5
3	4/6/00	5
3	6/6/00	5
6	7/13/00	4
3	8/15/00	5
5	8/26/00	6
7	6/15/00	3
5	4/25/00	6
8	5/1/00	2
18	7/6/00	2
8	8/4/00	7
45	3/3/99	1
22	3/6/00	3
45	6/17/00	1
54	7/1/00	32
22	8/6/00	2
26	7/15/00	4
45	8/5/00	10
30	9/1/00	3
42	6/8/00	2
126	6/4/00	1
52	6/2/00	1
177	6/21/00	11

Figure 28: Raw (Not Summary) Imported Customer Records

I used the labels Customer ID, Activity Date, and Units to represent the different types of data. You can use whatever you want, but the following description will use these labels. You might also have additional columns with names, addresses and so forth. I won't be showing those for the sake of clarity. Note there are multiple records for the same customer in this spreadsheet, so we have to figure out how to aggregate the units and select the most recent date. Also note for this example, we are using multiple units in a transaction – there was more than one visit, page view, or item ordered. If you are scoring orders, this column would probably be filled with 1's, except in the case of a customer placing multiple orders in the same day, which certainly does happen.

We're going to use a Microsoft Excel Pivot Table to aggregate all these individual transactions to the customer ID level and choose the most Recent transaction date for each customer. We will create 2 Pivot Tables, one for Recency and one for Frequency, and since both are sorted by customer ID, paste those results together to get a list of customer ID's, with no duplicates, each having the most recent transaction date and units (orders, items, visits, page views, surveys, downloads, etc.).

I'll say again, at the risk of boring you: this is the simplest and most accessible way for the average person to aggregate and create the spreadsheet you need to score your customers. It is NOT the most elegant way to do it, and if you have anything more than fundamental spreadsheet skills (how to write macros, use functions, etc.) you should be able to write a small program to handle this task. You could also use MS Access, or use the Drilling Down Software. But the point of the book was to show any hack with few basic skills how to do it, so that's what we're going to do. For the more talented, program away!

Put your cursor in a cell within the data, pull down the Data menu at the top of the spreadsheet, and click on Pivot Table Report. A wizard window pops up. Select "Excel list or database" from this Step 1 page, and then click on Next. If you put your cursor in the data table before you started the wizard, the data should be selected. If not, select the data as your range for the Step 2 wizard page. Click the Next button.

In the Step 3 wizard page, drag the customer ID box on the right side of the page and drop it on the diagram where it says "ROW." Drag the Most Recent Date box on the right side of the page and drop it where it the diagram says "DATA." Double click this box and you'll get a menu, with Count pre-selected. Select "Max" and click OK to close the box. Ignore the Units box for the moment. Click Next, and from the Step 4 choices, select the "new worksheet" radio button if it isn't already selected. Click Finish.

You should get a new spreadsheet. The date field may be converted to a computer language date; you can change it. Highlight the cells this row, choose Format > Cells, highlight Date on the menu, and choose a date format you prefer. Your data table should look something like Figure 29 on the next page, with the records sorted in ascending order by Customer ID:

Max of Activity Date	
Customer ID	Total
3	8/15/00
5	8/26/00
6	7/13/00
7	6/15/00
8	8/4/00
18	7/6/00
22	8/6/00
26	7/15/00
30	9/1/00
42	6/8/00
45	8/5/00
52	6/2/00
54	7/1/00
126	6/4/00
177	6/21/00
Grand Total	9/01/00

**Figure 29: Pivot Table of Most
Recent Activity Date, Sorted by Customer ID**

Go back to your first spreadsheet and click on a cell in the data.

Pull down the Data menu at the top of the spreadsheet, and click on Pivot Table Report. A wizard window pops up. Select "Excel list or database" from this Step 1 page, and then click on Next.

If you put your cursor in the data table before you started the wizard, the data should be selected. If not, select the data as your range for the Step 2 wizard page. You will get a screen asking if it's OK to base the new table on the previous one. Click yes. Click Next.

In the Step 3 wizard page, drag the customer ID box on the right side of the page and drop it on the diagram where it says "ROW." Drag the Units box on the right side of the page and drop it where it the diagram says "DATA." Click Next, and from the Step 4 choices, select the "new worksheet" radio button if it isn't already selected. Click Finish.

You should get a new spreadsheet, with Units summed at the Customer ID level. Your data table should look something like Figure 30 below, with the records in the spreadsheet sorted in ascending order by Customer ID.

Sum of Units	
Customer ID	Total
3	20
5	12
6	4
7	3
8	9
18	2
22	5
26	4
30	3
42	2
45	12
52	1
54	32
126	1
177	11
Grand Total	121

Figure 30: Pivot Table of Total Activity, Sorted by Customer ID

Now we're going to combine the two. Click on Insert > Worksheet to create a new worksheet. Go to the data from the first Pivot Table (Most Recent Date), highlight the Customer ID's and Dates (ignore the Total row), Copy, then switch to your new empty sheet and paste. Go to the second Pivot Table (Sum of Units), highlight the units (without Total), Copy, and then return to the sheet you pasted Most Recent Date to, put your cursor in the cell immediately to the right of the first record, and click Paste. You should end up with something like Figure 31 on the next page. Label your columns if you want. That's it! You created a Customer Scoring Spreadsheet (database) of your customers, with most recent date and total units of activity. Now let's score your customers.

Customer ID	Most Recent Activity	Units of Activity
3	8/15/00	20
5	8/26/00	12
6	7/13/00	4
7	6/15/00	3
8	8/4/00	9
18	7/6/00	2
22	8/6/00	5
26	7/15/00	4
30	9/1/00	3
42	6/8/00	2
45	8/5/00	12
52	6/2/00	1
54	7/1/00	32
126	6/4/00	1
177	6/21/00	11

Figure 31: Combined Recency and Frequency Pivot Tables

Chapter 17
How to Score Your Customers

OK, you have your Customer Scoring Database, and all the transactions are rolled up at the Customer ID level with the most recent transaction date and total units of activity.

We're going to use a statistical concept known as **quintiles**. A quintile is 1/5th (20%) of a **population ranked by an attribute**. All five 20% quintiles would cover 100% of your customers. The top (best, most recent or highest units) 20% quintile is usually labeled 5, the next 20% lower is labeled 4, the next 20% lower is labeled 3, and so on.

To produce the RF Score, we need to sort your customer database by most recent date, in descending order, and label each customer with a quintile score between 5 (top) and 1 (bottom) for Recency. Then we do the same thing for units, creating a second quintile score between 5 and 1 for Frequency. The combination of these two quintile scores is the RF score for the customer.

Again, there are those of you out there who could write macros or use functions to do this. Just sort, divide the total number of customers by 5, and use the result to count down the column and label the customers, or use the Drilling Down software. In a database of 100 customers, sorted in descending order most recent to oldest, or most units to fewest, the first 20 customers would get a 5, the second 20 would get a 4, and so on. So return to your programming. We're going to do it the easy (?) way.

Go back to your spreadsheet and highlight all the data (not the labels, if you created them). **Warning!** Highlight ALL data — the Customer ID, Most Recent Date, and Units, so they all stay together when you sort. Choose Data > Sort and you'll get a box with choices on sort order and sort by. Select the column your dates are in and choose descending order, click OK.

Now type in "Recency Quintile" at the top of the empty column immediately to the right of your data. Calculate the number of customers in your quintiles by dividing the total customer count by 5. Put a 5 in the cell next to your most recent (top) customer and copy it down until you reach the number of customers in a quintile (total number of customers divided by 5). Then type in a 4 and copy that down the same number of customers (total number of customers divided by 5). Repeat with 3, 2, and 1 (it's OK if it doesn't come out exactly even at the end). You should have something like Figure 32 below, shown in a 15-customer database. A quintile has 3 customers in it (15 / 5).

Sorted most Recent
to Least Recent

Customer ID	Most Recent Activity	Units	Recency Quintile
30	9/1/00	3	5
5	8/26/00	12	5
3	8/15/00	20	5
22	8/6/00	5	4
45	8/5/00	12	4
8	8/4/00	9	4
26	7/15/00	4	3
6	7/13/00	4	3
18	7/6/00	2	3
54	7/1/00	32	2
177	6/21/00	11	2
7	6/15/00	3	2
42	6/8/00	2	1
126	6/4/00	1	1
52	6/2/00	1	1

Figure 32: Recency Scores Added to the Scoring Spreadsheet

Now repeat this whole process with the units column, sorting in descending order and labeling with a Quintile number from 5 down to 1 as you did with Recency, only this time, call the column Frequency Quintile. Make sure you highlight your new Recency column when you sort or you'll lose the match-up. **Warning!** Highlight ALL data — the Customer ID, Recent Date, Units, and the Recency score so they all stay together when you sort. You should end up with something that looks like Figure 33 on the next page:

Sorted most Frequent
to least Frequent

Customer ID	Most Recent Activity	Units	Recency Quintile	Frequency Quintile
54	7/1/00	32	2	5
3	8/15/00	20	5	5
5	8/26/00	12	5	5
45	8/5/00	12	4	4
177	6/21/00	11	2	4
8	8/4/00	9	4	4
22	8/6/00	5	4	3
6	7/13/00	4	3	3
26	7/15/00	4	3	3
7	6/15/00	3	2	2
30	9/1/00	3	5	2
18	7/6/00	2	3	2
42	6/8/00	2	1	1
52	6/2/00	1	1	1
126	6/4/00	1	1	1

Figure 33: Frequency Scores Added to the Scoring Spreadsheet

OK, now the fun part! Type in "RF Score" at the top of the empty column immediately to the right of your data. Put your cursor in that column next to the top cell with data in it. Click on Insert > Function and a box pops up. Scroll down and select Text in the left box and select Concatenate from the right box. Click OK, a box pops up. Type the cell address of your Recency data in the top line, and the cell address of your Frequency data in the second line. Click OK.

It should create a new number with the Recency Quintile digit followed by the Frequency Quintile digit. Copy this RF Score cell in the spreadsheet down for every customer row, and Presto! The RF scores for each customer! Sort the RF scores in descending order (remember to highlight all the data, including the new RF Score, when you sort the data).

You did it! You scored your customer base! The spreadsheet should look like Figure 34 below. The customers with the highest scores are your most responsive, most valuable customers! So what?

Customer ID	Most Recent Activity	Units	Recency Quintile	Frequency Quintile	RF Score
5	8/26/00	12	5	5	55
3	8/15/00	20	5	5	55
30	9/1/00	3	5	2	52
45	8/5/00	12	4	4	44
8	8/4/00	9	4	4	44
22	8/6/00	5	4	3	43
26	7/15/00	4	3	3	33
6	7/13/00	4	3	3	33
18	7/6/00	2	3	2	32
54	7/1/00	32	2	5	25
177	6/21/00	11	2	4	24
7	6/15/00	3	2	2	22
42	6/8/00	2	1	1	11
126	6/4/00	1	1	1	11
52	6/2/00	1	1	1	11

Figure 34: The Completed Scoring Spreadsheet Sorted by RF Scores

All your customers now have a two-digit RF score, whether you did it yourself manually or got some whiz-bang programmers to do it for you. But what do these scores really mean? The RF scores tell you the "**who**" of High ROI Customer Marketing programs – who should I spend money on to keep as a customer, and who should I ignore? Generally, high potential value customers are worth spending on, while low potential value customers are not.

For example, let's look at response rates. The following average performance data is compiled from many different kinds of offline Data-Driven businesses, mostly catalogs and direct mail. These examples are for your information and are not related to the data we just used to create the RF scores above; I just wanted you to see what the power of RF scores looks like. Dig this crazy data, first on Recency (Figure 35), then on Frequency (Figure 36) on the next page:

Recency Quintile	Response Rate
Quintile R = 5	13.6%
Quintile R = 4	6.2%
Quintile R = 3	3.2 %
Quintile R = 2	1.1 %
Quintile R = 1	0.34%
Average Response	4.89%

Figure 35: Average Response Rate by Recency
For Recency, Quintile 5 is 40 Times More Responsive than Quintile 1

Frequency Quintile	Response Rate
Quintile F = 5	7.6%
Quintile F = 4	3.8%
Quintile F = 3	2.1 %
Quintile F = 2	1.4 %
Quintile F = 1	0.84%
Average Response	3.15%

Figure 36: Average Response Rate by Frequency
For Frequency, Quintile 5 is 9 Times More Responsive than Quintile 1

Are you starting to see why this is important? The response rate at the top Recency Quintile (5) is 40 times higher than the bottom quintile (1). 40 times higher! For Frequency, response at the top Quintile is 9 times higher than the bottom Quintile. Look at the tables above again. You have to understand how powerful this kind of modeling can be. Run the numbers yourself. Can you imagine how much money you could save if you targeted mailings using RF scores for choosing customers? Or using the Discount Ladder from the Recency Toolkit chapter titled "Turning Recency Data into Profits"?

What Recency, Frequency, or RF scores do is "spread your average" – they break down the average response rate into component parts, and show you where the highest and lowest responders are. In the case of Figure 35 above, the campaign averaging a 4.89% response rate is really composed of 5 different segments, each with very different response rates averaging 4.89%.

Online (e-mail) results will usually be higher at each level, descending in a similar pattern. The point here is not the actual response rates, but the **magnitude of the difference between the quintiles**. If you get an average response rate 3 times higher than the averages above, you will probably generate a response rate at each quintile level 3 times greater than those shown above.

For example, in the Recency table (Figure 35), the average rate is 4.89%. If your average response rate is twice that (9.78%), you could expect the response rate of your top Recency quintile to be somewhere around 27.2%. At each quintile, your response would be twice as high.

The response rate at each higher level is not simply a percentage increase, but usually a multiple of the response rate just below it. If you have generally higher response rates than the table overall, you can expect to see the same kind of "spread" between the quintiles. This isn't a promise, by the way. Your mileage will vary, and there are many other variables, such as type of media, offer, targeting, ad copy, and so forth. But on average, you can see how important this scoring can be to a successful promotion. If you need a quick sales hit, mail (e-mail) to your 55's. Guaranteed sales pop.

Remember the following dirty little secret of interactive behavior:

The customer lifecycle for interactive businesses is more exaggerated than for traditional Data-Driven businesses. The behavior ramps up faster at the beginning of the cycle, but then falls off faster into the end of the cycle.

On the next page, Figure 37 is what a combined Recency & Frequency (RF) breakdown looks like for TV shopping, where there is considerably more interactivity happening than in the catalog / direct mail behavior shown above:

Frequency Quintile	Response Rate
RF = 55	72.4%
RF = 44	3.9%
RF = 33	0.9 %
RF = 22	0.4 %
RF = 11	0.1%
Average Response	15.5%

Figure 37: Average Response Rate by RF Score in TV Shopping
Top RF Score is 700 Times More Responsive than Bottom RF Score

You can clearly see this effect in a comparison of the tables between the traditional catalog business and the TV shopping business. The behavior in TV shopping is much more exaggerated; much higher response occurs at the top of the table, and much lower response occurs at the bottom of the table.

If possible, create a field in each customer record for RF Score so you can create reports using them whenever you want. With customer records tagged this way, any marketer, service agent, or manager can just glance at the RF Score and know the value of the customer relative to all other customers. Used this way, RF Scores become an extremely powerful tool for customer management because they create a common framework across the company for understanding the value of a customer, and can drive (if any) special offers and treatments customers deserve. RF scores become "shorthand" for managing customers and can be used for everything from reporting to triggering automated campaigns.

Here's a quick note on RFM scoring. There are several different ways to generate RFM scores. Some approaches are quite complex and may be better than others in certain circumstances. This book teaches a simplified version of the RFM model originally developed in the catalog industry several decades ago, a new interpretation more suited to people approaching customer value management and CRM for the first time. The version of the model in this book is widely applicable across a variety of industries and easy to implement. If you want to learn more about some of the other approaches to RFM scoring used for specific situations in particular industries, simply search "RFM Model" on the web. If you're not particularly dedicated to the RFM model for some reason, I wouldn't worry to much about all these other versions. Like the previous models you have learned about in this book, the RFM model is just another stepping stone on the journey to really understanding how to Measure, Manage, and Maximize customer value. In the Advanced Toolkit section of the book, you will learn some of the shortcomings of the RFM model and how to create an even more useful behavioral tool using the "best of" all three models you have learned about in this book.

Speaking of approaching customer value management and CRM for the first time, your author is aware this book will be read by a wide variety of people with different interests and skill sets. Allow me to explain where we're headed now so that the various audiences can make some choices on how to proceed.

So far in the book, we have been focusing on tracking, execution, and measurement using simple, one-dimensional tools. We have been working in the single dimension of "Potential Value". RF Scoring adds the Current Value dimension to the mix, and with this addition comes the capability to actually **predict and manage** (not just track and measure) the **financial outcomes** of communications programs. You will be able to **predict** the sales and profits generated with a communication, and **decide in advance** about trade-offs between driving higher sales or driving higher profits. The capability to do this is very powerful – think about asking your CFO mid-quarter if the company needs more top line or bottom line at quarter end, and then delivering it.

However, this capability to predict and manage the outcome of communications involves some fairly tedious preparation. Not that it is particularly difficult, or requires a statistics degree. But it is a bit time consuming to do it right, and these ideas are probably not relevant to some business models.

So here is what we're going to do. We are now going to run straight through all the powerful programs you can create with RF Scores and the related LifeCycle Grids **first**. We will follow the same general format we have with the other models you have learned, focusing on customer tracking and measurement – the "let's get something done" part of Data-Driven marketing and management. After we have finished with the nuts and bolts stuff, we'll hear from some fellow Drillers who have read this book and are putting these ideas into action in the real world. And after that, we will address the science and math behind predictive financials and the capability to actively manage sales and profits.

The reason for this approach is clear to me – there are many different kinds of business people reading this book, and most (if not all) of them are not reading it because they love the science of database marketing, at least when in "first time" mode and just beginning to explore this area. These folks want to learn about relatively simple techniques they can use to increase business success. It is very important to understand how the numbers work to be successful in many forms of Data-Driven program design, but not all of them. Beginners, the focus of the book, are here to learn something, not to prove anything.

So, if you are most interested in what true Customer Value Portfolio management can do to improve your business results now, proceed to the next chapter. If you are an experienced Data-Driven program designer, longing for some predictive financial models to beat your brain against, proceed to the chapter titled "Predicting Campaign ROI: Set Up" and have at it. Read about Subsidy Costs and Halo Effects until you can't see straight. Then come back to the following chapter when you have satisfied the urge to "run the numbers" and want to learn some really cool marketing stuff.

Chapter 18
The Commerce and Content Examples:
Turning Scoring Data into Profits

Your customers are now scored, and you know the customers with higher scores are the most responsive customers. In this chapter, we're going to go through 2 very basic approaches to customer marketing using the scoring database you just created – using **Individual** RF Scores and using RF techniques on **Groups** of your customers.

Each chapter after this one adds a new level of capability to these basic approaches, providing additional knowledge about your customers and how to successfully market to them. By the Advanced Toolkit chapter titled "Straight Talk on LifeTime Value," we will complete the "profiling and scoring" part of the book and get into the "turning scores into profits" part of the book, where you will see how your customer scores turn into real bottom line dollars by using financial models to manage promotions.

In this way, you will first understand all the potential uses of customer scoring and the marketing possibilities they open up, sifting through the options and determining the right approach for your business. Then, after all the options are clear to you, we'll look at converting all these scoring methods into hard dollars by the use of financial models, to predict the profit or loss of any particular promotion before you even send it out.

Using Individual Scores: Targeting Most Responsive Customers

Let's look at two different angles on using individual customer scores to allocate marketing budgets and maximize the Return on Investment for a marketing promotion you send out.

Let's say you have 10,000 unique visitors, and you just started carrying a new line of products. You want to send out a marketing promotion to encourage customers to come back and make a purchase. This campaign is going to cost you 2 cents per e-mail sent, and your budget is only $100. This means you can afford to send out only 5,000 e-mails, because 5,000 x $.02 = $100 budget to spend on the promotion. Of your 10,000 uniques, which 5,000 would you pick to send the e-mail promotion to?

You know the answer. You are asking your customers to respond to a request for activity, and you know activity-based RF Scores are a ranking of the likelihood of a customer to respond. So you would start your e-mail list at the top of your RF Scores, the RF 55 customers, and move down in score, adding e-mails to the list, until you hit the 5,000 e-mail maximum.

Since the 5,000 maximum represents about half your customer base, you would probably finish adding e-mail addresses to your promotion at RF 34 or maybe RF 33 customers, the "center" of your spreadsheet in RF terminology.

Following this method, you will get the maximum response possible for the $100 you are spending. And that's ROI thinking. Your response rate will be much higher than any other method of customer selection for the e-mail, so your "cost per response" will be much lower than any other method. Driving activity higher while lowering cost, the Data-Driven mantra.

Here's a second way to approach this same situation, and will provide more insight into customer behavior for the newly minted Data-Driven marketer. You follow the exact same method as above, and choose the same people. But instead of dropping all this e-mail at once, drop it gradually, by RF Score, and look for response by RF score.

Perhaps the first e-mail group you send is only to RF 55 – RF 54 customers. You should be able to see real strong response in your items sold. Then send the RF 53 – RF 52 e-mail, and do the same thing. You should see response perhaps slightly lower than the first e-mail drop. Continue on down your list, watching for response metrics.

If you are using some kind of tracking system like personalized links, even better, because you will not only see purchase response but also visit response. If you track click-through on the e-mail, you should see a very smooth response curve, with the highest response from the top scores, gradually falling off as you move down the list in RF Score from the high end RF 55 customers down to the low end RF 34 customers.

Why is this important? It's the beginning of your ability to predict response rate by RF Score, a key ingredient in the building of your predictive financial models later on in the book. It is also a great reason to implement a tracking system, if you don't have one, so you can understand the response behavior accurately. Perhaps you don't use tracking because there was never a reason to track non-purchase (clicks, visits) response. You've got a reason now!

Using Group Scores: Looking at Trends in Overall Customer Behavior

I think you would agree that a customer who visited (or any activity – I'll use "visits" to cover them all) Recently and Frequently is more valuable than a customer who has not. No matter what a visit is worth, it's worth something, and customers who have less of them must be worth less than customers with a bunch of them.

You know something about Recency and Frequency now, and you know that high RF scores are tied to a high LTV. So we'll take a "more behavior is better" stance on visit activity. As the person in charge of generating traffic, your goal would be to increase the number of high RF visit customers, and convert low RF visit customers to high RF visit customers. That's customer retention. If you accomplish this goal, then whatever a visit ends up being worth, the value of the business is growing and you did your job well.

I call this technique Hurdle Analysis, and it's an application of the RF scoring technique for entire groups of customers. It allows you to get a sense of how some of the more macro trends are evolving on your site. It's particularly useful for measuring the success of broad changes in the site, like content changes, site redesigns, new features, or changes in policy on the site.

"Hurdles," or minimum levels of activity, are selected for R and F, then the entire customer base or a particular group of customers is evaluated against these hurdles **as a group. A Hurdle Rate** is simply **the percentage of your customers who have at least a certain activity level for R and F.** It's the percentage of customers who have visited (purchased) since a certain date or have visited (purchased) a certain number of times.

If you're looking for a simple way to track the overall health of your business, or track the success your various promotions on the business, you want to look at activity metrics over time. Just set up Hurdle Rates for these activities and look at their performance. You can use a combined view, as in "any activity at the site," or you can set up Hurdles for separate activities (visit, survey, etc.) individually. You'll be measuring the percentage of customers who are "over the hurdle" in your customer base. And fortunately, you already have the data set up to do this.

You can do this reporting weekly, biweekly, or monthly, as long as you do it consistently, and watch the trends over time. If the percentage of customers over the Hurdle is gaining, you're winning. If the percentage is dropping, you're losing the future value of the activity.

Let's start simple. Think about your site and the kind of business you're in. Do you have high repeat traffic, like a news site, where a lot of content changes daily? Or do you put up something new every week? Every month? Your answer is a logical Recency Hurdle for your customers. Think about their behavior, and set your Hurdle accordingly. I think in most interactive situations, 30 days without so much as a visit would be pretty bleak performance for a customer, unless for some reason you have a rigid monthly schedule that forces a different type of behavior. For purchases, you might use 60 days. It just depends on what your business is like and the kind of activity you're trying to measure and manage.

Once you start looking at behavior, you'll be able to see what is logical based on the actual behavior of your customers. I'll use 30 days as an example. You might want to use different time frames for different activities. Maybe visits get a weekly hurdle, surveys and purchases monthly, and downloads quarterly — whatever is right for your business.

So now go to your RF database for a specific activity, make sure it's sorted in descending order by Most Recent Date, and look 30 days back (either manually or with your software gurus). Count how many customers have a most recent date of less than 30 days ago. Divide this number by total customers, and you have your 30-day Hurdle Rate. Figure 38 on the next page is an example of what this looks like, based on a current date of 9/2/00 in a database with 15 customers to profile in total:

Thirty days back from 9/2/00 is 8/2/00. There are 6 customers more Recent than 30 days ago. You set the Hurdle Rate for this activity at 6 / 15, or 40%. This is a baseline rate, or snapshot, of **where you are now**. Unless for some reason you are at the peak of performance (maybe a seasonal blip), the percentage of customers who engaged in this activity in the past 30 days should rise over time as you bring on more customers if the business is a healthy and vibrant one.

Total 6 customers with Activity Less than 30 Days Ago from 9/2/00.					

Customer ID	Most Recent Activity	Units	Recency	Frequency	RF Score
30	9/1/00	3	5	2	52
5	8/26/00	12	5	5	55
3	8/15/00	20	5	5	55
22	8/6/00	5	4	3	43
45	8/5/00	12	4	4	44
8	8/4/00	9	4	4	44
26	7/15/00	4	3	3	33
6	7/13/00	4	3	3	33
18	7/6/00	2	3	2	32
54	7/1/00	32	2	5	25
177	6/21/00	11	2	4	24
7	6/15/00	3	2	2	22
42	6/8/00	2	1	1	11
126	6/4/00	1	1	1	11
52	6/2/00	1	1	1	11

Figure 38: Determining the Recency Hurdle Rate

If you are tracking activity by content area — visits, chat, and store area, for example — you can do the same kind of analysis across the multiple areas. Just count the number of customers with a Recency of less than 30 days (or whatever makes sense for a particular activity) **in the specific area** of activity, and as you did above, divide by the total customers visiting that area. This is the Hurdle Rate for the area.

If the next time you look at this, the percentage has dropped, then something has occurred. There were not as many new customers coming in, or older customers were not coming back – something happened. Did you change the site design? Was the content not as strong? Did you have a service interruption? Are all

your affiliates still on board? The following Figure 39 demonstrates what these
Hurdle Rates might look like over 8 weeks:

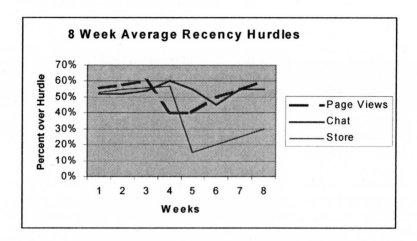

Figure 39: % Customers 30 Days Recent in Subject Area over 8 Weeks

Let's take a look at Figure 39 in detail.

There's a huge drop in Recent visitors around week 3, a spike in Recent users of
chat around week 4, and Recent visitors to the store dropped through the floor
around week 5. Then there's a recovery. What happened to this business?

The point is, something happened, and you've been flagged. Now you just have
to find out what it was. You may have operational systems that tell you about a
page serving glitch or shopping cart problems, and you already knew something
happened. If your site is hosted elsewhere, you may not have known it
happened at all. But now you know what affect the event had on your
customer's behavior.

Knowing customer behavior was affected is much more important than just
knowing something happened. Falling Recency is a serious problem, and has a
specific impact on your revenues. You can use this type of information to
predict how severe the impact on your business may be. But without this kind
of tracking, you'd never know, and it would probably get worse, until one day

you woke up and say, "Where's all my traffic gone?" This kind of erosion tends to snowball, so it's worth looking into if you see it.

Likewise, if the percentages over the Hurdle are stable or growing, you're doing something exceptionally right – Friction is falling. What is it? Better content, good promotion, new affiliates? Figure it out and do more of it, because your customers like it, and they're becoming more valuable as a result of it.

Yes, you can do the same thing with Frequency. Go to the database, sort by number of units, sum all the units, and then divide by number of customers. You get the average number of units per customer. I'd say that's a convenient Hurdle to use, and easy to calculate, as seen in Figure 40 on the next page and the calculations in the 2 paragraphs below.

Count down the number of customers with more units than the average, and take it as a percentage of your customer base. Then compare the percentage the next time you do the analysis. If it's rising, your better customers are still coming back and repeating visits. If it's falling, either your best customers are starting to slow down or your new customers aren't engaging in the activity as often.

Here is an example of calculating the Frequency Hurdle rate (see next page):

Total units = 121 divided by 15 customers = 8 units avg. per customer
Number of customers over 8 units = 6
Frequency Hurdle Rate = 6 divided by 15 = 40%

More than 8 Units
of Activity

Customer ID	Most Recent Activity	Units	Recency	Frequency	RF Score
54	7/1/00	32	2	5	25
3	8/15/00	20	5	5	55
5	8/26/00	12	5	5	55
45	8/5/00	12	4	4	44
177	6/21/00	11	2	4	24
8	8/4/00	9	4	4	44
22	8/6/00	5	4	3	43
26	7/15/00	4	3	3	33
6	7/13/00	4	3	3	33
30	9/1/00	3	5	2	52
7	6/15/00	3	2	2	22
18	7/6/00	2	3	2	32
42	6/8/00	2	1	1	11
126	6/4/00	1	1	1	11
52	6/2/00	1	1	1	11

Figure 40: Determining the Frequency Hurdle Rate

A more sophisticated version of this approach would be to set an activity threshold for the customers you count, reducing the "junk" customers you are counting and creating a more significant hurdle in the process. For example, if you include everybody who has only 1 or 2 visits (page views), it's going to bring the average way down and may not be helpful if your site has been around for awhile. It could be argued these low visit people are just "noise"; they are not really customers. So they shouldn't be included when you calculate an average to get your Hurdle Rate. New sites, or sites with just a few customers, probably should include them, at least for a while.

Here's an example. Let's say you have 1000 visitors (or buyers), but the bottom 10% of them, or 100, have only 1 or 2 visits (page views). These visitors probably don't mean much to your business, and if you include them in calculating your average visits, they will bring the average down, lowering the Hurdle Rate for your "real customers." So you would only count the total visits of the highest 900 customers, and divide the result by 900, to get the average visits. This Hurdle Rate is a much more "fair" representation of average customer activity, because it eliminates customers from the calculation who really aren't active and don't contribute to profitability.

> More than 11 units of Activity
> 5 / 11 = 45%

Customer ID	Most Recent Activity	Units	Recency	Frequency	RF Score
54	7/1/00	32	2	5	25
3	8/15/00	20	5	5	55
5	8/26/00	12	5	5	55
45	8/5/00	12	4	4	44
177	6/21/00	11	2	4	24
8	8/4/00	9	4	4	44
22	8/6/00	5	4	3	43
26	7/15/00	4	3	3	33
6	7/13/00	4	3	3	33
30	9/1/00	3	5	2	52
7	6/15/00	3	2	2	22

Figure 41: Determining the
Frequency Hurdle Rate without Inactive Customers

For the previous Figure 40, if we eliminated the customers with 1 and 2 units of activity, we would have 11 customers to count. The total activity for these 11 customers is 115 units. The average activity, eliminating the "noise" customers would be 115 divided by 11, or 10.5. See how this raised the bar? You now need over 10.5 visits (page views) instead of over 8 to be counted "over the average," or Hurdle. There are 5 customers of the 11 with over 10.5 visits (page views), so the new Hurdle Rate to track, excluding the noise customers who don't contribute, is 5 / 11 or 45%. Figure 41 above is a visual example of this approach. The same approach can be taken with buyers; many remote shopping companies don't even consider "1x buyers" to be "customers" for the purpose of profiling activity — they reduce from the accuracy of the analysis.

Keeping a chart of these percentages over the Hurdle can be extremely instructive. They'll rise and fall depending on things like seasonality, what's in the news, and so on. After a while, you can compare where you are this year to last year and have some solid information on the health and direction of your business, and make better sales or activity projections for the business.

And it's very important to have a handle on these stats when you do promotions or make changes to the site. You'll be able to tell right away if the changes are having a positive or negative affect. If you make changes that tend to affect customer behavior negatively, the Hurdle Rate percentages will begin to fall; positive changes will increase the percentage of customers over the Hurdle.

So now we know how to measure the effects of promotions or changes to the site on the health of the business. What kind of promotions can you do to drive these Hurdle Rates higher?

Well, almost any kind you do — contests, special offers, e-mail, new feature announcements — any promotion serving to encourage activity would be fine. But this time, instead of promoting it to all customers, target by RF score. Instead of spending time or resources on everybody, focus on spending more effort where you get a bigger bang for the effort, and a higher Return on Investment. Reduce the number of people you were going to promote to and use the money you save to provide a bigger, more effective incentive for those you do promote to. And then check your Hurdle Rates for the results, and see if the promotion drove activity.

Looking at Recency, you probably want to target a promotion at the "middle of the pack," the RF score of 33 – 44. Why? Your most recent people, with an R score of 5, are more likely to continue visiting if the content appeals to them at all. You really want to try and get an R4 or maybe an R3 to come back. Don't forget with Recency, if they visit just once they pop right back to the top as a 5, a most recent customer, with a new potential to remain a best customer, and a higher value to your business. We will cover the reasons why it may be more profitable to promote to R4 or R3 customers than R5 customers in the Advanced

Toolkit Chapter "Costs You Don't Know About: Measuring True ROI in Best Customer Promotions."

Frequency is a little more complex. Like Recency, very Frequent visitors are likely to continue as Frequent visitors, so you get more bang for the buck going after an F4 or an F3. There's an additional idea available however – the RF 51's. A very Recent but not Frequent customer is probably a new customer. If you can give them some special attention, it might be worth it to grow the customer's behavior.

The flip side of this RF 51 customer, an RF 15 customer, the Very Frequent but not Recent customer, is a "too late" case – you'll have a low response, and you obviously did something at one point to make this person unhappy – they're a **former** best customer. You win some, and you lose some.

One more thought on Frequency – there's no "popping to the top" like there is with Recency, where the customer becomes an R5 as soon as they visit or purchase again. Frequency is a tougher game, and an F3 has to become an F4 before becoming an F5. Also, Recent customers are likely to drive Frequency all by themselves, since they are happily visiting and engaging in activity. If you have limited resources, concentrate on driving Recency in the middle of the pack (RF 33 – 44) for the largest Return on Investment in most businesses. There will be more details on selecting specific scores as the target of campaigns later on in the book.

Chapter 19
Case Study: Non-Profit Scores
192% Increase in ROI using RFM Model

Cal Farley's Boys Ranch and Affiliates, a 501(c)(3) non-profit childcare organization focused on the raising of at-risk youth in a "ranch" setting, raises funds with direct mail. Each year, the Cal Farley organization serves more than 1000 children and families either in residence or through other outreach services. Today, more than 350 at-risk boys and girls from Texas and 15 other states are finding hope for a brighter future.

Basic-care residential programs and services are provided at the three Texas communities of Cal Farley's Boys Ranch, near Amarillo; Cal Farley's Girlstown, U.S.A., west of Lubbock; and Cal Farley's Family Program, near Borger. Current donors are contacted three times a year by mail and asked again for support. The average response to these mailings for the past 4 years has been a little less than 3%.

Cal Farley's decided to use one of the techniques outlined in my book - RFM scoring of their donors. First, they created a control group - a random sample of all donors - to test the scoring method against. This is extremely important, because they were also testing a new creative approach in the mailing.

If the RFM scored mailing ended up with a higher response rate, they wouldn't know if it was the new creative or the scoring that created the higher response without something to compare the results to. Having a control group allowed them to compare the effects of the scored mailing against mailing to a "normal" group of donors.

Next, using the RFM methodology, the rest of the donors not selected for the control group were ranked by their likelihood to respond to a donation solicitation using RFM. The top 10% most likely to respond were identified by RFM score and sent an identical mailer to what the control group of donors would receive, except for a different donation tracking code.

The response rate from the control group was 5.7% versus the average of just under 3% in previous years; the new creative approach had worked! But the real eye-opener was the response from the group of donors ranked most likely to respond by the RFM model.

The response rate for this group was 11.7% - more than twice the response rate of the control group, even though the same creative was used. This is a huge increase in response, and when combined with the average donation amount from this group, creates the statistic non-profit fundraisers look at most critically - the yield on a dollar spent. In this case, a dollar spent asking for donations from the RFM scored group generated total donations 192% higher than a dollar spent with the non-scored group.

After the success of this test, Cal Farley's is continuing to explore further uses for RFM segmentation of their donor base. For more information on Cal Farley's Boys Ranch and Affiliates, please visit www.calfarleysboysranch.org.

Advanced Data-Driven Marketing Toolkit

Chapter 20
Using Customer Characteristics and Multiple Scores

Time to add the other data you may have collected to your RF scoring process. Survey data, external data, content area data, subscriptions, geography, first visit date, type of browser, time of day – any and all of it can give you a heads up on more specific slices of your site using the RF customer scores.

Customer ID	Most Recent Date	Units	Recency	Frequency	RF Score	Pet
30	9/1/00	3	5	2	52	Bird
54	4/5/99	32	2	5	25	Bird
3	5/6/00	20	5	5	55	Cat
5	8/6/00	12	5	5	55	Cat
8	3/19/00	9	4	4	44	Cat
22	5/6/00	5	4	3	43	Cat
7	2/4/99	3	2	2	22	Cat
45	5/5/00	12	4	4	44	Dog
26	2/10/00	4	3	3	33	Dog
6	2/3/00	4	3	3	33	Dog
177	3/11/99	11	2	4	24	Dog
42	1/8/99	2	1	1	11	Dog
126	1/3/99	1	1	1	11	Dog
52	12/5/98	1	1	1	11	Dog
18	4/6/99	2	3	2	32	Horse

**Figure 42: RF Scored Customers
Sorted by a Characteristic: Favorite Pet Survey**

There's a couple of ways to do this. The easier way is to use your existing RF scores and characteristics to look for potential problems. I'm going to use surveys as an example data source. Look at Figure 42 above.

Let's say you have a pet site, and you have asked a favorite pet question. Each customer record in your spreadsheet or database has an indication of "dog," "cat," "bird" etc. representing their favorite pet. You do your RF scoring on all customers for total visits, then re-sort the RF score spreadsheet **by pet chosen**, and look at your RF scores. Are you thinking about where this could lead?

Which pet category has the most RF 55's in it? How about RF 11's? You could count up the scores at each RF level and compare the success of your categories within their own audiences. Or you can take a simple average of the RF Scores in each category and compare them. If you have generally higher scores in cats than dogs, then perhaps the dog section of the site needs a little work – Friction is high there. You're probably losing the dog audience to another site if they don't have frequent or recent visits.

The point here is people have self-selected a favorite topic, and so you would expect them to be equally enthusiastic about coming to read about it. The fact that there is a difference means the data is speaking to you again, and you should consider what the message is. Interestingly, you have more dog customers than cat customers, but the cat customers are more satisfied, based on their activity. Wow, what does this mean for your site? Should you market it as a cat site instead of a pet site? The Dog customers don't come back much anyway.

What if customers are generally recent, but not too frequent (RF 52, 53) in a category? Seems like providing more content (more pages to view) would be in order. What if they're frequent, but not very recent (RF 25, 35)? Sounds like you have to update the content more often. In comparing the categories with the help of RF scores, you may be able to see problems you were not aware of, tipped off by RF scores.

Another easy way to do this would be to create **Hurdle Rates by customer characteristic**, as opposed to **by area of the site** as we did previously. If the Hurdle percentages differ widely by characteristic from the whole customer population, you should be able to see at a glance which types of people (by characteristic) are strong and which are weak compared to the overall site. You could do Hurdle Rates for every characteristic you have in the database, creating a "customer satisfaction map" of your entire site, based on Recency, Frequency, and customer characteristics.

For example, you could take the same Recency and Frequency Hurdle Rates you are using for the overall site, and apply them by customer characteristic (see the RFM Toolkit chapter "The Commerce and Content Examples: Turning Scoring Data into Profits" for information on determining Hurdle Rates).

Are different customer groups by characteristic generally above or below the overall site Hurdles? Is the percentage of cat customers over the Recency Hurdle higher than the percentage of all customers over the Recency Hurdle? This technique can point out the types of customers who are either more satisfied or less satisfied than the "average customer."

More technically oriented sites might be interested in the types of browsers, IP addresses, and so on. The same techniques apply, and you can track the satisfaction of these groups by RF score or using Hurdle Rates on characteristics. Retail oriented sites can take an RF scoring on total purchases and re-sort by product categories instead of "pet," or set Hurdle Rates for different lines of merchandise.

If you have a large number of customers sharing the same characteristic, you can split them off and run the RF scoring process on just these customers. Looking at the group, try to determine why different customers **sharing the same characteristic** might have different scores. Are the lowest scoring customers unique in any way, perhaps they have been with you the longest? Or are they new customers?

Promotional techniques would be similar to those described previously for the general population, for either purchase or non-purchase activities, **but even more targeted**. Once you realize you have a problem with your dog content, make your changes, then shoot the marketing at "middle R dog customers" (R4, R3) to see if you can get them back and encourage them to stick. **You'll be able to measure your success by looking at the RF scores or Hurdle Rates** after the promotion has been executed. Compare to the Hurdle Rates existing before the promotion to measure any impact you have had.

Why is this approach important? When the whole customer file was scored, or you looked at areas of the site using Hurdle Rates, you were able to identify your high value, high LTV customers and low value, low LTV customers. At this point, we know who is likely to respond and who isn't. **But we have no clues to WHY they are likely to respond or not**; how did they get to be high or low value? You don't know the **underlying cause** of the high or low valuation these customers in the database have.

So the best you can do with this "general" score is make some kind of "general" offer to the lower value customers and hope it hits the mark. When you combine the RF score with some knowledge of the customer, you can draw a direct implication as to what the **specific** problem is, and why they are not coming back. Then you can take action to correct the problem.

The smart marketer or content manager, before redesigning the site or changing the products around, might **ask the marginal dog customers** in a survey what they think of the dog content. I don't think you would open up with "We noticed you're an R3 on dog content and were wondering why you're not in the top 20%." But a quick "what would you like to see" might be very instructive. If similar scoring people begin to say similar things, then you've got a pattern you know is viable and means something. Make your changes according to their input and then invite them back to your site. If you're on target, your first Data-Driven relationship marketing promotion will result in a loyal customer for some time. Congratulations!

Multiple RF scoring works in a similar way. How do you get multiple RF scores for the same customer? Any activity you keep track of with customer ID's, where you have a date of activity (R) and units of activity (F) can be used to rank customers against each other — purchases and visits (page views) are a good pair to look at.

In the first examples above, we used a static characteristic, such as "cat person," to enhance our knowledge of a customer's RF score. In the case of multiple RF scores, you are using a behavior-based RF score to enhance your knowledge of another behavior-based RF score, as opposed to using a static customer characteristic in the comparison.

What's the difference? In the case of using "Cat person" and the RF score, knowing "Cat person" allows me to speculate on why your RF score is what it is. However, your RF score doesn't tell me anything about why you are a "Cat Person" instead of "Dog Person." Cat Person is a given; it's a characteristic, not a behavior. There's a one-way relationship between the RF score and characteristic of the customer.

When using multiple RF scores, you will frequently find they are interrelated, because they are both about human behavior and activity. There is frequently a two-way relationship between RF scores for the same person; each can provide information about the other. Let's take a look Figure 43 below:

Customer ID	Visit RF Score	Purchase RF Score
3	55	55
5	55	54
30	52	33
8	44	34
45	44	42
22	43	53
26	33	42
6	33	44
18	32	33
54	25	25
177	24	22
7	22	25
42	11	11
126	11	11
52	11	11

Let's say you do RF scores on visits (page views) and purchases for all your customers, and put them in the same database so each customer has both. You sort by visit RF score, top to bottom, and notice that many of your highest RF visit score customers also have high purchase RF scores. Looking to the bottom of the list, you see the same kind of matching up between low RF visit score customers and low RF score purchase customers.

**Figure 43: Visit and Purchase RF Scores
in the same Spreadsheet (Database)**

Well, seems logical to me. Heavy users of the site would buy more products; light or defected users would not. If you look at visits, you can predict purchases. If you look at purchases, you can predict visits.

But then, near the top, you also notice a few customers with a high RF score for visits and a low RF score for purchases. These customers are shaded in gray in Figure 43 above. What does this mean?

Opportunity. You have seen the likelihood of a high **correlation**, or tendency for two things to move together, between high RF score visits and high RF score purchases, as demonstrated by the majority of your customers. Customers with **high** RF scoring visits and **low** RF scoring purchases are more likely to respond compared with customers with **low** RF scoring visits and **low** RF scoring purchases to a purchase promotion you deliver.

They are more likely to become a frequent buyer on the site; the behavior of all your other customers tells you this. The data is speaking to you. So give these customers a push, will ya, before they get interested in something else? Make them an offer.

In a similar way, you can compare categories of purchase or different content areas of your site. In addition to scoring total purchases or visits across the entire site, as we did previously, you would score the customers only on purchases or visits in a particular product category or site area. Any customer who has at least some activity in the area being studied would receive the RF score for the area in question.

Visits and purchases are pretty simple RF score pairs to work with; most customers of a commerce site would have both. Unlike a single RF score, there's a unique situation with pairs (or combinations with even more scores) you should be aware of and will need to address.

When you produce the RF score for a single activity, by definition, the customer has to have participated in the activity. When you begin to pair one or more RF scores at the customer level, you will find some customers who have participated in one activity but not the other. Hmm. That means literally the RF score is zero for that activity. Additionally, there may be a large number of people with varying activity in one area, but the same activity in the other. For example, visits are all over the place but purchases are all equal to one. So how do you create the RF scores on purchases for these people if they all have the same purchase level?

It's pretty simple. You cannot do multiple scoring on customers who don't have **significant** multiple activities. Intuitively, this works because if there isn't enough activity to create a score, there probably isn't enough activity to create a score useful in predicting behavior. Simply ignore these customers as it relates to a dual score approach and use their single most useful score for marketing, placing a "zero" in a column where there's no activity or activity is so low it is meaningless in terms of behavior.

For example, if you were using visits and purchases for the two RF scores, you would generate each score first by itself, as was done above. Then you put them together at the customer ID level. Since it's probably impossible for a purchase to occur without any visits, you will end up with good RF scores on the visit side for every customer, but a lot of blank scores on the purchase side. Not all the customers scored for visits made a purchase, and so were not included in the RF score process for purchases. For marketing and analysis purposes, you would only consider a dual-score analysis for people with good dual scores, and with the rest use only the single score for marketing and analysis. Their second score is zero.

If there's a ton of customers with 1 purchase, scoring them might not really make any sense. If there are so many people with 1 purchase that the people with similar activity end up getting different scores through the RF quintile process, the scoring method is breaking down. Just give all these people a score of zero and score the rest of the people, where the activity really means something relative to the score. We took a similar approach when we eliminated everybody with 1 or 2 visits for the Hurdle analysis (see RFM Toolkit chapter "The Commerce and Content Examples: Turning Scoring Data into Profits."

This doesn't mean you ignore the question brought up by the lack of a dual score. I mean, how is it a customer can be RF 54 on visits and have no purchases? Whassup with that? So even though you can't use a dual score analysis, the absence of the RF purchase score on a high RF visit customer **defines yet another target group**. Create promotions to address the "how come you hang around here all the time but never buy anything, is there anything we can do to help" issue.

At some point, you use your judgment. What if you are scoring across 5 content areas or product categories, and multiple categories have zero or one activity event in them? Use your judgment. Look at it, listen to what it says to you (you can do this now, right?). What does it mean that a customer is heavy in sports scores but never reads sports news and rarely listens to the live audio? Does the single activity event in a category really mean anything, or is it just "noise"? What would this person be like? Do they not like the news format, or the content? Formulate some answers (or better yet, survey the customers) and plan your marketing promotions.

Sure, it's a little more work to sort out the issues involved with using multiple scores. But the knowledge you gain is even more powerful than you had before. It allows you to really get inside the heads of people, and ask, "What are these people telling me through these multiple behaviors?" The more information you have, the better you can answer this question. You make some guesses, perhaps do a survey or a marketing promotion, and try to address the answers that make your customers happy.

The more RF scores you do on different parts of your customer's behavior, the more correlations you will see. If it gets too complex to spot this information by eye, there are a number of software programs that will do this for you. The programs go through the data and ask, "If someone has a high RF score in surveys, what else are they likely to score high in?" The software produces a "model" that tells you about **highly correlated scores**.

Then you go out and look for customers who match the profile the software delivers, but are weak in one RF score area they should be strong in. This weak area provides a window for a promotion they are likely to respond to, similar to the high RF score visits / low RF Score purchases example we reviewed earlier in this chapter. And once you start working with ideas like this, do you know what? You're building behavioral targeting models like the Ph.D. guys.

There are some huge implications here for those of you who can do any kind of customized page serving based on a database or spreadsheet lookup. It's not very difficult and can usually take place with a Perl script or similar tools. The idea is when someone comes to the site and you identify them, by a cookie, sign-in or other technique, you do a quick lookup to the RF scoring file or database and check for RF score on any number of variables (visits, purchases, anything) and serve pages appropriately. You've built your own personalization engine using RF scores!

To go back to the dog person example, a dog person with a low RF score on visits could be served a message telling the customer to check out the "newly revised and more in-depth dog pages." This works in the background without your intervention and is what I call "death by a thousand cuts" marketing. Each event by itself at the customer level is insignificant in the grand scheme of things, but 24 hours a day, 365 days a year, across several or dozens of RF scores serving custom pages – it has a major impact. And you don't need to take my word for it, it's been proven using the $500,000 personalization packages you have all read about.

At this point, you have built a VERY complete profile / model of the customer, one that will stack up favorably to a $200,000 job. You know how to mimic a $500,000 customization package. And you have done it all with a spreadsheet!

A few more words about using Recency and Frequency in promotions:

Recency, or really the lack of it, probably means you won't have a chance to speak to the customer at your site, so e-mail is probably the way to go to get them to come back, maybe snail mail (postcards do drive visitors if you mail to the most Recent ones) if you can afford it. This might be obvious to some people, not so obvious to others. Just putting up banners on your site is not going to solve a Recency problem. A derivative of e-mail if you don't have a list would be advertising in targeted newsletters. You may reach a few of your customers if you have a targeted audience. At any rate, a Recency promotion has to be put to work external to the site.

Frequency however, is perfectly suited for any kind of site customization methods you have, however crude they might be. If you can serve customized pages or content based on a low F score in the database, you can encourage Frequency at very little cost. This would be an excellent way to promote to the RF 51's or 52's – newer customers just discovering your site with the potential to become very good customers. Offer them something to encourage their behavior and make them feel like they're "winning," like links to parts of the site a new customer might not know about, or special offers.

Chapter 21
Customer LifeCycles: Tracking Scores Over Time

Ah, time. Time is the most overlooked and underutilized tool in the Data-Driven marketing toolbox but one of the most powerful. You can see the strength of time's influence in the importance of Recency, the most powerful of the modeling variables. Customer behavior changes over time and these changes are clues to the future.

So far, when we have done our RF scoring, we have been looking at a "snapshot" of the customer, their Recency and Frequency at a single place in time. But are you the same person now as you were last year? Have you not had experiences and thoughts and triumphs and downfalls in the past year that changed the way you think and behave?

Even though activity-oriented human behavior can be modeled at a point in time, it is far more powerful to look at it over a time period. This issue is lost on many who do "profiling" in today's environment, and even some of the pros from the catalog and TV shopping worlds where these techniques were developed don't grasp the power of time.

Think about this: in terms of understanding a customer's behavior, is it more powerful to know they are an RF 43 today, or to know they are an RF 43 today but were an RF 55 last month?

I think you'd agree knowing not only the current state, but also the path to this state, can provide critical additional clues to a customer's potential and future behavior, and provide powerful input into the marketing to be used to address the current state of the customer.

How is this accomplished? Well, you're probably ahead of me on this, since we've been making references to the idea all along. You need to store multiple RF scores for the **same variable** (purchases, visits, etc.) in your customer database, and extract trends from these scores over time. It's like a blend of the Hurdle Rate analysis from earlier in the book and the RF scoring technique. Instead of having one Hurdle Rate to watch over time, you look at the RF scores themselves over time.

It's tremendously powerful stuff. Imagine this. Each month (or week) you do the RF profile of your customers. But instead of replacing the old score, you keep it, and add the new one. Then look at the spreadsheet or query the database and ask, "Find everybody who has a lower RF score this month than last month, and find everybody who has a higher RF score this month than last month." Think of what you could do with that information.

Anybody who was a RF 55 and isn't anymore deserves your promotional attention, before they drop even lower, with visits or purchases. Anyone with a rising RF score should be encouraged.

Generally, anyone who is moving lower in RF score is in the process of **defecting** — of leaving you as a customer. The more dramatic the move, the more likely they are to be defecting. The mirror image is true for those climbing in score. The more dramatic the move, the more likely it is they are on their way to becoming a more valuable customer and adding value to your business. As I said earlier:

The customer lifecycle for interactive businesses is more exaggerated than for traditional Data-Driven businesses. The behavior ramps up faster at the beginning of the cycle, but then falls off faster into the end of the cycle.

The speed or rate of behavior change is incredibly important to modeling interactive behavior, much more important than in offline models. Small changes over time are to be expected; rapid and accelerating or decelerating changes are much more significant and signal a time for quick action.

For example, check out Figure 44 (next page) of new customer behavior over the first 13 weeks of being a customer:

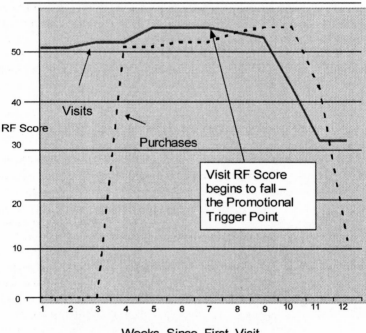

13 Week RF Scores - New Customer
Visits vs. Purchases

Weeks Since First Visit

**Figure 44: RF Scores, Visits and Purchases
of a New Customer over the first 13 Weeks of Contact**

RF scores for visits and purchases are on the y-axis (left side); the number of weeks since the customer made a first visit are on the x-axis (along the bottom). First day of contact is at the far left. Just look at it for a second. What does the data speak to you? If you saw this chart, could you instantly form a "new customer" marketing or service plan, particularly if the average new customer behaved in the same way? Can you **see the friction**?

You would certainly have a good idea of **when to apply the grease – it's when the visits start to fall**. If you can keep them interested in visiting the site, perhaps the purchases won't fall off as quickly.

In this chart, the customer starts off at RF 51 on visits, as all new customers would, with zero purchases. Then the visit RF score starts to rise, and in the 4th week, the first purchase is made (customer jumps from "0" to RF 51 on purchases). The visits peak in weeks 5 through 7 at RF 55, then start to fall off (Visit Friction rising). **Purchasing peaks 3 weeks after visits do**, in week 10, then falls off a cliff (Purchase Friction rising), ending with the RF for purchases even lower than the RF for visits. So you basically have 3 weeks in there somewhere to try to grab onto this customer and apply the grease before the lightning-quick defection takes place.

The first time you see this kind of data on your own customers, if you don't get a rush across your entire body, you need to be in a different line of work!

The marketing implications of this behavior are staggering. Can I get them to start purchasing a little earlier, when I see the visits ramping? Once I see the visits beginning to drop, can I extend the purchase cycle? What type of promotion would be effective to do either of these? You have to test your ideas and find out. But at least you now know a critical piece of information – WHEN to pull the trigger. The data will speak to you.

What we're talking about here is called the **LifeCycle** of a customer. RF scores over time. Every customer has a LifeCycle, and becoming familiar with the different types of customers you have and their LifeCycles is one of the most powerful marketing tools you can have at your disposal. Think of it. How powerful could your marketing be if you had an idea of what your visitors or customers were going to do **before they did it**?

The fact is, you can have this knowledge. LifeCycle analysis works. It's about human behavior. A new product or service excites people and then they get tired of it. They binge and then get exhausted. It has a lot to do with where they are in their lives and what's happening around them at the time.

For example, let's take a new mover, someone who has just bought a house. They have what seems like unlimited capacity to buy stuff for a while, and then they just stop. Perhaps they've reached their budgetary limit or they have everything they need for the new house. It's not bad service or faulty products that make them stop; they just stop, because they're all done. That's a customer LifeCycle in action.

You can't eliminate the LifeCycle, but you can take advantage of it, in two ways. You can try to bump activity up early in the LifeCycle, and you can try to extend the LifeCycle. This means trying to drive a few extra purchases or a bunch of visits in each customer, trying to maximize and extend the LifeCycle. Introducing new and "must have" products can do this, but everyone runs out of ideas after awhile, and people ultimately exhaust their behavior in any one direction. So you have to be creative with your marketing and sell harder at the beginning and end of the LifeCycle to maximize the amount of time people stay with you and continue to be active.

Some customers have long cycles, others have short ones. To benefit the most from LifeCycle analysis, you want to look at different groups of customers and see if their cycles are similar or different. **This means grouping similar people together and looking at their RF scores over time.** Cat people versus dog people. Headline readers versus full story readers. Frequent buyers versus light buyers. Compare and contrast how the LifeCycles for these groups are different. Do some last longer than others? Perhaps some groups could use a lot of marketing up-front, but other groups can be put off until later. The point is, there will be differences and you can use these differences to your advantage.

Over the years people have been studying LifeCycles, similar patterns have emerged across different kinds of businesses. The following "Big 5" LifeCycle ideas seem to be the most universal — you should definitely analyze your customers using these segments, since they have proven consistent and using them can drive revenues and profits for the Data-Driven marketer:

1. **LifeCycle by type of media used to bring in a customer.** New customers coming from the same banner ad will typically have similar LifeCycles, and they will be different from customers who come in from search engines. The reason? Different missions, different attitudes. Different LifeCycles. Generally, the more targeted the method of customer acquisition, the longer the LifeCycle **if you are the superior provider of the desired product.** If you're not the superior provider, the more targeted the acquisition method you use, the shorter the LifeCycle may be. A sophisticated consumer will become disappointed or find an alternative faster than an unsophisticated one will.

2. **LifeCycle by type of product experienced first.** This is a Darwinian, self-selection type of notion. It's hard to make generalizations or provide examples for this, since everybody is selling vastly different products and

content. But trust me, look at it yourself. It has to do with the overall experience of the first product, the "first test" of you as a source of information or products. If the product delivers a fantastic first experience for a particular type of person, it's likely to deliver the same experience for another person of the same type, and for the first purchase (visit) experience, a fantastic first experience tends to lead to another purchase (visit). You will find the item of first purchase will generally determine who will have a long lifecycle and who will have a short one. Same thing with content. Look at the number of pages new visitors view in certain areas, and look at their visit LifeCycles. You will find certain first visit areas create longer lasting customers. Makes sense, right? If the right customers match up with the right content, they're pleased and enjoy themselves, and stick around. If they don't find anything they like, or got to your site by accident, they don't stick around. Pretty simple idea.

3. **LifeCycle by the price of the product purchased first, or in the case of visits, the registration or other "actions" the customer took to get access to the site**. On average, the prices customers pay will fall over time, and for content, the "hurdles" they're willing to jump over to get what they want will fall over time. If the first purchase by a customer is a lowest priced product, there is no next purchase available with a lower price, and they just stop buying. Many one-time buyers fall into this category. For content, if there are no requirements at all for the customer to get access to content, and you ask for no commitment at all, well, there you go. You have a customer who lacks commitment to your product. These customers tend to have shorter lifecycles. You should always try to get them to customize or leave behind something to bump up that level of commitment. The highest value customers will generally be the ones willing to "do something" (register, fill out a survey, etc.).

4. **LifeCycle by the date and time of first purchase**. Sound crazy? It's not, because **time** is critically important, and anything affecting time is also important. Most businesses have some seasonality, and customers who begin at the low point of the seasonality tend to be worth less than customers who begin at the high point. That's why the holiday season purchasing cycle is so important. New customers acquired during the holiday season tend to have longer lifecycles than new customers acquired during the summer, for example. There's just a higher likelihood the customer will have a good experience and have needs fulfilled during the holiday season than in summer. If you're one of those that disappointed in

the holiday season, you have more than just immediate problems. You missed the opportunity to pick up long LifeCycle customers who would come back and shop with you again because of a positive experience the first time.

Time of day has a dramatic affect on customer quality in a 24 x 7 interactive business. Why? Because the audience shifts, and since audiences tend to be similar based on time of day, so does the customer quality and length of the LifeCycle. In TV shopping, on average, the lowest value customers tend to be those who buy from 2 AM – 4 AM. Are you surprised? Probably not. If you survey them, and ask them why they bought, a large percentage of them will say, "I'm not sure." This is a customer destined for a short LifeCycle. They have high return rates and are generally disloyal. In the TV shopping business, you should only sell low priced items in the middle of the night to lower the return rate and expense of serving these high maintenance customers.

When you group customers by initial (acquisition) marketing promotion, price point, and so forth, and then look at their LifeCycles, you can make decisions on which strategies and price points generate the most valuable, longest LifeCycle customers. Then allocate your resources more towards the winners and take resources away from losers. ROI thinking, folks.

5. **LifeCycle by affinity profile**. The affinity could be for products, content areas, or anything else where activity can be measured. Affinity can be defined any way you want, something like "spends 75% of their time reading sports" or "spends 60% of their money on accessories." The idea is to find something the customer seems to prefer over everything else. Decide your parameters based on your business; just think about behavior and use what makes sense.

Then take a group of **new** customers (less than 30 or 60 days old) and do affinity profiles on their activity. Look to see what their preferences are using parameters aligned with your business. Then wait 30 or 60 days and do another affinity profile **on the same customers**. If you are working with content / visits, you would probably profile every 2 weeks. Experiment to see where the changes in affinity happen.

What you will see is the morphing of customer affinity over time, over their LifeCycle. If you know these trends, they can be used in very powerful ways to market to customers by customizing offerings and marketing strategy. **Then you match this "Product LifeCycle" up with the "Behavior LifeCycle," represented by RF scores over time.** This matching up of changes in product or content preference (affinity) with changes in purchase or visit activity (RF scoring over time) provides a very strong action plan for not only when to promote, but also the context or content of the offer when the time comes to act.

Here's an example from TV shopping. Many new customers start off buying jewelry as a first purchase. When you profile these new customers at 60 days, they still show an affinity for jewelry.

When you profile these same customers at 120 days, an interesting thing has happened. First off, a bunch of them have stopped buying. This is normal, they've exhausted their needs for the time being, or got bored, or found an alternative source. The remaining customers have started to buy some fashion items. At 180 days, **they're buying mostly fashion**, and not purchasing much jewelry at all.

How powerful is it to know this? Extremely. The data is speaking! The data is saying the customer gets tired of jewelry at around 90 days, and if they don't become interested in fashion by 120 days, they simply stop buying. This has huge implications for the kind of marketing you would do to new customers at the 90-day mark. It gives you the WHO, WHEN, and HOW of an affinity promotion set-up.

You would try to go with the flow, extend the LifeCycle. A deep discount on a hot fashion item delivered at 90 days, when customers begin to get tired of jewelry, would do the trick. If they continue on in fashion after the promotion, their activity will easily pay for the discount. So how do you tell who will make it by themselves to fashion in 120 days, who will need a marketing push at 90 days, and who won't make it at all?

If you guessed RF scores, you were right. By looking at the RF scores on purchases, you can tell who is not going to make it to 90 days and begin conversion to fashion. **At 60 days after becoming a new customer**, low RF score customers won't make it to 90 days, middle RF score customers need a push to get to 90 days, and high RF score customers will make it to 90 days without any prodding. Using this method, you can cut the expense of this "conversion from jewelry to fashion at 90 days" promotion by two-thirds, by

leaving "will never make it to fashion" and "will make it to fashion by themselves" customers out of the promotion.

And it works like a charm. You end up making a huge pile of money by converting only a few jewelry buyers into fashion buyers, because the marketing was targeted, and the fashion buyers **have very long LifeCycles**. How do you know that? You studied the LifeCycle of fashion buyers, of course, and found they stick around 3 times longer than jewelry only buyers.

The content or visit version of affinity profiles is a similar idea. You might look at new customers and find they mostly read content on the site. Later on, you re-profile and find many of them gone, but those that stick are now spending more time in chat. If you look at high RF visit customers and find they have an affinity for chat, and low RF visit customers do not, you have made a major discovery. You need to push people towards using chat at some point before their score drops too low, they split on you, and never come back. Make sense? You want potential best customers to discover chat earlier in their LifeCycles, ultimately resulting in more people sticking with the site.

Will these LifeCycle ideas work with every single customer? No. But customers in the aggregate, when looked at as a group, yes. They are general rules of thumb to get you started on looking at lifecycles. You will undoubtedly find others. But if you're not capturing every possible piece of information about the first contact with your customers, storing multiple RF scores over time, and doing affinity analysis, you're missing out on a huge marketing opportunity. So do it already, will ya?

Plus, you need to know your customer's LifeCycle in order to do an accurate job of determining LTV, or LifeTime Value. We'll get to that soon, I promise. But first we want to take a look at modifying our RF methods a little, by using your new understanding of LifeCycles.

Chapter 22
Customer LifeCycle Grids:
High Performance Behavior-based Modeling

You now have a pretty darn good method of estimating future customer behavior — the RF scores. RF scores answer the question "**who**" do I promote to. You also have the answer of "when" to promote, using RF trends over time. The "why" and "how" of promotions are gathered from characteristics and RF scores from different areas for the same customer, or from affinity profiling. Not a bad toolkit for a humble spreadsheet jockey.

Using quintiles to determine RF scores is handy, because it's easy and forces even sized groupings, perfect for marketing promotion testing. But something bothers me about quintiles, and it's this – the "forcing" of the customer ranking doesn't tell me as much as I want to know about behavior. Here's an example. Let's say someone is RF 55 in the current month. Next month, because of a big promotion, a bunch of new customers come in. Since they are all newer customers than the RF 55 customer mentioned above, on the next scoring, this customer drops to RF 45. The newer customers are forcing the older customer down in the rankings, but does this really mean he's less of a good customer? I mean, the customer isn't as Recent as all these new guys, but he's a pretty **decent** customer, right? It's this effect that got me thinking about Hurdle Rates again, and resulted in the development of a tool I call LifeCycle Grids.

Remember when we discussed Hurdle Rates? The idea is you set a cut-off for Recency and Frequency, and measure the percentage of your customer base above the cut-off. This gives you a quick read on the health of your customer base, be it rising or falling. It's only a single point though, and we might want to know about multiple points in time, because we really want to zero in on the customers a little tighter, and squeeze out some extra marketing profit. And we want to avoid "mislabeling" a customer, like the one above, who fell from RF 55 to RF 45 because of an external event (adding new customers) rather than because the customer's behavior had changed.

So we use LifeCycle Grids, which contain multiple Hurdles. The position of each Hurdle, instead of being based on an average or guess about the business (as it was in the beginning of the book), is now based on actual behavior changes we see in the LifeCycle. The LifeCycle Grid is similar to a spreadsheet, with columns and rows. In this example, on the horizontal (x) axis we put Recency, and on the vertical (y) axis we put Frequency. The resulting LifeCycle Grid looks like Figure 45 below:

Recency
Days Since Last Action

Frequency (Units)	181+ Days	91–180 Days	61–90 Days	31–60 Days	≤ 30 Days	Totals
25 + Units	45	97	178	245	374	939
10 – 24 Units	102	312	489	634	721	2258
4 – 9 Units	154	435	678	768	934	2969
3 Units	478	532	897	978	1217	4102
2 Units	1073	1267	1543	1876	2389	8148
1 Unit	1578	1971	2245	3543	4245	13582
Totals	3430	4614	6030	8044	9880	31998

Figure 45: The LifeCycle Grid

The row and column boundaries are set based on the customer LifeCycle. Any significant change in behavior along the LifeCycle curve, in Recency or Frequency, gets a new boundary set for the behavior change. Customers are then placed on the grid at the intersection of their Recency and Frequency parameters. It creates a **Customer Friction Map,** if you will; you can look at it and instantly know where the dynamics of your customer base are taking you.

The shaded box at the upper right would be read like this: There are 374 customers who have taken action (made a purchase, visited, downloaded, whatever action you want to profile) in the last 30 days (Recency) who have acted at least 25 times in total (Frequency). The shaded cell in the center would be read like this: There are 897 customers who have taken action between 61 and 90 days ago (Recency) who have acted exactly 3 times in total (Frequency). Please look at the table and understand how this works before reading on.

The 374 customers in the upper right-hand cell are your most Recent, most Frequent customers, the "55's" of the RF scoring system. But under this new LifeCycle Grid system, we don't arbitrarily choose the cut-off to separate customer rankings at 5 (quintiles); we decide how many rankings there are and where to place them on the grid.

As a customer becomes less and less Recent (more days have passed since an activity, Friction rising), their "location," or the intersection of their Recency and Frequency, moves across the grid from right to left though consecutive "cells." As they become more and more Frequent (Friction falling), they move from the bottom to top of the grid. Best customers are in the upper right of the grid; worst customers are in the lower left of the grid. In the middle are the great "unwashed," customers who don't seem to be either best or worst.

Does the LifeCycle Grid sound and look familiar? It should. The LifeCycle Grid is in fact a more detailed and action-oriented version of the Customer Value Portfolio, shown below:

↑ **=** **Current Value**	Low Potential Value, High Current Value Grow These Customers	High Potential Value, High Current Value Keep These Customers
	Low Potential Value, Low Current Value Should You Spend Money Here?	High Potential Value, Low Current Value Grow These Customers
	Potential Value Ⅲ➡	

Figure 46: The Customer Value Portfolio Revisited

The middle customers are generally your most profitable promotional targets, for the same reasons the R4, R3, F4, and F3 customers were in our previous discussion (at the end of RFM Toolkit chapter "The Commerce and Content Examples: Turning Scoring Data into Profits"). Customers who are already Recent and Frequent will tend to stay that way; customers who have slipped far away in Recency and stopped acting are very unresponsive to promotions. Generally, you want to promote to the middle-ground customers, driving them up and to the right on the grid, and let "worst" customers slip away down and towards the left of the grid without spending a lot of time or money on them.

OK, so how do you decide where the breaks in the grid should happen, where the "boundaries" on the cells should occur? Glad you asked. This takes a little work on your part, but once you do it, it's done.

Use the LifeCycle, your RF scores over time. Look for trends and changes in the customer LifeCycle, and set your gridlines where you see important shifts in behavior, for both Recency and Frequency. Or, if Latency better defines the Customer LifeCycle, use Latency and Frequency. Hard-cores can include Monetary Value if you want to see a 3-D LifeCycle Grid customer map. Imagine what a 3-D customer map looks like! Send it to me if you do one and I'll put it up on the Drilling Down web site (http://www.jimnovo.com).

Here's an example of pegging the grid boundaries to the actual LifeCycle of a customer segment. Recall the example from Figure 44:

"The visits peak in weeks 5 through 7 at RF 55, and then start to fall off. **Purchasing peaks 3 weeks after visits do**, in week 10, then falls off a cliff, ending with RF for purchases even lower than for visits." For this example, you would set your Recency Hurdles at 5 weeks, 7 weeks (the Promotional Trigger Point), and 10 weeks. With this setup, you would "see" (in your LifeCycle Grid customer map) the number of customers about to cross over any of these critical behavior boundaries and you should take action, if need be. Define your LifeCycles first, and then use the information to choose LifeCycle Grid boundaries for your Customer Friction Map.

Using this method, the LifeCycle Grid becomes customer defined, or "reactive" as opposed to the pre-defined method of quintiles. It will be more "alive" for you because the grid is based on actual customer behavior. Once you start doing this on a regular basis, you'll be able to pick up the monthly or weekly Grid, and just by glancing at it, **forecast** whether you are going to have a good next month or not. If you are really "into" behavior, there's hardly a bigger high than seeing a healthy LifeCycle Grid (OK, maybe we should get out a little more).

Do you see how this is a more elegant solution than "forcing" people into quintiles? If you use actual LifeCycle behavior to set the score boundaries for Recency (Latency) and Frequency, then it really **means something** when a customer crosses over a grid line into the next cell. Not that the quintiles don't mean anything, because they do and they work. But if you **know something to be true from the LifeCycle**, like a customer who doesn't visit for 3 weeks usually doesn't come back, you want to SEE that event on the customer map. If you use LifeCycle Grids, you can include these important milestones as Hurdles (boundaries) right in your spreadsheet, and see how you're doing against the milestones. If you're still struggling a little with the LifeCycle concept, or don't have enough data to plot the LifeCycle yet, you can still begin to use LifeCycle Grids. The LifeCycle Grid in Figure 45 is a good "default" position if you don't yet have the Recency or Latency stats to create the behavior boundaries. Let's first take a look at how to read the LifeCycle Grids; perhaps that will help you decide how to define your boundaries. Then we'll look at defining default boundaries perhaps more relevant to your business than the ones in Figure 45.

LifeCycle Grids in Action

Let's say you are using a default LifeCycle Grid like the one in Figure 45:

Recency
Days Since Last Action

Frequency (Units)	181+ Days	91–180 Days	61–90 Days	31–60 Days	≤ 30 Days	Totals
25 + Units	45	97	178	245	374	939
10 – 24 Units	102	312	489	634	721	2258
4 – 9 Units	154	435	678	768	934	2969
3 Units	478	532	897	978	1217	4102
2 Units	1073	1267	1543	1876	2389	8148
1 Unit	1578	1971	2245	3543	4245	13582
Totals	3430	4614	6030	8044	9880	31998

It's likely these "customers" are not customers anymore	If they move to this area, they're not following the "average" pattern (no 2nd action within 30 days – market to them	New customers who have acted once

Figure 47: First Action Behavior in the LifeCycle Grid

In Figure 47 above, let's say the **average new customer or visitor** repeats the action being tracked within 30 days after they first act. The first boundary is at 30 days and all customers who have "acted" in the past 30 days are located in the ≤ 30 Days column (towards right). Customers who have acted only once (probably the largest customer group) who "roll over" the 30-day boundary to the left (have acted only once, **more than 30 days ago**) are not behaving like the "average customer," and deserve some marketing or service attention before you lose them completely. The further customers move to the left in this grid, the more likely it is you have lost them as customers. As they move, they are becoming less Recent (Friction rising), and therefore less likely respond to promotions or service offerings you use to get them to act a second time.

Now refer to the LifeCycle Grid below:

Recency
Days Since Last Action

Frequency (Units)	181+ Days	91–180 Days	61–90 Days	31–60 Days	≤ 30 Days	Totals
25 + Units	45	97	178	245	374	939
10 – 24 Units	102	312	489	634	721	2258
4 – 9 Units	154	435	678	768	934	2969
3 Units	478	532	897	978	1217	4102
2 Units	1073	1267	1543	1876	2389	8148
1 Unit	1578	1971	2245	3543	4245	13582
Totals	3430	4614	6030	8044	9880	31998

It's likely these "customers" are not customers anymore, no action in 6 months

If they move to this area (no 3rd action by 60 days), they're not following the "average" pattern – communicate with them

Customers who have acted twice, at least 1 action in the last 60 days

Figure 48: Second Action Behavior in the LifeCycle Grid

Let's say of the customers / visitors that do act a second time (those in the row labeled "2 Units"), the average customer or visitor who acts a total of three times does so within 60 days after the second action. You put a boundary at 60 days, and watch for people at the second action level (row labeled "2 Units") to roll over (move left past) the 60 day boundary. If targets at the second action level roll over into the Recency cell 61 – 90 Days, they are not acting like the average customer who acts for the third time 60 days after the second action. So the 1,543 customers or visitors in this cell are prime targets for some kind of promotion or service offer; you would be communicating with them **only when you have to, and at the point of maximum impact**. That's High ROI Customer Marketing, folks – the right person, at the right time, with the right message. If you let them slide and roll over into the next two cells to the left, it will probably be too late. They're already gone, and now you will waste a lot of money trying to get them back.

That's not to say, of course, that the 1,543-customer cell in the example above is the **most profitable** cell to go after. But it's pretty likely, if the average customer who acts a total of three times does so within 60 days after the second action. What you need to do is test different cells and promotions / service offerings and find out which ones drive the highest response or customer retention at the lowest cost.

Get it? Good. You want to see a gradual increase in customer counts upwards and to the right in the LifeCycle Grid (Friction falling). If this is happening, your customers are becoming more Recent and more Frequent, passing through a series of Hurdle boundaries based on behavior. This means the value of your business – now, and **in the future** – is rising. You can also look at these cell counts as a percentage of your customer base and track the rise and fall in the percentages of good customers versus "bad" customers.

As you might guess, LifeCycle Grids are perfect for driving so-called "lights out" marketing programs. As a matter of fact, that's exactly what we did at Home Shopping Network in the early 1990's with our interactive retention programs. Every month, we would "sweep" the database and find every customer who was "rolling over a boundary" in the LifeCycle Grid, and do a High ROI Customer Marketing promotion to them; this massive program was almost totally automated. After years of testing, we had 126 different "rollover cells" that received 126 different messages. It was like printin' money, I tell ya; very high incremental sales versus the control groups with very little cost.

When we ran a new LifeCycle Grid after this promotion you could **see** the effect of this retention effort "pop" all the best customer cells while "draining" the targeted roll over cells in the Grid. Customers migrated up and to the left, meaning they now had a higher Current Value and a Higher Potential Value. Of course, we were using a Unisys A series box with dumb terminals. For those of you who now have "rules-based" CRM or communications management systems, LifeCycle Grids can be the raw data engine you need to power these newer technologies towards measurable impact on the bottom line.

As with RF Scores, you can create a field in every customer record for a LifeCycle Grid "ID" of some kind. For example, you can number the cells in the grid, or come up with names for them based on their behavior. It doesn't really matter what naming convention you use, as long as it can be understood across the company. Trust me, when you create this kind of segmentation and people begin to understand the power of what it can do, **everybody** who has contact with customers or is involved in customer management strategy is going to want to use these LifeCycle Grid Cells for reporting and decision-making.

Determining Default "Time" Boundaries in the LifeCycle Grid

For Recency, a good default is even blocks of time – a week, a month, a day if you like. For convenience, set the boundaries to coincide with some other event, like weekly reports or monthly financial statements. By the way, if you have investors, this kind of stuff will make them very happy (if it is positive) because it really shows the "guts" of how the business is doing and the future potential.

The other way to determine the "time" boundaries is to study **Intra-Activity Latency (IAL)**, the average amount of time between purchases or visits (or whatever action you are tracking / forecasting), and use this data as boundaries. Look at a 10% random sample of customers and find out how much time, on average, passes between their first and second action, second and third action, third and fourth, and so on. Set your "time" boundaries in the grid at these points. If most customers make a second purchase within 30 days of the first purchase, place a boundary at 30 days in the LifeCycle Grid.

By the way, you really should study IAL anyway, even if you don't use it in the LifeCycle Grids – it's a superior trigger point for marketing. If a customer is taking more time than the average customer to repeat an activity, they are raising a hand and saying something is wrong. So use the IAL time span between each of the first few purchases or visits as a trigger point for a "we want you back promotion." If the customer rolls over the boundary, send the promotion. Obviously, you'd use a tighter scale on visits, perhaps a week or even a few days, depending on your content and activities at your site. This concept is covered in the Latency Toolkit chapter titled "Trip Wire Marketing."

These time-oriented metrics (Recency and Latency) are most critical to track in the beginning of a LifeCycle, and not so important later on, so your grid divisions should be finer for earlier (more recent) time and after some threshold (say 90 days), you can begin to group them into larger chunks. The reason? Once the behavior has been established, it tends to continue, so you don't need as much detail over longer lengths of time. The default Grids used in the examples above follow this convention, check them out again; finer segments earlier in the LifeCycle (right columns for Recency, bottom rows for Frequency). Ninety days without activity in an interactive environment is a darn long time, so if you're still clueless, at least put a break there. See what works for you and your business. Or just use evenly spaced blocks of time to start, see what it looks like and how it changes over time, and modify going forward.

Determining Default Frequency Boundaries in the LifeCycle Grid

Frequency is a little tougher to do without using the LifeCycle information. You kind of just have to "eyeball it" by producing a list of the targeted action by customer and looking for places where there seems to be different behavior taking place. This list would be the total number of customers making 1 purchase, total making 2 purchases, total making 3 purchases, and so on, all the way up to the top buyer (or visitor).

As with Recency and Latency, early behavior is most important, so finer detail is good there. You would definitely have breaks for 1, 2, and 3 purchases, since this is where a ton of customers will sit for some time, and you want to see if they're moving up. After 3 purchases, if you see "clustering" on your purchase totals list, use the clusters to define the boundaries in the grids.

For example, let's say you don't really have many customers making 4, 5, 6, 7, 8, or 9 purchases, but then they seem to kick in again at 10. The next bunch seems to kick in over 25, and then it trails off. This would make you think that many people get satisfied at 3, but good customers run right up to 10, and best customers run to 25 and over. So you would use 1, 2, 3, 4 – 9, 10 – 24, and 25+ as boundaries or behavior breaks. It depends on the business and how the average customer behaves.

On visits, looking for behavior clusters is a great piece of analysis, but you would obviously use much wider scales, like under 25, 26 – 50, 51 – 75, and so on, depending on what kind of a site it is and the behavior demonstrated by the visiting customers. Otherwise, you'll get too much data and it won't really be meaningful. Really, is there a meaningful difference in value between 12 and 15 visits? If so, then by all means, set a boundary. If not, aggregate into chunks.

Generating the LifeCycle Grids

Once you set these boundary parameters, just query the spreadsheet or database for the number of customers who fit the parameters of each cell on the LifeCycle Grid, and put the total in the cell. Programs can be easily written to do this, and once it's done, it's done, since behavior-based boundaries shouldn't change much over time. Then just run your program or series of queries each week or month, and compare the numbers. Using the LifeCycle Grid default example in Figure 45, your queries would look like this, starting with the upper right-hand corner, moving down the column, with R = Recency and F = Frequency in the simple equations below:

$\leq$ 30 Days Column

$R = \leq 30$ days, $F = \geq 25$ units
$R = \leq 30$ days, $F = 10 \leq F \leq 24$ units
$R = \leq 30$ days, $F = 4 \leq F \leq 9$ units
$R = \leq 30$ days, $F = 3$ units
$R = \leq 30$ days, $F = 2$ units
$R = \leq 30$ days, $F = 1$ units

31–60 Days Column

$R = 31 \leq R \leq 60$ days, $F = \geq 25$ units
$R = 31 \leq R \leq 60$ days, $F = 10 \leq F \leq 24$ units
$R = 31 \leq R \leq 60$ days, $F = 4 \leq F \leq 9$ units
$R = 31 \leq R \leq 60$ days, $F = 3$ units
$R = 31 \leq R \leq 60$ days, $F = 2$ units
$R = 31 \leq R \leq 60$ days, $F = 1$ units

These are the first 2 right-hand columns before the totals. You get the idea. While you are at the programming, don't forget to figure out a way to get some kind of "LifeCycle Grid Cell Code" into each customer account so they can be used systems and company wide for reporting and customer management.

If you're a real glutton for spreadsheet punishment, try doing a **Delta Analysis** on your LifeCycle Grids. This simply means you take 2 consecutive LifeCycle Grids (calculated 30 days apart, or 2 weeks apart, or whatever your time frame is) and net the numbers between them, cell for cell. Taking the upper-right hand corner in Figure 45 as an example, (R = ≤ 30 days, F = ≥ 25 units), if the next month there are more than 374 customers in that cell, the Delta analysis will show a positive number in the cell. Check out this Delta LifeCycle Grid:

Recency
Days Since Last Purchase (Visit)

Frequency (Units)	181+ Days	91–180 Days	61–90 Days	31–60 Days	≤ 30 Days	Totals
25 + Units	-33	-19	9	18	25	0
10 – 24 Units	-43	-13	12	30	42	28
4 – 9 Units	-37	-25	15	42	67	62
3 Units	-102	-77	84	187	236	328
2 Units	-228	-109	132	267	400	462
1 Unit	-389	-234	5	15	-89	-692
Totals	-833	-477	257	559	681	187

Figure 49: Delta LifeCycle Grid
Demonstrating Healthy, Growing, Profitable Business

You will see both positive and negative numbers in the Delta LifeCycle Grid, depending on whether the number of customers in the cell grew or got smaller. Then you begin to really understand how customer "value flows" are moving, where Friction is rising or falling, and whether your customer base is getting stronger (positive Delta Grid numbers generally towards the upper right-hand corner, negative generally towards the lower left-hand corner) or weaker (negative Delta Grid numbers upper right, positive lower left). Figure 49 above is an example of a Delta Analysis showing a customer base getting stronger, with growing future sales potential. Let's look at this for a moment. Remember, these are **"net change"** numbers.

The cells referred to in the following discussion are shaded gray in the LifeCycle Grid above. You had a **net gain** of 187 customers (junction of the **Totals** row and column, far lower right). You added a total of 681 customers to the ≤ 30 day Recency column (bottom of ≤ 30 column), hugely bullish. You lost 833 customers from the 181+ column (bottom of 181+ column). Very bullish, but hope you didn't pay too much to get them to purchase or visit; they're pretty dead customers, and never should have made it there. Can't win them all, though; there always will be SOME customers there, and it will grow over time. Your number of 25+ customers stayed flat (right end of 25+ row). You had a net loss of 89 1-time buyers in the ≤ 30 day Recency (junction of F = 1, R = ≤ 30), which probably means they bought a second time (moved up), but maybe moved left. This loss might be amplified by a lack of new customers to replace those moving out of the cell. Gotta check into that! Generally, customers moved up and to the right, creating positive cells in more Recent and higher Frequency cells, leaving negative cells in the more distant Recency and lower Frequency cells. This is an example of a powerful customer base, not only growing in size but also in future value. Friction is falling throughout all the important areas of customer base. Call the money guys!

Let's take a look Figure 50 below for a more problematic Delta Analysis.

Recency
Days Since Last Purchase (Visit)

Frequency (Units)	181+ Days	91–180 Days	61–90 Days	31–60 Days	≤ 30 Days	Totals
25 + Units	120	50	12	-66	-111	5
10 – 24 Units	99	87	14	-77	-121	2
4 – 9 Units	125	95	-25	-102	-83	10
3 Units	130	120	-57	-187	5	11
2 Units	263	169	-89	-113	-227	3
1 Unit	235	198	-203	-254	45	21
Totals	972	719	-348	-799	-492	52

Figure 50: Delta Grid Demonstrating Poorly Performing Business

Think about it for a minute before you read my explanation. Hey, you can do this stuff now, can't you?

You're right, this Grid is just terrible; it's what the death spiral looks like — the old "RF – LTV death spiral." They obviously haven't been keeping track of RF scores or doing LifeCycle Grids at this under-performing mess of a business. Who's the captain around here?

The cells referred to in the following discussion are shaded gray in the LifeCycle Grid above. Where to start? Well, on the bright side, they gained 52 customers (bottom of Totals column). Recent activity is not too bad in the mid-level Frequency area, and stayed positive at the 3 purchases level (junction of F = 3, R = ≤ 30). A couple of buyers are moving up, that's pretty good action.

But look at the massive customer defection going on. There are negative numbers up and to the left of the LifeCycle Grid, while positive numbers are down and to the right – Friction is rising among most valuable customers and it is out of control. Look at the total numbers across the bottom, from right (most Recent) to left (most distant). Customers are bolting! The right-most columns (more Recent) are shrinking while the left-most columns (Less Recent) are growing. Perhaps this site has been aced in their category. Customers are rolling over into the more distant columns, and not being replaced by enough new Recent customers generating some activity.

So that's what Delta Analysis on consecutive LifeCycle Grids looks like. Hey, by the way, remember the Recency of Visit graphs we looked at way back in the beginning of the book? There was one for a good business (Figure 11), one for a poor business (Figure 13). You probably didn't really get it back then. So go back and look at them again – they are in the Recency Toolkit chapter titled "Predictive Marketing." Then think about these two Delta Analysis Grids above. One of the Visit Recency graphs and one of the Delta Grids represent growing, healthy businesses, and the other of each, a poorly performing, headed for trouble business. The Visit Recency graphs give you a good snapshot of Potential Value, but lack the Current Value information to ensure you are taking action against most valuable customers. A Delta Analysis of LifeCycle Grids give you a "heads-up" on defections **by customer value** and provide directly actionable targeting information before defection gets too serious.

And of course, you can add characteristics to the LifeCycle Grid toolkit, just as we did with the RF scores. This is where LifeCycle Grids start to get really interesting, and provide the deepest insight into customer behavior; this is the approach we used at Home Shopping Network to develop our 126 most profitable "roll over" cells for automated targeting.

You can approach this task in two ways:

1. Take any cell and explode it out by other variables or characteristics

2. Do the LifeCycle Grid using a targeted customer population to start with

An example of #1 above:

Remember the first LifeCycle Grid we looked at with the 374 customers who were ≤ 30 days Recent, and had 25+ purchases (Figure 45)? Well, just who the heck **are** these 374 customers? Query the spreadsheet or database for their cell data (last purchase date less than or equal to 30 days ago, total purchases 25 or more) and produce a summary of the other characteristics of these customers. They're your best customers; you should see what they're made of! Do they take surveys? Are they cat people? Purchase categories? Use this information in your marketing. Find others like them, and grow them up and to the right in the LifeCycle Grid with your astoundingly smart and targeted promotions.

Customers who show similarity to your best customers, but are not yet there, are the easiest targets for turning into best customers. If your best customers are cat people, then cat people who are not yet best customers will be the easiest to "push along," and they will be more likely to follow through on your promotional or service efforts.

And an example of #2 above (use a targeted population):

Before doing the grids, break the customer base up into segments with known characteristics. Then run a grid on each segment separately and compare. Run the LifeCycle Grid on **just** cat people, and compare it with the LifeCycle Grid on **just** dog people. Compare headline readers with full story readers; compare book buyers with CD buyers, visitors form Overture to visitors from AdWords. If the resulting LifeCycle Grids demonstrate clear differences between the customer groups, you should be able to draw conclusions about where marketing budgets are most effectively spent.

For example, if the cat people LifeCycle Grid shows a higher percentage of Recent and Frequent customers in comparison with the dog people LifeCycle Grid, you could decide either to focus your business on the more profitable cat group, or work harder on making the dog group happy.

Exploding the LifeCycle Grids using characteristics is only one way to approach the business. You can produce LifeCycle Grids using any variable as a base, by running it with **only** those customers who fit or participated in that variable. For example, use the same "Big 5" variables we talked about when examining LifeCycles by different customer attributes and affinity profiles (see the middle of the Advanced Toolkit Chapter titled "Customer LifeCycles: Tracking Scores over Time for this discussion of the "Big 5").

Run LifeCycle Grids by customer acquisition source (banner, search engine, direct mail, newsletter ad, etc.) Run them by product or category of first purchase. Run them by price range of first purchase. Run them by date and time range of first purchase, by discount usage, and by product affinity. Any variable or characteristic is fair game. Just collect a group of customers who share the attribute in question, and run your LifeCycle Grids. You will learn more about your customers through this process than you ever thought possible – and this process guarantees you will have a job for as long as you can stand it!

You will understand which media brings in the most profitable customers, the products and pricing you should use to attract high value new customers, and the days of the week or months of the year generating the highest quality customers. And using this information, you should be able to drive marketing costs down while driving revenues up. Because you're a Data-Driven marketer now!

Chapter 23
Straight Talk on LifeTime Value

LifeTime Value. The promised ground. We've arrived, having made it through all the background information you needed to really understand this concept. And interestingly, I think, you probably already get it by now. Almost like it's not worth talking about. But talk about it we will, so you get the whole picture.

There are two kinds of LifeTime Value measurement - **absolute** and **relative**. The first can be difficult to calculate; the second, very easy to calculate and in many ways more powerful than the first. The most difficult part of calculating LTV is deciding what a "lifetime" is. LifeTime Value is the value of the customer over the LifeCycle (if you don't know what a LifeCycle is, you really should read the chapters on LifeCycles before reading this one). Lifetime Value doesn't exist without a LifeCycle; the LifeTime is the amount of time a customer will stick around and create value before defecting. We will get into some details on calculating **absolute** LifeTime Value in a moment, but first, we need to go through some clarifications.

The LifeTime Value concept has been horribly abused and misunderstood over the last several years. It is not necessary to figure out an absolute LifeTime Value for a customer or wait "a lifetime" to find out the value to use the concept in managing customer value. If you are new to this LifeTime Value stuff and have not tracked the appropriate parameters, or your company is new and lacks meaningful operating history, you can look for "**relative** LifeTime Value," link it to customer behavior, and still get leverage from using Lifetime Value / Lifetime Customer Value in your business model to manage customer value.

Here's a very simple example. Say I run the same ad in two different newsletters and get response from both. When I look at these responders, maybe a week later for a content visit or 30 days later for a purchase, I find a high percentage of repeat visitors or buyers from one newsletter, and a low percentage from the other. Repeat behavior indicates higher LifeTime Value, and predicts future repeat behavior, regardless of the absolute monetary LifeTime Value is. I can switch money out of the low repeat newsletter into the high repeat newsletter and get higher ROI without having to measure anything but repeat behavior.

As you know, using customer behavior to predict the relative LifeTime Value and loyalty of customers is a 40-year old technique still used by mail order and TV shopping companies today. Large sites with CRM analytics are using this technique, to predict customer value and response to promotions. If you'd like to read more details on using relative LifeTime Value to make ad or product decisions, see the Recency Toolkit chapter titled "The Ad Spending Example."

But let's say you're not satisfied with using relative LifeTime value as a proxy for absolute LifeTime Value. You're a glutton for punishment, or your boss wants a hard number. No problem. If you have studied customer LifeCycles, you know what a LifeTime is, and that is the first step towards understanding Lifetime Value. Here are a couple of issues we need to put on the table when discussing the calculation of LTV:

1. If you haven't been in business long enough to know the Lifetime of a customer, just put a stake in the ground by looking for defected best customers. Look at customers who have spent or visited the most with you and then of these, look at the ones who haven't made a purchase or visit in some time (6 - 9 months, for example). In all likelihood, the last purchase or visit was the end of the LifeCycle when considering best customers who have stopped buying or visiting for some time. When best customers stop, they're usually all done. Then look at first purchase or visit date for these customers, calculate your Lifetime, and use this length of time as the "standard" customer LifeTime, realizing the average lifetime is probably much shorter.

2. Frequently, a customer will defect for a few years and then come back. This is cool, and normal. Their life changed somehow and they left, and now they need you again. Many Data-Driven marketers would call a customer who has had zero activity for over 2 years a defected customer. Online, it's more like 6 months for the average customer, unless you are in a classic seasonal business. In many businesses, if the customer starts up again they would be a "new customer" for marketing and RF scoring purposes. They will more likely behave like a new customer than a current customer. The behavior will ramp and fall off all over again, just like it did in their previous LifeCycle.

That doesn't mean you can't use the same customer number, or combine the old behavior record with the new behavior record in the customer service shop. In fact, knowing how long a customer defects before they come back on average can be a useful promotional tool.

But there has been a significant break in behavior, and this customer is more likely to behave as a new customer than a customer who has been with you the whole time. That's just the way it works. They're likely to be interested in different products, for example, or use a different payment method. You decide if it's a new lifetime or not based on your business. In most cases, from a Data-Driven marketing perspective, and for the purposes of LifeTime Value, they should be treated as a new customer. **Otherwise, all your customers will have "infinite" lifetimes**, and analysis will be futile.

I am **not** saying from a service standpoint they should be treated as a new customer and assigned a new customer number or not recognized as a customer. You should "welcome them back" like an old friend. But realize their behavior is likely to be different now from a marketing standpoint and don't brand them with any old labels.

Perhaps the customer had a low RF score for most of the LifeCycle the last time; this customer could turn into a high RF customer the second time around. Things change, and the customer announced it by defecting and coming back. Appreciate the potential for a change in behavior, from a marketing perspective, and act accordingly. Let them demonstrate their new behavior. Start a new RF file on them. **This is particularly true in interactive businesses**. Remember the following dirty little secret:

The customer lifecycle for interactive businesses is more exaggerated than for traditional Data-Driven businesses. The behavior ramps up faster at the beginning of the cycle, but then falls off faster into the end of the cycle.

This means a previously defected, returning customer is more likely to behave like a new customer with a new LifeCycle. And as I said before, if you don't determine a place to cut-off, your LifeCycle and LifeTime Values become "infinite." There's only one reason you would want to look at customers this way — if you have to justify outrageous acquisition costs.

LifeTime Value properly applied is the net profit a customer contributes over their Lifecycle. A calculation of LTV allows you to decide how much to spend to acquire a customer in the first place. If the LTV of a customer is $100, you don't want to spend $120 to acquire them as a customer; you would end up losing $20 in the longer term on the customer. If you acquire a customer with an LTV of $100 for $80, you will make $20 on the customer before they defect. Some people will take the "Net Present Value" of this $100 in order to get an idea of what this stream of future profits would be worth today. To me, this practice simply confuses the issue. If may be very appropriate in some businesses, particularly very long-cycle, high ticket retail and B2B, but for the average person out there, forget about Net Present Value. Deal with dollars that will hit the bank account sometime in the next year or so.

LTV is a pretty straightforward calculation. Define the length of time you will use, measure sales, subtract cost of goods, subtract directly related service and admin overhead, subtract promotional costs and you get LTV. If you are not a commerce site, you have to imply the value of customer revenues by using a proxy, say (total revenue / unique visitors) or (total revenue / uniques with at least 10 visits). We will use purchases in the following discussion as the measurement of revenues.

One challenge to calculating LifeTime Value can be this: perhaps much of the data you need to complete the simple calculation is not available, or can't be agreed upon by all the players, especially if you are in a big company. If you don't know what the average unit returned costs you in terms of overhead, you can't do the calculation. If you don't know what the average number of customer service calls per unit shipped is and what the calls cost, you can't do the calculation. This is a particularly difficult problem for offline retailers, who don't have a database that captures nearly enough relevant data.

Here's one way to approach it if the operational data you need is unclear:

Try to focus on the average unit sold or a unit of revenue like a CPM for ads, and break up all the revenue and cost components that comprise the unit. Once you get to a profit / unit, just multiply by units sold to / generated by a visitor over the "lifetime," minus overhead and promotional costs, and you get LTV.

Average price, cost of goods sold, gross margin...should be easy to find. To get customer service costs, look at how many units you move annually, and divide by annual customer service cost. Do the same thing for returns, and so on, until you know the costs / unit sold of all the elements going into a sale. Don't forget credit processing, after sale support, fraud, etc.

If you find this impossible, a proxy might be found in your company's annual financial statements. Depending on the kind of business you are in, you would take your annual net income or cash flow and divide by units sold. This number will be contaminated by all kinds of adjustments; perhaps your accountant or finance department could help you "add back" to income or cash flow items not really related to selling units. These things might include goodwill, tax-related items, acquisition costs, depreciation, etc. If it doesn't directly affect the sale of a unit, back it out. This will no doubt be a lively discussion, but it is at the heart of a company-wide agreement on how to define LTV — what costs should be allocated to the sale of a unit, and what the real profit of a unit sold is.

For example, would you define the company web site as a "cost of good business practices and servicing our customers"? If so, then it would exist anyway, regardless of whether sales were made on it or not. If this statement is true, then allocate only the costs involved in generating and processing sales, not the costs of "the whole site." This exercise is great fun and if you're in a big company you'll finally get to bond with that finance guy you eat lunch with.

Many times this discussion will be about fixed versus variable costs. What costs would you have anyway, regardless of the next marginal unit sold? If a cost is difficult to attribute directly to the sale of the next unit, it probably doesn't belong in a LTV calculation. The cost to add another HR person to hire more customer service reps to keep up with growing sales is probably a stretch for an addition to the LTV calculation. The cost of the service reps is another story, and would probably be added into the LTV calculation.

Frequently "step costs" enter into the picture. A step cost is a cost occurring at "thresholds" of activity. Data storage is a good example of a step cost. For each unit sold or each visit made, the storage needs don't vary directly with the activity. But at some point you have to add more storage, and wham! You get a huge increase in cost occurring all at once on the last marginal unit sold that caused the need for the additional storage. These effects need to be smoothed out for an LTV calculation, if infrastructure is to be included as a cost.

You shouldn't add anything you can't measure – the value of an e-mail subscription, pass-a-long referrals, etc. – just assume any positive or negative contribution it makes is already reflected in sales. After all, if you include the entire value of a pass-a-long referral in a customer's LTV, what is the customer they referred worth? It's double counting. If you know pass-a-long exists, it's fine to add the effect in when looking at customer acquisition programs, but it's not part of LTV. For example, let's say you find the average LTV to be $20, and on average, the new customer recruits 3 other customers who also have an LTV of $20. This first customer's LTV is not $80; it's still $20. But the amount you can spend to acquire a customer is $80 at breakeven, knowing the customer will "create" 3 more customers each worth $20. Every dollar less than $80 you spend to acquire the customer is profit; every dollar over $80 is a loss.

If you're trying to segment LTV's for different groups, make assumptions and adjust. Web based customers make less or more calls to customer service when compare with offline customers? Return rates are higher or lower? If you can't break this out, use the sales / COGS / gross margins unique to each group, and assume the "overhead" (customer service, warehouse, etc.) is the same across all other customer groups you will be measuring.

And finally, subtract the cost of promotion to each group, advertising, discounts given, etc. and you'll have profit per unit. If you don't track these variables, allocate as in the examples above. Once you have the net profit per unit sold, which at this point should include all overhead and promotional costs, multiply by the number of units sold to a customer over a "lifetime," and you have it – LifeTime Value. Don't be surprised if you find some customer groups have negative LTV's – it's very common. This is the part of LTV analysis usually forgotten, because it literally means you would be more profitable if you had fewer customers. And explaining that to your boss (if you have one) is often a challenge, even on a good day. The following Figure 51 is what a unit profit analysis might look like:

Average Sale Price	$40.00	100%
Cost of Goods Sold	(36.00)	90%
Gross Margin	4.00	10%
Credit Clearing	(.80)	2%
Cost of Ship & Handle	(4.00)	10%
Revenue Ship & Handle	6.00	15%
Call Center (1 call every 5 sales)	(.80)	2%
Returns and Processing (5% of Sales)	(2.00)	5%
Fraud / Merchandise Loss (1% of Sales)	(.40)	1%
Promotional Costs / Discounts / Ads	(.80)	2%
Net Profit per Unit	$1.20	3%

Figure 51: Unit Profit Analysis for LTV Calculation

LTV Calculation and Customer Acquisition Cost Calculations:

The average customer buys for 2 years, then stops for at least 1 year. Therefore, we are defining the LifeTime of a customer as 2 years.

Over 2 years, the average customer makes 16 purchases.

16 x $1.20 Profit per Unit = $19.20 LTV of the average customer

The average customer recruits 3 other customers. The maximum acquisition cost of a new customer should be 4 x $19.20 = $76.80 to breakeven on the customer acquisition.

This process should be carried out across different groups of customers. The "average customer" is really a meaningless concept, from the marketing point of view. You should at least do LTV's by the media source of the new customer, by affinity for content and product, by price point of first purchase, etc. This is pretty easy, since the only variables are really how much you spent on promotion and the number of purchases the customer makes. The rest of the internal "operational" parameters – such as profit per unit – should be pretty much the same. Since you are a Data-Driven marketer now, you know all this.

If you want to get fancy, high RF customers may have lower return rates, or they may be higher. Fraud is probably lower. Backend customer service might be higher. Just adjust for the variables as you study different groups. This is where you really find out how your business works, and where profits are coming from down in the guts of it.

Here's a final thought on calculating LTV – **there is not one right way to do it across all businesses. The most important issue about LTV is everybody agreeing to the way it is calculated, and everybody knowing what goes into LTV and what does not.** LTV is an extremely critical concept to all Data-Driven businesses, because it drives much of the internal decision-making. Hash it out and agree to a standard measurement.

Once you have LTV's for your different customer groups, what next? Are they actually good for something other than determining what you can pay for customer acquisition costs?

Well, sure. Remember that RF is a proxy for LTV, but RF only talks about potential for revenue and current revenue. LTV includes both revenue and cost for a net number more closely related to net income or cash flow, depending on how you calculate it and what kind of business you are in.

So here's the short story – you can use LTV with all the RF techniques we have discussed so far in the book. Profiling, modeling, RF Scoring, and LifeCycle Grids all benefit by including LTV as a characteristic, or using it as the primary focus of an analysis.

For example, you can do the LifeCycle Grid and then look at the LTV's of the customers in a cell, just like you would look for "cat people" or other characteristics in the cell. You can take all your highest LTV customers and put them through a LifeCycle analysis, looking at RF scores over time. Compare this analysis to a low LTV customer group, looking for clues on how to market successfully to each group.

Or you can combine customer origin analysis with LTV. Looking at the LTV's of customers by source of advertising that brought them on as new customers is hugely beneficial. It's a direct comparison of what you pay out in ads versus what you get in LTV, a profitability analysis. I guarantee you will see staggering differences in LTV by marketing source, differences so large you will immediately cancel the ads pulling low LTV customers and beef up the ads pulling high LTV customers.

LTV by first product purchased or site area frequently visited can be very powerful. It will determine which products or content you feature to new customers, and which you never feature, because it creates low LTV customers. In a similar direction, LTV by product or content affinity will tell you which products or content you want to get new customers hooked on before they defect and stop spending.

In TV shopping, there is a huge correlation between time of day of first purchase and LTV, as was pointed out earlier regarding buyers between 2 AM and 4 AM. There is also a strong correlation between LTV and product of first purchase. You could tell what the LTV of a new customer would likely be by just looking at what they bought and when they bought it.

It's very highly predictive in the aggregate, over large groups of customers. LTV by price of first purchase has always been predictive across many different kinds of businesses, with high first purchase price generating high LTV's, on average. Check to see what the relationship is in your business.

Now you know how to calculate LTV and use LTV in designing marketing promotions and measuring the value of your customer base. We'll finish up on LTV with an example of how important LTV can be to your business.

Let's say your sales are growing because you are bringing on boatloads of new customers **from a new marketing approach.** Everything looks great. The problem is, you don't know these new customers have low LifeTime Values, lower than your existing customers. You haven't measured LTV by media the customer came from, or by first purchase offer, or by product of first purchase, so you don't know you're generating low value customers. For whatever reason (usually the media and the offer used have a lot to do with it), these new customers are generally not repeat buyers or visitors, meaning they have low LTV. You are not even RF scoring the new customers, so you don't know they are not generally repeaters.

As the percentage of these new low LTV customers as part of your customer base grows, the **average LTV** of your customer base begins to fall. Recall that LTV represents future profits from your customers. This is happening **while total visits and total daily sales look great**, because of all the new customers from the new marketing promotion. Your existing high LTV customers are becoming "diluted" with your new low LTV customers. When looking at reports, and projecting future profits and activity **based on past performance**, everything looks great. **Overall activity** is "ramping," and you figure all these new customers will make a contribution to future profits similar to your current customers. Activity **at the customer level** is a different story; average profit per customer is falling. And all of a sudden, sales growth goes flat, even though you are bringing on more and more new customers. And profits start to tank even though sales are staying flat. Average profit per customer begins to fall because the **future profit potential of the low LTV customers fails to materialize as you thought it would based on past experience. You were thinking the future profit potential of the new customers would be the same as your current high LTV customers, and it's not by a long shot.**

I have seen this slide in action, and it's not pretty. It may take 6 months to a year to get to the day when sales go mysteriously flat and the profit slide effect kicks in; but once the slide starts, it accelerates. It typically takes as long to correct the mistake as it did to create it in the first place. You have to double your efforts to attract high LTV customers just to stay even, and while you are spending time and resources pursuing this, profits continue to slide.

This is the "RF – LTV" death spiral I have referred to previously in action. "Death spiral" because it sneaks up on you and you don't even know it is happening until it is almost too late. By the time you realize what is happening, you are so deep into the vortex of the spiral you can't get out, you're trapped. It takes a tremendous focus and plenty of resources to reverse this process. Only when you have acquired enough high LTV customers will profits begin the slow climb back to where they were.

And now you can **truly** understand why the dot-bomb happened. It was not really a matter of "spending more money than you bring in", almost all new businesses spend more money than they bring in. The key is most dot-coms spent more money acquiring visitors / customers then the LTV of these visitors / customers. Put another way, these visitors and customers had **very low Potential Value**, particularly when people realized how low the value of an average unit of display advertising (page view) on the web is. Conversely, when people realized how much higher the average value of a Search advertising unit was, the advertising model finally clicked and the money followed.

Why does the average unit of search advertising have a much higher value? Because search advertising is driven by behavior, not by demographics or content like display advertising. People using Search tend to have high Potential Value. "Page Viewers" only have characteristics, they are of a certain age, or enjoy a certain lifestyle. But these characteristics have extremely low Potential Value relative to knowing a person is likely to buy, knowing they are likely to click, etc. That is why so-called Behavioral Targeting in the display ad area is so hot now, isn't it? Behavioral Targeting is the display advertising universe's attempt to get as close behaviorally to the Search model as they possibly can. And the early studies seem to indicate it is working. No surprise there, right?

Be a smart Data-Driven marketer. As soon as you are able to, pay some attention to LifeTime Value. Learn what you can afford to pay to acquire a customer for each source or segment. When you start using RF Scores or LifeCycle Grids to track retention and defection by customer value over time, determining "true" or absolute Lifetime Value is really not very far away. You now have all the raw materials and tools you need to get there.

You're welcome.

Chapter 24
Lifetime Value, I'd Like to Introduce You to the CFO

All-righty then. All that said on Lifetime Value, and particularly if you work in a larger company, at some point you are going to have to explain how this "long-term value of the customer" stuff fits into the reality of corporate finance. I wrote this article for the annual Customer Retention issue of a trade magazine called The Customer Report. This article should be very helpful to those staring customer value management or CRM straight in the eye, because at some point, you are going to have to deal with these issues. Might as well be prepared...

And then there was Lifetime Value, the mysterious, near impossible-to-figure Holy Grail of Customer Marketing. Is there more to Lifetime Value (LTV) than just a ruse for keeping a consulting contract open-ended? Customer behavior expert and author Jim Novo thinks so – if you transform LTV into a concept your CFO can reconcile with the existing financial reporting system.

Conflicting Values

Why is this idea of Lifetime Value (LTV) so difficult for a firm to absorb, never mind to calculate and implement? Because it is a "fish out of water" relative to the way most firms are managed. The idea of LTV contradicts the entire structure of a firm driven by periodic financial statements. When profits, security prices, compensation, and budgeting are all tied to the quarterly income statement and balance sheet, then how would you expect a firm to embrace the idea of a customer Lifetime? Where is the incentive? What value will implementing the use of Lifetime Value measurement bring to the firm? If you don't have a way to reconcile the notion of LTV with the internal financial yardsticks of the firm, it is not likely you will find a lot of support for managing the business based on longer-term customer value.

But Lifetime Value is a central idea in customer retention and Customer Relationship Management (CRM); after all, if you cannot extend and increase the value of a customer, then why bother with CRM at all? There may be some measurable operational efficiencies and cost reductions to be had with a properly planned CRM installation, but without a measurable increase in customer value and profitability tied directly to CRM itself, CRM will continue to be a bitter pill to swallow for many involved – unless you can prove bottom line impact. Operational efficiencies and cost reductions are certainly welcome, but the majority of CRM ROI is on the customer side, not on the business side. If you can't measure this **customer-side ROI** – the net increase in customer profitability attributable to CRM – you're not going to be able to lay claim to it. And the traditional periodic accounting statements your company uses to measure profits are not going to provide you with the information you need to make your case.

Even before you get started planning for CRM, you are faced with a conflict between the customer accounting approach of LTV and the periodic statement accounting approach of the CFO. **It is this conflict, buried deep in the heart of the firm, which I believe ultimately results in "CRM failure."** Unless this conflict is resolved prior to the implementation of CRM, it will grow and begin to manifest itself in the CFO's eyes as lack of Return on Investment (ROI), viewed through the lens of the periodic statement system. You must prove you know how to track customer value and establish benchmarks if you ever expect to forecast and measure the customer-side ROI of a CRM implementation.

Question of Time

The critical difference between customer accounting and periodic accounting is the way **time** is handled. Customer accounting based on Lifetime Value is forward looking; the periodic statement system is at best a snapshot of the current situation, and more frequently backward looking. The Lifetime Value system is constructed using mathematical predictions of customer value based on historical data; the periodic statement system is based on a "best guess" forecast of what revenues and expenses will be, or by taking past performance and incrementing it by a percentage. It is not based on customer value "facts."

These different accounting treatments often result in different management styles. Firms using customer accounting (as many direct and database marketing entities do) understand and believe in the concept of Lifetime Value; they know as long as they continue to incrementally increase the ROI of mailings and acquire customers of higher and higher Lifetime Value, the periodic statements will take care of themselves. Firms managing by periodic statement can only rely on what they transact, and are loath to trust "future value." They are also frequently surprised when profitability shifts in either direction due to operational or marketing changes.

In order for CRM to be successful, there has to be a reconciliation of these two accounting systems and management styles in order for costs and benefits to be aligned and ROI proven out. The best time to do this is in the "pre-CRM" phase, before any serious discussion of organizational changes or software occurs. The firm should undertake a significant study of customer value and be very clear on how customer value accounting relates to periodic statement accounting as the very first step of a CRM effort.

Periodic Error

Does the whole customer accounting versus periodic accounting premise sound quite fantastic to you? Allow me to relate a true story I believe clearly demonstrates the difference between the customer accounting and periodic accounting measurement and management styles, and offers some insight on the value of a pre-CRM customer accounting effort.

A direct-to-customer retailing company I was doing work for generated new customers with an average Lifetime Value of $120 (profit, not sales), and the LifeTime of the customer was about 2 years. These numbers could differ substantially by customer acquisition method and category of product sold, but the averages related above had been stable for over 5 years. Revenues and profits were quite predictable based on the number of new customers acquired using these metrics. If you know every new customer is worth on average $120 in profits over 2 years, it is quite a simple matter to project the financial health of the firm out into the future. This is an example of the forward-looking nature of customer accounting in practice.

New management came in to run the company, and as new management frequently likes to do, changed the marketing and merchandising approach. The new format was to emphasize the marketing and merchandising of products generating higher volumes of new customers. Unfortunately, this change was made without concern for the **value** of the new customers attracted by this change; we predicted these new customers would have significantly lower Lifetime Values based on past experience with these methods and products.

As the changes in marketing and merchandising took hold, sales remained flat to slightly higher, and the number of new customers acquired started growing faster than before the changes. From a traditional periodic financial reporting view, the changes appeared to be successful. But on the Lifetime Value ledger, after studying the new customers generated by these changes for several months, we saw the dramatic drop in the value of new customers **relative** to the "old customers" we had predicted.

When examining customers three months after their first purchase, customers acquired under the previous business format spent on average about $200. The new customers attracted by the current format had cumulative sales of only $100 at three months after first purchase. Further, under the previous format, 50% of customers would still be active buyers at 3 months. For the new customers attracted by the current format, this number was 25%.

We flagged this situation immediately to management. At this rate, we predicted sales for the firm would drop significantly **12 months in the future.** Under the old business format, we could depend on customers acquired in one year to still be buyers in the next year. Under the new scheme, it appeared the average new customer stopped buying sooner and spent less overall.

You can probably guess the response from management to this prediction.

According to the periodic financial statements, everything was just fine. Sales were flat to up, and new customers were coming on even faster than before – proof the new strategy was working. We warned **a** high percentage of the current sales activity was coming from **old customers** who would be "rolling off" next year, and that the new customers replacing them would not purchase as much. In fact, it looked like we would have to double the number of these new customers we brought in if we wanted to replace the sales of the old customers rolling off – the new customer value looked to be about half the value of the old customer, based on our **relative value** tracking studies.

We were summarily tossed out of the room at this point.

About 6 months later, year over year sales started sliding, gradually at first, and then at an increasing rate. A short 6 months after this, the company was on the verge of going out of business, management was replaced, and the original marketing and merchandising format put back into place. How long do you think it took for this company to build sales and profits back to the level of performance before the change in format? It took as long as it took to destroy the Lifetime Value of the customer base in the first place.
Sales and profits initially continued to erode under the reversion to the old format. The rate of new customers coming in dropped significantly, back to

levels consistent with the old format. This was not a comforting sign for the new management, because the periodic financial statements presented increasingly bad news - for a time. But the new management believed in the concept of Lifetime Value, and our analysis showed the new customers coming in were indeed twice the value of the new customers created by the rejected format. We advised management stay the course. The rate of decline in sales started to slow, then reversed and sales began to grow month after month.

Just as we predicted using the customer accounting approach.

It took a full year for the low value customers created by the new format to be replaced with higher value customers created by returning to the original format. Once this customer value replacement cycle was complete, the company surpassed the old sales and profitability level it had achieved before the initial change in format – and kept right on growing at double digit rates.

The periodic financial accounting statements failed to provide vital management input on two occasions. They could neither tell of the future decline in business due to a faulty change in format, nor could they predict the future rise in profitability due to a beneficial return to the original format. Only an accounting system based on measuring and managing the future value of a customer can do this. Customer value accounting is forward-looking and predictive of sales and profitability in the future.

Pre-CRM Analysis

Where does all of this leave us? On the one hand, managing by customer value is in direct conflict with the well-established periodic reporting accounting system used to manage the majority of firms in operation today, and all the definitions of business success are tied to this system. On the other hand, managing a business by customer value allows for an unmistakable advantage – the ability to predict future profitability and the effects of changes to the operation **before** they create any significant economic impact.

I believe management must clearly understand and implement a customer accounting system before implementing CRM, for it is this accounting system that CRM implementation decisions and ROI calculations should be based on. The use of periodic statement thinking to measure and manage CRM is simply not appropriate, and the CFO has to feel comfortable in understanding how to reconcile these two accounting systems. If you are the champion of the CRM effort, it is your job to deliver this reconciliation capability. After all, your system is late to the financial and management party.

Note this: in the example above, we did not actually measure "Lifetime Value" in the traditional, **absolute** sense. We looked at the **relative** value of customers, and determined the direction value was moving in. This idea of tracking relative customer value is one way to convert the concept of Lifetime Value into a more tangible number aligned with the periodic accounting statement system. There will be more on this idea of tracking relative value later in this article

Employee Incentives for CRM Failure?

Accurately tracking the customer-side ROI of a CRM project is only one good reason to implement a customer accounting system. The second is employee incentive plans. You can talk the customer-centric talk all you want, but if your CRM ROI relies on customer accounting and your incentive plans are based on periodic financial accounting, you could end up sabotaging the CRM effort by actually rewarding employees for CRM failure. You know a company is not just paying lip service to customer-centricity when employee incentives are not based on sales or profits, but on increases in customer value. To create such an incentive plan, a customer accounting system is needed.

Here is why. In B2C markets, the long-term value of the customer is often directly related to the method used to acquire the customer – the media, offer, and product can be used to predict long-term customer value. Marketing campaigns can be designed to generate lots of sales in a short time, but these promotional campaigns tend to generate customers of low value. Conversely, highly targeted non-promotional campaigns will generate sales at a slower rate but tend to generate customers of higher value. A Marketing VP reaching millions of consumers with these campaigns has a choice to make between the two approaches. With a bonus system tied to quarterly sales, which approach will be chosen? And when the time comes to look at the customer value increase from CRM, what do you suppose the result will be?

In B2B markets, the long-term value of the customer is often related to the difficulty of selling to them. Large companies have large budgets but large companies can also take forever to make purchase decisions. A VP of Sales for a B2B company is facing a sales shortfall six months into the fiscal year – along with a shortfall in annual bonus. While reviewing the list of prospects, the VP realizes the prospects with the highest long-term total sales potential will be the most difficult to close, and those with lowest long-term sales potential will be the easiest to close. Which prospects will the VP have the sales team focus on? And then people will wonder why the new sales force automation system did not increase customer value.

If a customer value accounting system cannot be established, the first warning shot has been fired. The CRM project, if it relies on customer value enhancement to succeed, will fail. By deciding a customer accounting system is not possible to implement, management has demonstrated they do not have the will to look beyond the periodic accounting system, and in doing so, have made it impossible for the CRM project to generate adequate ROI.

Once customer value accounting has been established, the firm must then reconsider the composition of employee incentive plans. If these plans remain financial accounting-centric as opposed to customer accounting-centric, the firm is literally creating an incentive for CRM failure, and encouraging employees to participate in and drive this failure through their action or inaction.

Sample Customer Accounting Reports

The customer accounting system does not have to be a piece of software running on a piece of hardware. It can take the form of customer value reporting, designed to track the value of new and current customers over time. As long as the CFO understands and approves of how the metrics are constructed, this approach to customer value reporting should be good enough for financial people to reconcile customer accounting with periodic accounting. Generally, two types of customer accounting reports are valuable - an overall view of customer value status and a campaign or project specific view.

The **overall value view**, which could be constructed every 30 days or every quarter to match the periodic accounting cycle, divides customers into value segments and tracks the growth or shrinkage of these segments. The important idea conveyed here is the direction of customer value – is it increasing or decreasing over time for the entire customer base?

The **campaign or project specific view** is just that – a simple analysis of each individual activity funded to drive customer value. Each activity has certain costs, generates revenues, and has a profitability associated with it. The revenues should be measured over a length of time agreed to by the CFO, and a target ROI should be decided upon. If an activity cannot generate an acceptable

ROI, it should be discontinued. This approach does not mean you stop testing new ideas; it does mean you don't repeat low ROI mistakes. For example, each new customer campaign should be tracked over time to determine the value of the customers generated relative to other campaigns.

The idea behind both these reports is simple. As long as customer value at the macro level and ROI at the campaign or operational project level are tracking incrementally in a positive direction, a CFO can be confident this value will eventually flow through to the periodic accounting system. The CFO may not be able to "see it" in the periodic accounting statements, but you have proven in advance the value you created is "in there." These reports become the base or benchmark by which the CFO can be convinced CRM or a customer retention program is indeed contributing value.

I won't be completely resolving this question of periodic versus customer accounting systems for you in this relatively short article. I can offer you two examples of "overall value view" reports you can use as prototypes for the pre-CRM effort to begin the examination of these issues. The following should be fairly simple to accomplish, even if you don't have a data warehouse and a bunch of Ph.D.'s on staff, and should be relevant to most businesses.

The primary difference between a periodic accounting system and a customer accounting system is in the treatment of **time**. Any customer analysis you do pre-CRM should lean towards breaking down the variable of time into component parts aligned more closely to the periodic statement accounting system and creating a comfort level for the CFO regarding the concept of tracking customer value. If you can accomplish this and get "buy in" at a basic level, you can move on to more sophisticated reporting later on when you have the CRM tools.

The easiest customer behavior components for most firms to access and report on are total sales and customer start date - the first purchase or billing transaction with the customer. Here are two simple reports using these metrics that will allow you to start building your case.

Report 1: Sales by Customer Volume

Take any periodic statement time frame – a month, a quarter, a year. Gather all the customer revenue transactions for this period, and recast them into the **total sales by customer** for the period. Decide on some total sales ranges appropriate to your business, and produce a chart showing the percentage of customers with sales in each range, including non-buying customers, for the chosen periodic accounting time frame. For example:

Sales per Customer during Periodic Time Frame by Sales Volume	Percent of Customers in Sales Volume Range
Greater than $1000	2%
$750 - $1000	6%
$500 - $749	12%
$250 - $499	15%
$1 - $249	25%
$0	40%

Figure 52: Sales by Customer Volume

Run this report each period, and compare with prior periods. In general, you want to see the percentage of customers contributing high sales per period to grow over time, and the percentage of lower revenue customers to shrink. This means you are increasing the value of customers overall. If the numbers are moving the other way, this is the type of customer value problem you would expect CRM or a smart retention program to correct, and if you are successful, you should see the shift in customer value through this report.

Report 2: Sales by Customer Longevity

Take any periodic statement time frame – a month, a quarter, a year. Gather all the customer revenue transactions for this period, and recast them relative to the **start date** of the customer. In other words, when looking at the revenue generated for the period, how much of it was generated by customers who were also newly started customers in the same time period? How much revenue was generated by customers who became new customers in the prior period? How about two, three, and four periods ago? More than 4 periods ago? Depending on the length of the period you use, you may end up with a chart looking something like this:

Customer Sales Began in this Period	Current Period Sales by Customer Start Period
Current Period	40%
One Period Ago	30%
Two Periods Ago	15%
Three Periods Ago	7%
Four Periods Ago	5%
More than Four Periods Ago	3%

Figure 53: Sales by Customer Longevity

In many cases, customers who have previously defected and then come back should be considered "new"; use the most recent start date you have for the customer. There is a reason to account for the revenues this way: it is likely you deployed new money or resources to get these customers to come back, and eventually, you will want to match up those expenditures with the revenues generated by the customer to prove out ROI and calculate LTV.

You can run this analysis at the end of each period and track the movement of value in your customer base. Generally, you want to see increasing contribution to revenue from customers in older periods, meaning you are retaining customers for longer periods of time and growing their value.

Relative or Absolute Value?

The fundamental idea driving relative customer value tracking is this: future or potential customer value is ever changing, and there really is not much point in trying to come up with an "absolute LTV." What you most want to know is this: is the **potential value** of the customer growing or shrinking, and at what rate? Knowing this, the firm can allocate marketing and financial resources to their highest and best use – to accelerate rising potential value and to slow down shrinking potential value in the customer base. You might use a 2-year LTV to benchmark your acquisition costs, but during this 2-year period and beyond, you want to look at **changes in potential value.** This can be done using one or more simple customer behavior modeling techniques. The use of these models is beyond the scope of this article but described in my book *Drilling Down: Turning Customer Data into Profits with a Spreadsheet.*

One final note. There are plenty of consultants who will be glad to throw stones at these simple models of customer value tracking, and tell you why you can't possibly manage a business using reports like this. All I can say to this is you have to start somewhere. The problem with many if not most CRM efforts so far is the firm launched into them without any idea of where they currently stand in regards to customer value. Without establishing benchmarks for tracking customer value, how is one ever to prove the ROI of CRM to the periodic accounting world? This idea of using relative and potential customer value measurement to bond customer value to the income statement is the driving force behind my Simple CRM workshops and consulting practice.

Endless navel-gazing on the subject of "true Lifetime Value" is simply a resource drain, and is not going to matter one bit if you can't reconcile it with the real world of periodic reporting statements. Trust me, I've been there and back, and lived to tell you the story!

#

Jim Novo is an interactive Relationship Marketing, Customer Retention, Defection, and Loyalty expert with over 15 years of experience generating exceptional returns on customer marketing program investments. More on Jim's background and consulting services can be found on his web site.

Chapter 25
Fellow Drillers at Work

Over the past 4 years, I've received a tremendous amount of e-mail from visitors to my web site and people who have purchased the book. I deeply appreciate all the interaction and feedback on these topics, especially given the subject is a bit ahead of the popular curve. Thanks for all your support.

I firmly believe exposure to business issues outside the immediate realm of your own expertise has a funny habit of "turning the lights on" in unexpected ways. I encourage you to review the exchanges in this chapter. You simply can't know whether your own Data-Driven "Eureka Moment" is trapped just beneath the surface of your consciousness, ready to be set free by a surprising revelation from somebody in what you think is a completely different business than yours.

I see this happen almost every day. The following conversations are the most insightful and interesting I have received to date. Take advantage of them.

Definitions and Background Information

CRM Definitions

Q: I am working on a project and analyzing the key variables of CRM and Relationship Marketing (RM). After reading extensively the only main difference I see between the two is that CRM involves systems (technology) which makes RM a part of CRM. I am also in search of diagrammatic models to simply explain the same. Can you please advise me?

A: Well, I don't know of any sites with diagrams because I'm not sure many people have come to this conclusion yet, which by the way, I think is correct and have said so. I wouldn't use technology as the "boundary" though, because good RM programs make heavy use of technology. To me, if you take RM and add Customer Service integration to it you have CRM, so RM is indeed a component of CRM. RM itself is made of components, or is the outcome of adding enhanced technology and strategic purpose to previous efforts.

At the lowest end of individual customer contact marketing you have direct marketing, which simply means you have a "list" of people and you send them something, frequently the same thing to every person. If you have more data than just the name and address, you can send different versions to different people based on this other information.

Now, if you collect the results of this effort and attach them to individuals and change your mailings based on the activity of a customer over time, you have entered the "database marketing" world, which would include simple customer marketing models like Latency, Recency, and RFM.

If you further modify your efforts by determining the LifeCycle of customer segments and change your marketing based on the LifeCycle stage of the customer, you have entered Relationship Marketing, at least according to the original definition of it.

And I would argue, if you add the integration of Customer Service and Sales Force Automation on top of this (if either is applicable), you now have CRM, or CMR, or CVM, or whatever they are calling it this month. I really don't care what they call it, for me it's simply about using data to increase profits. The trades can call it whatever they want. Specifically applied to customer marketing, it's all the same thing.

Anybody / any company who uses rigid definitions of the differences between all these shades of gray to create a pitch on "expertise" probably doesn't have a lot of expertise in the first place. It's easier to look like an expert when you create a microscopic market.

Jim

Best Books on Relationship Marketing

Q: I'm putting together a college course on Relationship Marketing, but find sources on the subject conflicting with each other. Is there any quality material out there on this topic worth using as a college textbook? And here's a confusing issue for me doing this research: is there a difference between Relationship Marketing and CRM?

A: There are quite a few opinions on the definition of Relationship Marketing, and I have to state at the start I am not part of the "new thinking" group (mostly CRM "experts") who believe something has fundamentally changed about customer behavior in the past 9 years. This is where a lot of the confusion starts.

There is a big difference between a new channel and a new behavior. Customers may do things faster or more often now with the web, but that does not mean the overall behavior or even attitude has changed. Customers have always wanted sharp pricing and good service. Just because it is much easier for a company to fail to provide what the customer wants on the web, and this failure is so much more obvious, does not mean customer behavior has changed.

The fact is, many companies never had customer data before and now they do, and they don't like what they are seeing. People who claim things have changed are simply seeing evidence for the first time of what was always there, and calling this evidence "new." Many CRM experts focus on the "intangible value of the customer relationship" and spend a lot of time theorizing on the future value of a "loving customer" having a "relationship" with the company. Even if this mattered, you can't measure it, so this track is a perfect excuse to expand billings with endless navel-gazing.

I believe customer loyalty is measured in sales and profits, and the customer isn't interested in having a "relationship" with a company. I don't need abstract theory to make the ROI work out - I have always proved it with hard data. As soon as you start "estimating the intangible value of the customer relationship" to bolster your ROI, you are entering into never-never land, in my opinion.

Relationship Marketing, as originally defined, is not about having a relationship with the customer. It is a strategy matching the marketing approach to the ebb and flow of the Customer LifeCycle, and creates very high ROI customer retention and value-enhancement programs using this information. Anything else is a dream, in my opinion.

You appear to be teaching this course at several difficulty levels. Now that you know where I am coming from, I will provide the fundamental list of books every serious student of this area should read.

Personally, I follow the original definition of Relationship Marketing as defined in this book:

Relationship Marketing - Successful Strategies for the Age of the Customer by Regis McKenna (1993).

McKenna is a true visionary who "got it" way before CNBC created visionaries every day. The essence of this book: Marketing has a much higher ROI if it is "tuned" according to the Customer LifeCycle. For more on the Relationship Marketing concept, see the link below:

http://www.jimnovo.com/Relationship-Marketing-more.htm

FYI, CRM as most "experts" describe it is not Relationship Marketing, it's just a jumble of "happy speak" and wishful thinking. In the end, what customers **do** is what matters, and except in very rare cases, don't want to have "a relationship" with a company. More on this below.

This next book essentially provides real world examples as proof the core ideas McKenna put forth actually work and are very profitable:

The Loyalty Effect : The Hidden Force Behind Growth, Profits, and Lasting Value by Frederick F. Reichheld (1996)

Let me be clear: the intent of this book was not to prove McKenna was right, but that was my take on it. If you read the examples carefully you will notice high retention / high customer ROI companies intuitively change their approach to the customer as the LifeCycle plays out.

The next book takes some of the ideas from the previous books and updates them for the web; it is lighter on background and theory, more organizationally and implementation oriented, making it the perfect 3rd book to read:

The Engaged Customer: The New Rules of Internet Direct Marketing by Hans Peter Brondmo (2000)

Brondmo "gets it" and delivers it straight without the navel-gazing. This book is the right one for the VP level people who need to understand how things fit together at the macro level but don't need all the gory implementation details.

This next book is mine and focuses on executing the specific tactical elements of a Relationship Marketing strategy: defining / tracking the Customer LifeCycle, and turning this information into higher profits through the development of highly targeted, High ROI marketing programs:

Drilling Down: Turning Customer Data into Profits with a Spreadsheet by Jim Novo (3rd edition 2004)

My book is for the Director level people who have to implement. It uses simple customer models to identify customer value issues early in the LifeCycle, and shows how to proactively address these issues in two ways: by fixing customer acquisition campaigns so they increase initial customer ROI, and by creating high ROI customer retention programs that increase customer value.

Good luck on putting together your courses!

Jim

What is the story with Data Mining?

Q: We're trying to develop an action-oriented customer retention program and are starting to build our trip wire metrics. I've been "hit up" by some of these firms that specialize in data mining - all of the neural networks stuff - can you help me understand why I should NOT go with one of them, versus develop this internally using your approach?

A: I don't know that my approach would be superior without understanding your objectives and a bit more about your data. But I can give you some "need to knows" about data mining in general that should help you decide...

Note to the data mining community: please don't hate me for stating the case in plain English. People really need to understand this stuff. If you are different, then simply prove it to your prospects. Love ya, I really do.

Understand that mining was originally developed for use by highly advanced modelers, not beginners. These are people who have used every human-based tool to do modeling and have squeezed every bit of info out, but want more. The only way to get more is to use a machine to look for patterns. The fact these services are sold to people just beginning the data modeling process is not particularly honest, in my opinion.

Here is what may happen: you will pay the money and spend the effort and they will come back and tell you that the Recency and Frequency of the trades are key to defection - and say their miner figured it out. And it did. The fact you could easily have already known that with a few simple tests is beside the point.

It is the ability of mining to improve on human modeling by 1% that is valuable, the ability to "go granular." If you have never done any human-driven modeling, you will see a tremendous benefit in using your first models generated by the miner. But the real question is this: could you have generated something nearly as good yourself, at a fraction of the cost, using "universal" behavior models?

Mining works best (meaning, delivers highest ROI) under these conditions:

1. Your data is super clean.
2. You have an enormous amount of data, and no logical way to aggregate it.
3. You have done everything you can to understand the data on your own.
4. You have tested theories and generated results that can be analyzed.

Reasons the above are true:

1. It's a machine; it can't distinguish between bad and good data. Dirty data = dirty results.

2. This one is tricky. You probably think you have more data than you really do, and that it is more complex than it really is. Example: Do you really think what stock was traded and how many shares were traded is meaningful to your end objective of predicting customer defection? Doesn't it make sense that a slowing in aggregate volume of trades or the number of months since last trade would be more relevant to spotting customer defection? I think so, and this approach means you would have much less data to analyze and the data is a lot less complex that you thought. If you are convinced the detail is important, use data mining. This is really a question of scale, and what data you believe is relevant, which leads to #3:

3. You have to "train the miner." This can take months. Basically, it keeps running scenarios and you tell it when it is wrong. This continues until it gets something right. In order to provide these instructions, you have to know what is wrong and right, you should have already run some analysis. When it comes back and says "customer defected because they traded 100 shares of SUN in Sep

1999" you have to say, "Um, I seriously doubt it." If the mining company says they "already have the training done," fine, but it's not on your data, so the granularity that is the real benefit of mining is lost.

4. If you are looking for direction on "what to do," there has to be "outcomes" for the miner to analyze. If you have not done any customer retention or targeted promotional programs and generated results from these programs, there is no "result" the miner can tie to "why."

So my advice is this: I think it is always best to make sure you have generated enough meaningful data for the miner to analyze. To do this, you have to do some basic modeling yourself and try some things, see how it goes. Doesn't have to be very complex, just generate some activity along the lines of the objective you have. Then if you are not satisfied, call in the miners. At least you will then have the kind of data that the miner can use, and will know enough to be able give the miner instructions.

Another alternative: hire a real human modeler for a time, and see what they come up with (not me, I use universal models or hire a modeler myself). I guarantee a hand-built regression model will be much better than using RFM, and much better than what the miner will come up with, because human intuition plays a huge role at the beginning of the modeling process. At the end of the process is where mining comes in, when it becomes an issue of "brute force." And if you do hire a modeler, be prepared for the first question they are likely to ask: do you have any results I can look at from universal models like Latency, Recency, or RFM?

Jim

Customer Loyalty and Retention Definitions

Q: Just wondered if you could answer a question I can't ever seem to find an adequate answer for.

A: I'll give it a shot. I have a pretty good track record so far...

Q: Are customer loyalty and customer retention the same thing, the terms are used so interchangeably with one another, I presume they're not - so how do they differ and conversely how are they similar?

A: They can be the same, in a broad sense. If you don't have customer retention, you don't have customer loyalty, and vice versa. I think most "old guys" like me think of customer retention as the very tactical and targeted to individual customer actions you take to keep customers on board. "Loyalty" is the end result of these programs.

Personally, I don't think any customers are "loyal." They may be loyal at a point in time, but it seems to me this is more like "infatuation." It isn't loyalty, which to me implies a long-term affair. Your best friend is "loyal." Harley Hog buyers are "loyal," and Harley Davidson is one of the very few companies that can claim loyal customers in the true sense of the word.

For most companies, they will be lucky if they can get "retention" - a short term, tactical idea; never mind loyalty - a long term, emotional idea. While we're at it, let's throw in "customer satisfaction." This is the weakest sister; customers can be satisfied and neither "retained" nor "loyal." The fact that some pretty famous "experts" use these words interchangeably tells you they really have no practical knowledge of consumer behavior.

Q: Also, what's the best way to measure customer retention - as customer satisfaction surveys will never provide a good measure?

A: Retention is really easy to measure if you have direct contact with customers. There's a ton of stuff about it on my web site - in fact, that's just about all my web site is about.

If you don't have direct contact with customers, well, that's another story completely. I'd have to know more about what industry you are in and the role you play in that industry. Describe your situation and perhaps I can help.

As far as satisfaction surveys, they can be used as a proxy for retention if you create a hard behavioral linkage between the two. For example, do your satisfaction survey, and then track the retention rates of the actual people in the survey. If you find a hard match between satisfaction and retention, then satisfaction = retention, simple as that.

You want to recheck this kind of proxy at the very least each time you have a major change in product, service, marketing, and so forth. At the high end of confidence, if you repeated this matching of satisfaction and retention every year, you could be highly confident it holds true over time.

Hope this answers your question, and if you need additional direction, please just let me know.

Jim

Affinity and Loyalty Program Definitions

Q: Jim - interesting site.

A: Thanks for the kind words!

Q: How would you define the difference between an affinity program and a loyalty program?

A: Well, I'm not sure they are all that different from a customer perspective, but one could think of the difference in this way:

In a loyalty program, you are going directly to the customer and want them to be directly loyal to you. In an affinity program, you are typically going to an *organization* the customer is already loyal to and hoping some of that loyalty rubs off on you. This often involves cutting a special deal for the organization's members, and even giving the organization a piece of the profits.

Affinity deals tend to work if there is a strong relationship between your products and the mission or make-up of the organization. If I can imply the underlying business we are talking about from your e-mail address, that means knowing that tech types make great cell phone customers and going to a software association and making a deal. Search the web on the phrase:

Association "preferred vendors"

or

Association sponsors

and you will probably come up with examples of affinity groups.

If you think pet owners make great cell phone customers, you go to the ASPCA and do a deal. When a non-profit is involved, affinity is usually called cause-related marketing.

I'll say again, for affinity to work, you have to know of a logical bond between your best customers and the group. For a product like wireless, something that universal, affinity may be more expensive to execute than loyalty and not provide the same bottom line benefits.
Finally, for an interesting blend of affinity and loyalty, check out the case study on my site, which in fact in on wireless:

http://www.jimnovo.com/download.htm#cellone

It's a classic loyalty program, with an affinity twist: many of the rewards were locally based. In this case, the affinity was to the Philadelphia / NJ area, and we used local rewards to fulfill and reinforce this affinity.

Hope that helps!

Jim

Survey Bias

Q: I have really enjoyed reading your newsletters. Keep up the outstanding work on them!!

A: Well, thank you for the kind words.

Q: Typically, most marketers offer an incentive for their customers' valuable feedback on a survey. I am interested in knowing if studies have proven or disproven that this offering skews the results of the survey. Any insight you can provide on this topic would be greatly appreciated.

A: I don't know of any "tight" studies on this I can link to. In general, rewards of any kind skew results, so I'm not sure anybody would bother studying it. How much skew occurs depends on the objective of the survey, the product, and the offer, so any study would have limited application in different situations.

The whole question of bias in surveys keeps the academic community alive with perpetual white papers. The key is to be consistent with your approach and look at trends. The first survey doesn't mean much as a stand-alone effort; the real question is, are things getting better or worse? The important number to look at is not the "absolute" level of any parameter, but the relative change in a parameter - the change over time.

With or without reward, you will introduce bias - it' the nature of this work. Some types of people answer, others don't; you always get bias! What you want to do is *control* the bias, and one of easiest ways to do this is to use the same survey method (and incentive, if you use one) each time you survey. The real issue is to set up something your company feels comfortable being consistent with, and look at the trends. If you ask if people are "satisfied" and 20% are, this is meaningless. What matters is the next time you ask, is it 25% or 15%?

Hope this answers your question.

Jim

Database / Prospect Quality

Q: I have a large client with an opt-in e-mail campaign. We found that the majority of customers who subscribe to these e-mails have never clicked on the offers they contain, and about one third have never even opened an e-mail. Can you direct me to any industry best practices and tactics for dealing with these inactive populations?

A: Well, I don't know about any "industry best practices" on this topic for e-mail, but I can tell you what is done offline - threaten 'em and then purge 'em. There is evidence for this working online, as it has been done successfully by people online wanting to maintain high list quality and responsiveness (the same reasons it is done offline).

There also seems to be some evidence that a "hey, if you're not going to read the e-mail, we're going to stop sending it" threat in the subject line, when applied with a "click here to confirm you want to keep getting this e-mail" in the body, actually converts people who were previously inactive to active openers, readers, and responders.

Again, this is what is seen offline. That's why you get catalogs with the similar "This is your last catalog if you don't buy" threat. It's a winner either way for the marketer; you make some additional sales from dormant targets and you stop spending effort on the ones who really don't care about your offers in the first place. More revenue, less cost. The Drilling Down mantra, for sure.

Q: You seem to provide practical methods for turning data into useful customer information. Do you think the lack of this expertise is the biggest reason why data-driven marketing is not more widely used?

A: Well, I don't know about not widely used. The $110 billion catalog industry is built on data-driven marketing. There are some people on the web doing a good job with it, though most of those are catalog operations. But yes, in general people are confused about which data is important and how to use it. There just are not many people around with practical hands-on experience.

Dealing with data is also highly math-oriented, and a lot of people don't feel comfortable with running numbers. These are the reasons I wrote the book. Techniques like mine are explained in some books, but either at too high of a level to be of practical use or with such mind-numbing detail and math you go crazy reading it. One day I thought to myself, Hey, you can strip this all down into a very basic approach, and really show the average person how to make a lot more money in customer marketing - by giving them the "dummies version" of advanced database marketing techniques. And to get rid of a lot of the math, I use graphical displays of behavior so "getting the results" is much easier.

Jim

E-Mail Costs a Lot More Than You Think

Q: What do you suppose the per piece rate for e-mail is? We are not sending out direct mail at all, just permission emails. How can we use RFM if our costs are nil for a campaign?

A: Well, I don't know what kind of business you are in, and that would help in answering this question. But generally, two things:

1. There are probably costs other than the cost of the e-mail involved

2. RFM isn't just about reducing cost, it's about increasing profits based on knowing who to communicate to and when, and perhaps what you should say.

1. Opportunity costs are all around us, and can be very steep, for example:

* the cost of giving away product margin with a discount when you really didn't have to – this is called subsidy cost

* the cost of over-communicating to someone and having them unsubscribe

* the cost of sending the wrong messages at the wrong times and depressing response or losing the customer completely

RFM allows you to measure and control these costs, maximizing profits.

2. RFM "standardizes" what you know about customers by ranking them against each other for present and future value. This allows you to test programs and repeat successes over and over and over. If customers with a certain score or range of scores respond well to a certain promotion, customers with this score or range of scores will respond well next month, the following month, and as far out as you can see. The RFM scores tell you where the customer is in their LifeCycle with you and allow you to tailor the most effective contact. Once you find something that works, you can repeat that success over and over just by looking at a customer's score, and constantly optimize for higher and higher levels of profit.

So RFM is about more than just reducing the cost of communications; as you pointed out, that is more of an offline play and an example of the "Old RFM." The New RFM is about optimizing the marketing mix to customers who are in different stages of their relationship with you, in order to squeeze out the highest possible profits from each customer.

I know that last statement probably makes some factions of the CRM community cringe, but business is business. You can still treat customers with respect and earn their admiration while increasing profits. Those having a "moral problem" with increasing per customer profitability won't be around for long in this business.

Good question!

Jim

Data Enhancement

Q: Jim, do you know anything about "geodemographics"? We have vendors calling us that want to "enhance" our database with demographic information based on the physical location of our customers. Will this help our marketing efforts and increase the response to our campaigns?

A: Hmmm...it might. Geodemographics, for those that don't know, consist of census and other information coded to the zip, zip+4, or census tract level. The idea is if you know where your customer lives, you can apply the "average demographics" of the neighborhood to your customer and perhaps learn something valuable for targeting campaigns.

As with any other database marketing technique, you have to test it. Don't do anything without getting a sample of your database enhanced and testing it versus an un-enhanced version for performance. Reliable and honest vendors of geo-dems would never refuse such a request, because if they are pros, they know the answer to the above question is "it all depends on your business and customers" and will let you test.

That said, here are some issues to consider:

1. Customer behavior will always be a better predictor of future profitability than any kind of demographics, so using customer behavior to drive high ROI campaigns will always be more efficient than demographic enhancements ever will be. And besides, behavior data is free to you; geo-dems will cost you money and lower your ROI. In other words, the profitability of a campaign

based on geo-dems has to improve enough over the un-enhanced campaign to at least pay for the cost of all the enhancements to your database.

2. If your customers are concentrated in certain zip codes, geo-dems may be helpful. If they are spread thin over many zips, it probably won't. Think about it. If the geo-dems are the average for the geographical unit, if you only have one customer in the zip (zip+4, census tract), what is the likelihood your customer really looks like the average? Think about zips in your neighborhood - is there at least one elderly complex in the upscale zip, one warehouse in the retail zip, etc.? The lower your customer penetration, the higher the likelihood the geo-dems won't represent your customer.

3. Geo-dems are most helpful in an advanced modeling environment, where you have already constructed basic models of customer behavior (like the RF technique described in my book) and are looking for extra "lift" to these models. Adding geodemographic information to the modeling mix, particularly when you are using data mining, can help improve response rate, average sale, etc. because even if the dems aren't completely accurate, they can be predictive (I won't go into why in this space). We did a project like this at Home Shopping Network and it turned out just fine.

4. Geo-dems are really hot for retail applications like choosing sites for stores or creating sales territories, where a large percentage of the population are likely customers. I used them to estimate the TV Shopping sales value of a cable franchise with great accuracy. These applications work because the average demographic becomes very meaningful when the customer penetration potential exceeds 50% - 60% of total households in the geographic unit.

I know there are people on this list who work at geodemographic enhancement companies. Equal time for you in the next newsletter if you'd like to challenge or augment what I've said here.

Jim

RFM and the Customer LifeCycle

Q: I have a small sampling of the RFM scores that correspond to the various lifecycle stages. For instance, 111 & 112 correspond to the acquisition stage,

333 & 443 to the growth stage, etc. However, I'm looking for a complete listing of all 125 possible RFM scores and their corresponding lifecycle stages.

Can you please send this my way?

A: Wow, I certainly hope you didn't get this idea from me; if you did, I have done a terrible job of explaining something somewhere. I would be very interested in the source of this idea, that a LifeCycle stage can correspond to a single RFM code or score.

An RFM code or score is the ranking of a single customer against all other customers for likelihood to respond and future value. High scores equal high future value; low scores equal low future value.

A single RFM score represents this ranking at a fixed point in time - the day the scores were created. There is no "cycle," which implies "over time," inherent in an RFM code. Only if you knew the previous code or sequence of codes could you imply a "LifeCycle stage." This is, of course, what my book is about - using a modified version of RFM to track and profitably act on customer LifeCycle behavior. If you know the LifeCycle, you can predict behavior. If you can predict behavior, you can dramatically improve marketing ROI.

If a customer is a 333, you don't know if they are falling or growing into it. They could be coming from above it - falling in value, or coming from below it - rising in value. For example, most new customers start at a 51x - they have to, because by definition, they are "new" (R = 5) but have bought once (F = 1). But this same customer 3 months from now might be a 555 or a 222 - either ramping up or sliding into oblivion. If you don't know what their score used to be, you can't imply anything about a "cycle" or any "stage" in the relationship.

That said, customers in the 111 and 112 are typically old, defected customers - not new or "acquisition stage" customers as you said. All customers start in the high numbers and work their way down into the low numbers throughout their lifecycle. The question is how long will it take to get from high to low, and can you do anything to slow this process or stop it. The scores tell you if what you are doing is working, and how to drive profitability following the two fundamental rules of High ROI Customer Marketing:

1. Don't spend until you have to
2. When you spend, spend at the point of maximum impact

If you are looking for some generalized system, I wouldn't worry about the detail of 125 RFM codes, there is really no meaning there unless you have millions of customers. The most important variable, from a LifeCycle perspective, is usually Recency, so you could roughly categorize the LifeCycle of customer into 5 blocks using the R score. The second two variables, F and M, have nothing to do with the lifecycle of the customer, but the value of the customer. These are two different issues. Any customer with a low R value but high "FM" value is a very valuable customer that isn't a customer anymore. In terms of Lifecycle, they are at the end. In terms of value, they are at the top.

Jim

Customer Loyalty and Retention

For University Students

Q: It is clear that retention of students is a complex issue. The students' satisfaction with the university will be partly determined by their experience during their first semester with the university. I have identified that each service encounter will contribute to the overall impression that the student has of the university. Some encounters are 'moments of truth' and will have a major impact on the student's perceptions of the university.

A: Hmm....interesting.

You just got very lucky, I happen to have first-hand experience on this topic, which is very rare, as not many educational institutions are thinking this way. You should be congratulated for making this connection, though it will be a difficult battle dealing with the university administration on making changes, in my experience...

Q: I would much appreciate if you could advice me on the retention strategy and what approach the university should take to retention. Also, any ideas on management of moments of truth, particularly what enhances and detracts from the customers' encounters with the university.

A: Please consider this business maxim: Only attempt to control what you can actually control; otherwise you will end up not having an effect on anything.

It very well may be that the various "touchpoints" exist and can be defined, but can you reasonably control any of them? Which ones, and how will you control them? This is where you need to focus your efforts.

In my experience, a university is not the kind of place where you can undertake a "customer service education program" with employees and expect compliance at all the touchpoints. So what you have to do is pick the major points of influence where you know you can exert some control and seek to prove your case with facts and testing.

The best way to do this is with (no surprise here) data. What you need to do is take a population, e.g. "first semester students in January 2003" and then segment them into two groups - those who continued and those who did not. Then compare - what is it about the "not enrolled" group that differs from the "still enrolled" group?

I can tell you from experience some likely differences between the segments. Please be aware these are based on US experience and may not apply in your culture, but they provide good examples:

1. The courses taken in first semester - this is very highly predictive of continuing enrollment.

2. Within a single course, the professors teaching it. For example, you may find students taking Calculus are very likely to drop out after first semester, and will think "Calculus" is the problem. But when you look at Calculus by Professor, you find the drop out rate is concentrated around one or two professors within the subject.

3. Financial aid amounts and qualifications

4. Involvement in non-academic pursuits - clubs, sports, student government

In the US, this last segment is also highly predictive of future donations to the institution, which is an important funding concern - in the language of CRM, the "Lifetime Value" of the student is positively correlated to participation in non-academic university activities.

Are any of the above "controllable"? In the US, if you value your job, you don't even bring up any of the results of #2. This is a losing battle, the politics are thick and the issues not always clear. #3 is likewise surrounded (in the US) with a lot of uncontrollable and often legal and marketing issues.

But on #1 and #4, you may be able to actually "do something." You can change marketing materials and "first semester required courses" to promote specific courses which tend to generate long-term students.

Once students are enrolled, you can boost the promotion of non-academic pursuits by having educational and recruitment events. A further refinement of this strategy would be to single out students enrolled in courses showing a high "first semester defection rate" and put extra effort into getting them into non-academic pursuits.

The amount of effort required to address #2 & #3 is enormous because there are huge institutional barriers to changes in these areas. Addressing #1 & #4 can be a more "under the radar" effort and not nearly as costly, either personally or monetarily. Once you know the most critical "touchpoints" that you also **can have some control over**, make your changes and measure your results. When you can prove first semester retention rate increases, you will get a seat at the table for going further and asking for control of other important touchpoints.

Jim

In Banking – Using Data to Debunk Myths

Q: Are you familiar with (or can you refer me to someone who is familiar with customer satisfaction around queuing up for service?

A: Frequently Asked Question for sure, and not one there is a lot of statistically believable data on...at least that people are willing to release. Kind of a sensitive subject, as you might think...

Q: I work for a large bank. We have perceived queuing problems in some of our branches - generally due to layout restrictions. I say perceived because although a queue is long, it moves fairly quickly with the actual wait time to see a teller often less than 5 minutes (considered at par with our competition).

However, customers grumble when they walk into the branch and see the line and continue to grumble out loud until they reach the teller and then continue to communicate their dissatisfaction to the teller. Do you know if any work has been done in this area with other large companies that tend to have long queues (like airline ticket counters, large retailers)?

Thanking you in advance for your response.

A: I think this issue is an illusion. Let me tell you what I mean. For e-commerce, somebody like Gartner does a survey that says people hate shipping charges, and every web site kicks in "free shipping." Guess what? People have always hated shipping charges since 1850 when the catalog business started. And why not? It looks like extra cost to the customer. But if you run your business correctly, you price with shipping in mind and manage costs so that you still make a profit.

It's just the way the business works. Given the choice, which do you think consumers would select of the two alternatives, higher product prices or shipping charges that are fair and reflect what the consumer knows is tangible cost of delivery? Sure they complain - but they still buy.

People have always hated queues. And why not? They are frustrating and perceived as a waste of time. And the alternative is? Raise prices to the consumer to cover extra staffing? But if you run your business correctly, you price with queues in mind and manage costs so that you still make a profit. It's just the way the business works. Given the choice, which do you think consumers would select of the two alternatives, queues or higher prices?

So perhaps "queues" are being raised as an issue to deflect other service problems that are the real cause for whatever angst the company has, something to blame which is not really the causation.

Regarding "solving your problem," I don't like benchmarking as a solution. Your bank has a unique persona created by advertising, staff training, corporate initiatives, the kind of customers it attracts, and so on. How can you benchmark against other companies who have a completely different persona?

And - most importantly - does benchmarking really provide any insight that is financially relevant and actionable? What action do you take knowing this information? What if their bank queues up low value customers, and you are queuing up high value customers? A disastrous decision could result.

Sounds to me like this issue is location-driven, which is perfect for an internal study. What the real question is here, I expect, is this: are these queues costing the bank money, and how much would it be worth spending to fix it (ROI)?

If this problem is specific to branches, set up a simple metric and use it to compare branches with no/short queues to branches with frequent/long queues. Perhaps annual churn of high total value customers? Annual churn of multi-product customers? Percent defection of whatever-you-call-best-customers?
Take three branches with long queues and compare them to three branches with no queues. Do the queues make a difference where it matters - on the bottom line? What if your best, most profitable customers never are in a queue, and so do not churn at a higher rate in branches with queues versus branches with no queues? And then what does the bank think of solving queue problems?

Let me know if you have any other questions or need further help with this issue. A great question, and a perfect example of one that needs to be asked in the context of customer value rather than customer volume.

Jim

In Retail – Overt versus Covert Program Features

Q: Jim, do you have an opinion on overt versus covert customer benefits? What I meant by overt vs. covert... have you seen clients do programs where they TOLD their customers they are a valued (Gold, Platinum) customer and provided tangible benefits, vs. others who have just covertly treated these customers specially in some way (i.e. priority routing, better reps, thank you calls, etc.)

A: Well, a program won't be very effective if everything is completely covert. I mean, it's nice to get great service and that certainly contributes to customer retention, but recognition is much more powerful. The customer needs to know they are being treated specially at some level.

Something like call routing is a good example. If a customer is getting priority call routing and they don't know it, they may think the service is good. If you tell them they are going to get it and then they get it, it's an entitlement they earned. More powerful, and more effective in keeping the customer. Let's say they are thinking of defecting. If they don't know they are getting priority routing, they could suspect the service might be as good at the competition. If they know they are getting priority routing, the question becomes "Does the other guy do this to? And if so, will he give it to me?" See what I mean? It's much more powerful for the customer to know they are getting special treatment than not to know.

Generally, a "surprise and delight" approach or philosophy is the most effective and highest ROI way to treat customers. Putting them in a program where they know all the benefits, a.k.a. "Gold Member" is fine, and may be a surprise and delight the *first* time, but wears out. If you go with a program like that you have to constantly refresh it and add benefits to it or it gets stale. This is what happens to most loyalty programs. Have you read my case study on loyalty? This program was about as "anti-stale" as you can get. 252% ROI in the cell phone business, about as tough a biz for loyalty as you can get.

http://www.jimnovo.com/download.htm#cellone

But you can do surprise and delight as one-off ideas, they don't have to be "programs"; it's the timing that is critical. You want to do the events near life-cycle events. Certainly the first one is the initial order - what is in the box, how is it packed, how easy is it to put together, etc. After that, things like just calling a customer to tell them you appreciate their biz, sometimes silly stuff like "1st purchase anniversary" cards - which can also be used to smoke out customer service / product problems - are effective. Anything you think will "surprise and delight" the customer. Use control groups and look for lift in sales or a slowing of defection, just like you would with any direct marketing program. If you can synch these promotions to known LifeCycle issues, all the better, because your marketing actually surprises and delights the customer.

For example, lets say you have a segment of top 20%, very valuable customers. You notice there is a pattern, probably Latency or Recency based, in this type of customer. So you anticipate and make some kind of offer that really lines up with what they would do anyway - but with a twist.

Say people in this segment typically upgrade service 6 months after initial purchase. You anticipate this and send a promotion that says "if you upgrade XXX to ZZZ you can also add this related service or product for 25% off." This way you don't subsidize the planned purchase, but you augment with related service / products and drive the transaction ticket higher. Or you give something really soft, like extending the warranty or months of service by a year if they upgrade - but they have to upgrade to a higher level than what is normal behavior for the segment.

Surprise and delight - for the customer. Not for you, because you knew the upgrade was going to happen anyway, you made it a surprise and delight for the customer - and made a couple bucks at the same time.

Jim

Customer Segmentation and LifeTime Value

Automobile LTV

Q: Do you happen to know approx. calculations of LTV for the car-industry? I wonder what this might be for a person that buys every a new car every 3 - 5 years, including service profits, etc.

A: The only published, verified study I know of on this was done by General Motors for their Cadillac division. To quote:

"Each new customer that comes through the door of a Cadillac dealership represents a potential LTV of more than $322,000. The figure is a projection of the number of automobiles the customer is likely to purchase over his or her lifetime, as well as the services those automobiles will require over a lifetime."

Take that number and extrapolate based on the average margin on sales and service for any other car, and you should get pretty close. Looks to be somewhere around 6x - 8x the original purchase price, perhaps?

Assuming service costs on a car are basically the same whether the car is cheap or expensive (perhaps a bad assumption, in the case of Jaguar, for example), there is not a direct relationship between initial price and LTV; it's a bit more "flat" than direct. That is, for lower priced car lines, the LTV is higher than implied by 6X – 8X price; for higher priced cars, the LTV is lower than implied by 6X – 8X price.

I'm not a fan of it, but some would include the value of customers recruited by the original customer in LTV. If you include the value of the recruited customer in the LTV, then what is the recruited customer worth? It's double counting.

However, if you are looking at cost **to acquire** a new customer, then you can factor recruitments in, because the sum of the original LTV and the recruited LTV's represents the maximum you can pay for new customers. The point is, both the original customer and the recruited customer each have their own LTV, which can be summed when looking at the cost to acquire a new customer. When asking the question, "What is the LTV of the customer?" the recruitments should not be included.

Jim

Modeling with Category Information (Retail)

Q: Hi Jim, I'm a great fan of your work!

A: Well, thanks for your kind words.

Q: I have a basic question for you. We are an online retailer and thus use email as the primary marketing communication channel (we do use Direct Mail to our best customers around holidays).

A: That's smart. I've seen some stats on using direct mail to drive lapsed online customers either back online or into a store that are very encouraging, real money-makers for retail. Definitely worth testing, though in both cases, the product mix averaged higher ticket than your category typically does.

Q: However, we don't have a set customer segmentation technique and thus no specific customer segments. One outside consultant, a statistician, had suggested looking at a new customer's activity in the first 30 days and then classifying them into High Spender, Frequent Transactor, etc. segments. Not sure how well it works.

A: That's quite unusual, I think. It would work in the first 30 days, but I think you would have to re-classify every 30 days using a scheme like that. Considering web-only behavior, the typical retail lifecycle beyond 2nd purchase (many buy only one time) is a ramping to a peak and then a more gradual, but still steep, falloff in purchases. The model above would not take this into account, and while the initial label might be accurate, it soon would not be. That's not to say these kinds of models don't work, but it usually takes years of testing and study to perfect them. "Data miners" often believe the numbers will simply tell them things like this, but they don't take into account the human behavioral and other mitigating factors which may not be in the data.

For example, Recency and Latency are really "meta-data" about customer behavior; they are data created from other data. You can't just look at the first 30 days of transactions and give a customer a label; customers have LifeCycles and you drive the highest ROI when you take advantage of knowing these cycles and acting on them to increase profits.

Q: I feel that we target our customers primarily by their category purchases, and not by any kind of behavioral model.

A: Category is often a secondary indicator, and probably more useful along the lines of writing copy than the timing of a promotion or offer. Your industry is full of stories about mis-targeting by category, e.g. I bought a book as a gift about something I have no interest in and you keep making offers to me like I want to buy every book in this category. But it really comes down to "when" first, and then "what." The highest ROI promotions are always about "when" - the timing of delivery. "What" is pretty much secondary, since a dollar is a dollar no matter what category it comes from. Put another way, if in the end, you want me to buy a book - any book - and don't really care which category I buy from, then I'm not sure "category" is anything other than information you can use in copy.

The exception to this would be if you find **known patterns** of category trending and are using those to generate incremental sales. For example, let's say you know on average, people who buy gardening books eventually either stop buying altogether or continue on and buy interior design books. Given this choice, I would screen for people who are decelerating in their purchases of gardening books and start making interior design book offers to them. Some will stop buying altogether, but some will convert to interior design buyers. If you use a control group with this kind of test you will find out how many people you transitioned to interior design that *would not have transitioned without your promotions*. These people represent incremental sales and profits due to the promotions - their defection was prevented, and that has a very high value.

Q: My marketing management thinks that segmenting customers is not worth the effort, since the cost of email is so low! We have over 15MM customers, with about 5MM active (have bought in the past 12 months).

A: Well, that's a typical attitude, and there is some truth to it if you only look at the cost of delivery. There are two other costs, one tangible and one intangible. The most common tangible cost in online retail is subsidy cost, that is, the cost of a discount you didn't have to give to induce purchase, which impacts margin. Do you remember the "ramping" after 2nd purchase I mentioned above? It is common for online retailers to blow a ton of margin discounting to people in this ramp who would have bought anyway. If you use control groups you can literally see it happening before your eyes.

For example, let's say you take a group of customers who made their first purchase in the same month due to some promotion or ad, and they have all made more than one purchase. You split this group 50/50 into two groups, the control, which gets no e-mails, and the test, which receives e-mails with discount promotions. Over the next 60 days, the control group spends an average of $200 per person and the test (promotional) group also spends $200 per person - except you gave them $20 in discounts, so their sales are really $180 for the period. Multiply that $20 times a million customers and all of a sudden you are talking about real money, know what I mean? That's subsidy cost, and it is as real as e-mail delivery is cheap.

The second cost is more intangible, but it manifests itself through declining response rates and unsubscribes. It's the cost of a shorter LifeCycle caused by delivering too many promotions too often. In other words, the cost of irrelevance. By the time the customer is preparing for defection, they are ignoring your e-mails because there have been so many of them that were not relevant to the customer. So just when you need to make that big splash to retain the customer, they are no longer paying attention and defect.

Q: What's your suggestion on a good way of segmenting them and how many segments do you normally recommend? Also, how often do we re-run the segmentation technique you recommend? Once every 6 months, e.g.

A: Hmm... Well, I rarely try to guess these things and simply let the data speak to me. Whatever the right segmentation is will be revealed by the behavior of the customers themselves in the data. Since you're somewhat familiar with my stuff you probably know that the heart of it is either Recency or Latency, and everything else from there is just a further sub-segmentation.

But even if the population on average is mainly driven by Latency, you will certainly find sub-segments where Recency is the primary driver. In the end, it's about increasing profits, and as I said above, the profits in High ROI Marketing are usually a function of timing. One of the components in the equation is reducing subsidy costs to active customers; the other is squeezing more profits out of defecting customers on their way out the door.

How can you figure this out? Start looking for patterns. Here's a very simple example. What is the average number of days between purchases? Let's say it is 40 days. When you do your promotions, make smaller offers to those with a purchase less than 40 days ago and larger offers to those with a purchase more than 40 days ago. Two segments, the offer is correlated to days since last purchase occurred.

After this promotion, inside each of those two segments, you have two sub-segments: responders and non-responders. Aggregate the members of each of the four groups and compare: what is similar or different about them? Categories, time of day, day of week, price point? Ad they responded to?

This is a Latency-based approach, which often works better when the sales process is not completely controlled by the customer.

If the customer is in control, as she is in most retail situations, a Recency-based approach is probably better. Recency looks at time *since last purchase* rather than time *between purchases*. Do the same thing as with Latency above. When you drop your promotion, look at response by 30-day segments - last purchase <30 days ago, last purchase 31 - 60 days ago, last purchase 61 - 90 days ago, etc. You will see the customer LifeCycle right before your eyes. Then look at responders versus non- responders for each 30-day block. Are they similar?   Different?   Similar / different within a 30-day block?   Similar / different when comparing between 30-day blocks?

You're looking for patterns. When you start to see them, they form the basis of the next test, where you specifically target a known segment of people with specific characteristics who exhibit a known behavior. Then sub-segment, and so on. Two segments become four, four become eight, etc. You stop creating new segments when you can't find a reason to create another one, there are no significant differences left to group people by. Again, the data itself tells you when you have reached the end of the segmentation possibilities.

Of course, with 5 million actives, that could take a LifeTime! The bigger question of course is this: how do you increase the number of 12-month buyers? The answer is slow down the defection rate by looking for it early, recognizing when it is beginning, and attacking it specifically. Most of the people "defecting at 12 months" really defected a long, long time before that, you just are not measuring it correctly

Jim

Analytics for Starting a Retention / Loyalty Program (Cellular)

Q: I have taken up a new assignment in this new financial year in my company in India (Cellular / Mobile connections). I would like some direction from you; also I have suggested your book to my management.

A: Well, thanks for the plug on the book and I'll give the "direction" a try...

Q: Objective: To create loyal customers who become brand evangelists

Areas covered:

1. To drive customer loyalty to ensure 80% of the customers recommend our brand to others.

2. Customer Behaviour Profiling: Create an action oriented customer profile, use profiles to create marketing & service programs to retain & increase value of our customer base.

3. Predictive Marketing / Promotions: To predict the likelihood of future events based on customer models & to predict the profitability of a promotion to encourage customers to do what we want them to do & achieve the highest ROI (Return on investment). Predict when a customer is about to defect & leave us.

4. Life Time Value: To find what a customer is worth in the future and based on this to find how much you could spend on retaining them & still make a profit. Please reply on how to start this activity?

A: Yikes! That's a pretty long list of "areas to be covered," you are going to be very busy! Some of it sounds pretty familiar too, like I've read it on my web site...you might want to get that book after all...

The creation of retention programs always starts with customer segmentation; you have to understand the behavior you have before you can create programs to modify behavior.

That probably means starting with #4, LTV. You want to look at LTV by segment of the customer base.

Get records of defected customers, put them in a spreadsheet or database, and then run analysis to determine:

* Average length of time as subscriber
* Average spending over that time
* Percent of this spend that is considered "profit," which you can use as a proxy for LTV in the early going.

In the beginning, you can use a company "profit" average for LTV until you get more sophisticated. In communications, the number often used is EBITDA Margin; ask your finance people what you should use to determine % of spending that is LTV.

Once finding the average, it is time to segment by different dimensions and determine the same 3 variables above for all the different customer segments.

For example:

Spending quintiles - highest 20%, high 20%, middle 20%, low 20%, lowest 20% of defected customers; what is average length of subscription, spend, LTV?

Product / service bundling - identify levels of service / tiers / add on services of defected customers; what is average length of subscription, spend, LTV?

Source of customer - which ads / offers / selling methods originally attracted the defected customer; what is average length of subscription, spend, LTV?

Geography - using transmitter locations or other natural boundaries dividing the defected customers; what is average length of subscription, spend, LTV?

Hardware - group defectors by type of phone or terminal or other hardware; what is average length of subscription, spend, LTV?

Contract details - if contracts vary widely as to their basic nature and terms, group defectors by contract type; average length of subscription, spend, LTV?

After running these studies you should have enough data to logically and critically construct your other 3 initiatives in profitable ways.

Jim

Multi-Channel Behavioral Modeling (Conference / Publishing)

Q: Jim, could you give me some guidance and opinion on two matters?

A: I'll try!

Q: The first is very simple. I recently attended a seminar in which XXX of XXX Associates discussed his new technique, Dynamic Segmentation Analysis. Have you come across this and if so, what are your thoughts on it? I have found only little information on this subject on the web.

A: Hmm...sounds like XXX has been reading my web site or book, the use of phrases like "relative lifetime value" and describing RFM as a "snapshot" I believe are ideas unique to my method...at least they were...

He's right about the weakness of traditional RFM analysis, and the "Customer LifeCycle" portion of my book addresses this directly, by enabling you to track relative LTV on an ongoing basis. In other words, each donor gets two scores, one based on past giving, one based on likelihood to donate in the future. Falling likelihood to donate scores, especially among best donors, are a warning sign and this "segment" needs to be addressed in a unique way. I suspect since XXX only needs "four fields" to do his segmentation and they are the **same ones** I use, he is probably doing something quite similar.

By the way, I don't have a problem with that, I want people to use the techniques I created. He also may have come to this position on his own.

Q: My second point is rather more long winded and I've tried to summarize it as best I can below. I am looking into whether RFM is suitable for our organization in terms of better marketing our paid for seminars and conferences, given the limitations we have:

The transactional data we hold is, whilst complete, is very limited. I estimate that even our best customers attend only one paid for event per year. As I understand it, RFM is best geared towards analyses where there is a large flow of regular data. Is RFM applicable here? Do we really have enough data?

A: Well, it would help to know a little more about your product, but in general, if you have long cycle times, you simply score over longer horizons. I've seem variants of RFM used in the auto business, for example, where the cycle time between purchases is 3 years and the scoring period 10 years.

Q: Regarding best practice, should we or should we not mix other types of purchase behaviour in with these stats? For example, we have a publishing arm where contacts can buy books and copies of proceedings. This of course is a totally different type of purchase activity from buying a place at a seminar or conference. My feeling is that these transactions should be defined separately in order not to distort the findings. Any ideas?

A: This is really a strategic decision and a LifeCycle issue; it would help to know a bit more about the business. If it is your intent that conference attendees be targets for retail activity then I would say mix it up. In reality, there are probably 3 segments: attendee only, attendee / retail mix, retail only. You are right to think about scoring each by itself if you perceive them to be unique relative to each other and there is no **strategy** that says you want them to crossover for a specific reason.

My guess is the attendee / retail mix is the most profitable segment, and the others should be cross-sold into this segment. For example, the purchase of a certain retail product probably is more likely to generate conference attendees than other retail products. This is the LifeCycle; if the end game (the "back end") is to create customers who buy both retail and conference, then on the "front end," you want to push retail products or conferences that generate new customers most likely to cross over.

Q: My third point is a question of who actually owns the transaction. What I mean by this is that a decision to attend an event is quite often a financial one, over which in many cases the contact has no real control. He may want to attend an event but his being able to do so is dependent on having the funding from the company. RFM looks at purchasing behaviour, which leads me to question again whether RFM is useful here. If the purchase behaviour is in many cases actually down to the company's accountants, how can his decision to attend be attributable to him? Can it?

Or should we be looking at two models here, RFM behaviour on an individual (contact) level, and a second model that groups behaviour by company, i.e. adding all contacts from one company into one group and then looking at purchase behaviour in that way. We might then be able to determine (at a rather cruder level) the purchase behaviour of individual companies. This may for example illustrate that (large auto manufacturer) appears to be more inclined towards paying for events than (another large auto manufacturer). Of course we could then go further and group each company by SIC code etc.

A: Sounds to me like you understand the application of scoring models very well. Scoring by company is an excellent idea in this case, since there is external control over the end consumer behavior. You could employ 2 scores, a macro (company) and a micro (person) and use them in a matrix. For example, a person who is highly likely to attend but works at a company with low likelihood to fund may be a weaker target than a person with medium likelihood to attend in a company with strong likelihood to fund. This you will only know though testing, but a matrix like this would allow you to discover "score pairs" with highest response to completion.

In addition, within each matrix cell you would have sub-segments - for example, is the person in the country where the conference will be held or would it involve a trip overseas. Some of this variable may be embodied in the "likelihood to fund" variable at the company level, depending on how you define "company" - as an international entity or on a country-by-country basis. If defined country by country, you will probably see "likelihood" rise on conferences in country, and fall on conferences out of country. Then you have SIC code and so on. It's important when thinking about these ideas to get the hierarchy correct. For example, is "likelihood to fund" more or less predictive than SIC code? This you find out through testing.

Finally, if you do campaign sequencing, Latency would come into play. For example, let's say you mail a brochure and follow-up with a telephone call, and have limited resources for phone calls - you can't afford to call everyone you mail. There is some number of days after the mailing where non-responders will start becoming less and less likely to attend any specific event. You need to find this "trip-wire" point and make sure calling begins prior to it for best response. On execution, you start the calls with non-responders that have highest macro and micro scores (perhaps a weighted or combined score?) and work down the list. In this way you allocate the resource to highest and best use, increasing the ROI of the effort overall.

Modeling is not a magic bullet; it's a process, a journey. You take your best ideas based on available information and test them. The data will tell you when you are right or wrong, and the models are simply a way to create reference points and breadcrumb trails along the journey to increased ROI.

Hope the above was helpful!

Jim

Scoring Travel Agency Customers

Q: Just read your book and I say full marks for such a practical and sensible approach!!! Start small and grow is the way to go.

A: Well, thanks for the kind words!

Q: I am a part owner of a travel agency (not been the best area to be in lately).

A: Eeeeek!

Q: My first focus for Drilling Down is on our leisure customers. But my head is spinning a bit with all the ideas I have from your book. I can electronically access our: customer names etc., an ID number, when they purchased, how much the product cost, the supplier, the category (i.e. air only, cruise, tour etc.) and the final destination. If you would be so kind as to give me a little steer in the right direction in setting up the metrics and scores.

A: Hmmm... I of course don't know your business but would think that particularly in leisure, there is a natural cyclicality caused by vacation timing, anniversary events, and such. So in terms of timing, you use a classic Latency approach, e.g. if a customer took a trip last July they are somewhat likely to take one this July. If they took one last July AND the July before, they are very likely to take one this July. If they have taken a trip the last 5 July's in a row, they are extremely likely to take one this July.

So you can rank customers by likelihood to travel each month, and if you want, could assign them a "score" to represent this likelihood, in the case above, extremely likely = 5, very likely = 4, etc. People who have not booked with you for a year might be a 2, not for 2 years a 1.

Then you add a Frequency / Monetary component and you have a two-digit ranking quite similar to an RF score, but customized for your business. My guess is due to the variance in prices on travel (e.g. plane flight versus ocean cruise) using monetary or total sales rather than frequency is the ticket, so to speak. Even better would be margin dollars or profit, since as I understand it a person could take 10 flights and not deliver the profit you might make on 1 cruise; the profit margins vary enormously, so "sales" or "number of bookings" is probably not tracking the real issue, which is to identify most profitable customers. Rank customers by value then divide customers into 5 equal "Quintiles" on this score as discussed in the book.

Once you have your rankings, first digit = likelihood to purchase, second digit = value of the customer (the RF score), you proceed with marketing as suggested in the book, using the scores to identify customers likely to buy and customers likely to defect.

For example, under the "likely to buy" approach, you may have an idea of how many days a person books travel in advance of the trip (or you can get this from your records, date of sale versus trip date). Let's say it averages 8 weeks. It is currently June, so 8 weeks from now is August. Find all customers who traveled last August, and look at their rankings. If you were going to call them but can only make a few calls a day, start with the ones with the highest ranking - the ones who are most likely to buy and are also best customers, and work down the list towards the less likely to buy.

This average number of weeks between booking and trip probably differs by type (cruise versus plane), so you might want to approach it like that, e.g. in June you call people you traveled by plane last July (plane = average 4 weeks booking to trip), and people who traveled by cruise last August (cruise = average 8 weeks booking to trip). Follow? Identify the behavior and then follow it, try to get it to repeat. This is the "when," the "timing." The "who" to market is defined by your rankings; given limited resources, start with the ones most likely to result in a sale.

On the defection side, look at people with high rankings who failed to book when they were supposed to. Back to using June as the current date, this would be customers with high rankings who booked last May. They are now Latent, past the "trip wire," they failed to book when they were most likely to. So you call them and find out if the trip was taken with somebody else, or perhaps delayed (highly likely) and would they like help with organizing the trip for later on in the year?

The above approaches (both sales and defection work) combined create a very systematic and directed way to just gradually push the whole thing forward every week, by specifically identifying customers who are likely to buy and likely to defect. You end up concentrating your work where it is likely to be most effective, and as long as you are taking advantage of every opportunity to predict a sale or recapture defecting customers, all customers will eventually make it to your radar screen as an opportunity for increased profits.

Hope that helps!

Jim

Estimating CRM ROI (Contract Facilities Management)

Q: Our industry is facility management services where a headquarters with chain locations contracts with us to manage their facilities in all their markets.

The President is interested in a "CRM Solution" but is concerned about the ROI he might expect from implementation. Do you know of any number that I can pass along to him that would placate his insistence on knowing in advance what the ROI will be?

A: Bad news: No, not really.

Good news: You can figure it out, which is something nobody did in the past and is why so many "failed" at CRM. You might not even need any new software to "do CRM," though it depends on what you have now and what the objective of the CRM program is (you do have one, correct?). But the software required is certainly not millions of dollars and if you only have 1000's of clients you can probably do it with some combination of ACT! or GoldMine, MS Access, and MS Excel.

The key question to ask: do you really know how your customers behave? In this kind of contract business, I imagine the central issue is this: Can you predict which customers are likely to re-up a contract, and which ones are not? And then can you use this information to focus on the ones less likely to re-up, and take steps to make them more likely to re-up?

Sometimes it is just a matter of better customer service. In this case, what you need is better service practices, not "CRM." From a distance, it is very difficult to know what the issues might be in your company.

Here's a test you can do to find out where you might be on the road to answering the CRM question. If you cannot accomplish one or more parts of the following, you are not ready to even talk about "CRM," and need to do some more internal research. These steps, by the way, are the ones everybody skipped on the first round of CRM and will pave the way for a successful implementation if you decide to go with a CRM approach:

1. Define a "best customer." It's not just sales; you have to take into account margins, service costs, etc. Don't worry about finding exact financial numbers. Think about best in relative terms - these customers are better than those customers, and you are pretty sure it is true. If you can't get to this point, you probably need better data collection before you think about a CRM project.

2. Once defined, how many of these customers left you in the past year or 2 years or whatever the right time frame is for your business? If you typically

sign 3-year contracts, then it might be "in the past 4 years." Also identify best customers who stayed with you and renewed. If you can't get to this point, you probably need better data organization before you think about CRM.

3. Group best customers who left and best customers who stayed and compare the two groups. Look for similarities and differences. Is it the kind of business they are in, geography, number of "trouble calls," billing disputes? You will almost always see patterns that will lead you to conclusions on what circumstances create a best customer who stays and one who leaves. If you can't get to this point, you probably need better data analysis before you think about implementing a CRM program.

4. Now that you know what causes customer defection and retention, figure how much more money you could make if you could keep a certain percentage of these best customers that would otherwise leave. If you can't do this, you probably need better customer reporting before you think CRM.

5. Figure out what it would cost to keep this certain percentage of best customers that would otherwise leave. Is it better targeting in sales upfront, better customer service, better billing practices? If you can't do this, you probably need better financial reporting before you think about a CRM project.

6. Calculate your ROI and either decide to do it or not. If you can't do this, don't invest in CRM, because it is going to cost you more than you will make!

Sorry I don't have "a number" for you, it simply does not work like that. But you can find that number, a number that is right for your business, with a little detective work. If you get hung up with any of the above steps, perhaps I can help. Many businesses can get great results following the above plan.

Jim

Segmentation in Financial Services / The Mutual Fund Scoring Model

Q: I have been enjoying reading your tutorials. I am interested in the financial planning market particularly and have developed an application for segmentation of market and clients by attitudinal factors. Having provided my clients (advisers) with the tools to turn the qualitative data into quantitative measures and slice and dice their client base appropriately, the next question from them is "How do I use this and what to do with the information?"

A: You betcha, that's the hard part. A common question when people get into analysis; the "what do I do with this" should really come first so the metrics produce an actionable outcome...

Q: I would be interested in providing links on my web space to access your papers and content. Do you have any content or case study examples for marketing and client servicing for the financial planning industry?

A: Well, I don't think I have a page on my site specifically on this area, but let's create one, OK? I'll include this example in my newsletter and it will go up on my site next month.

Characteristics and attitudes are interesting but frequently not particularly actionable because they are not "behaviors." When people speak of "doing something," they are typically thinking of increasing or decreasing a behavior of the customer. If you are trying to figure out what to do about a behavior, you really need to use behavioral metrics, which will tell you "who" to do something to and "when" you should do it for best results.

These are the hardest parts of "doing" because "who" and "when" get to value of the customer, time management, resource allocation, and ultimately ROI. The attitudinal stuff comes into play after you identify behavioral metrics and provides more insight into "how" you should approach the customer.

For example, from the prospective of a financial planner, let's say it is desirable to have customers buy and sell securities, and it is undesirable when they stop or slow down this activity. First, you must come up with a measure of this behavior. Then, you can connect this behavioral measure to certain attitudinal types. If you find certain attitudinal types consistently behave in certain ways, then you can predict the behavior (buying and selling securities) based on attitudinal profiles.

And certainly, this is part of what planners and brokers have always done intuitively. They know which clients are prone to trade and so on. The challenge occurs when the number of clients is too large to remember what these behaviors are, and also in the fact this intuitive system is backward looking - it does not "predict" anything, and a customer could one day defect to another planner without advance warning - even though the warning signs were there all along. But the planner has no "system" to recognize these warning signs and act on them - the "who" and "when."

What kind of system? Well, let's take the analogy fully into the world of securities trading. There are dozens of different technical indicators that are commonly used in trading - 50-day moving average, MACD, On Balance Volume, Relative Strength (RSI), etc. Now, think of customers as securities.

You can apply these technical indicators to whatever customer metrics you are looking at - volume of trades, balances on accounts, and so forth. Customers can have "Relative Strength" against each other. They can be engaged in a number of trades that are above or below their 50-day moving average, and above or below the 50-day moving average of the "index" - the entire customer portfolio. Do you see where this is going?

With securities trading systems, you can set stops or trigger alarms based on changes in the behavior of the security that violate or penetrate certain indicators like the 50-day moving average. You could also do this with the customer portfolio. Much like in securities trading, if a customer's trade volume or balance drops below the 50-day average, there could be cause for concern.

And what happens, for example, when a stock owned by a lot of mutual funds drops to the 50-day? It is often "supported" by mutual fund buying at that level - as long as there isn't something "wrong" with the stock, in which case they just sell and abandon the stock.

If a customer drops to the 50-day in trading volume, they too should be supported, in the form of a phone call or other contact, to try and "lift" them off the 50-day. To allow them to "plunge" below the 50-day without "doing something" is to accept the fact the customer is defecting and just abandon the customer. If the customer has low value, you might want to let them go - especially if you also have high value customers dropping to the 50-day who need attention and this requires resources. This kind of resource allocation increases revenues while at the same time reducing expenses. The trigger is the behavior, the "how" or approach taken can be influenced by known attitudinal factors collected on the customer.

Is this making any sense to you?

So, let's say a large group of customers fall to the 50-day moving average in their trading volume (or commissions, or whatever). This is unusual behavior versus the rest of the customers. As a financial planner, you don't want this happening because it means you are losing out on income.

You could then look at the attitudinal measures on this group and see if there are any similarities. If there are, you can draw conclusions and do something about it. Exactly what would depend on the metrics and attitudes used, but it is probably at least a contact of some kind. But you now have the most critical part of the equation - "who" needs attention and "when."

You can use a drop to the 50-day - or an On Balance Volume break through zero, or whatever. And then you analyze the results of your contacts and see what worked the best with this behavior on customers with specific attitudes. Further, you now know something about predicting the future behavior of customers with this particular attitudinal set. When you see customers with this set begin to fall towards the 50-day, you can be proactive and anticipate the move, using best practices learned from the past.

Finally, since you are familiar with my work, the Latency and Recency metrics are just two more ideas, which happen to be particularly good at enhancing the power of other measures of human behavior. For example, a customer who has dropped to the 50-day AND the last trade was less Recent than the average of all customers is somebody who is in a heightened state of probable defection. Likewise with someone who trades on average every two days and both drops to the 50-day AND their trade Latency expands to a trade every 7 days. If either of these customers is valuable, action should be taken immediately to try and save the customer right away.

Hope I didn't go to far out of the world on this for you. Customers can really be looked at as a portfolio of assets with differing future potential for returns, and as such, can actually be "managed" in the same way as a securities portfolio. "Managing a portfolio of customer assets" is often talked about in CRM circles but rarely implemented in any meaningful way. I find it to be one of the best "templates" for managing customer value out there.

Let me know if you have any questions!

Jim

Cycle Times for Calculating Metrics (Casino / Hospitality)

Q: I am reading your e-Book and I am trying to relate the material to work.

A: That's a good idea! Especially if work paid for the book. If you paid for it, then work is lucky to have you....

Q: I am involved in Data Warehousing and I am looking at defining some data marts for our Sales people.

A: Perfect application for the book, it will give you and the sales department some "common ground" to work from.

Q: Could you please help me with a question that has been nagging me...Over what period of time should we calculate Frequency?

a) 30 days prior to the last sale
b) 12 months prior to the last sale
c) 36 months prior to today
d) All of the above

The data calculated by each method is different however they all look useful.

A: If I can imply from your e-mail address that you work for (large casino and sports betting organization), and the business we are talking about is the casino / sports bet business....

Well, they all are useful, in their own way. Generally, you want to use long cycle models with long cycle events and short cycle models with short cycle events. For example, retail purchases are pretty short cycle events, with supermarket probably the shortest of them all. Enterprise Software and heavy-duty truck purchases are long cycle events. But within both of these long cycle events, there are short cycle events, such as software upgrades, replacing tires and exhaust systems, etc.

One way to "pin" the cycles down is to look at inter-event Latency - the average number of days or weeks between the events. If you are profiling casino visits and they happen on average twice a year, the "cycle" or Latency is 6 months. Running an RF model at 30 days doesn't get you much traction with a 6-month cycle. I would run it over 12 months, or twice the cycle rate.

The closer you get to the actual latency in the cycle, the more accurate the model can become, but the more erratic it can get over disparate groups. This begs a question: can you split the population and run the RF model on each segment by itself? Sure!

Say you have a top 20% group, and these people visit on average every 2 months. Then you have everybody else, they visit on average 1x a year. So the model for best customer would be over 4 months (twice the cycle time) and the model for the others over 2 years (twice the cycle time). That way you adjust the model to hang more closely with the behavior, and increase accuracy.

Q: P.S. Like your book.

A: Great, that's good to know. A little surprising, but IT people like the book quite a bit. From what I gather, the book helps IT people "get" database marketing enough to work on requirements, and provides a tangible platform to discuss behavior modeling issues with marketing folks. Hope I answered your question, and feel free to keep asking - you're a customer now!

Jim

Uncovering New Segments (Retail)

Q: I recently purchase your book "Drilling Down." Really enjoying reading it!

A: Well, thanks for the kind words.

Q: I had a question about the implementation of the RFM model against email campaigns. Say we have a client that has done this:

- Has sent out 2 emails to entire database (in June and July)
- Has sent out 3 targeted emails to a specific segment of the database (June, July and Aug)

From my CTR and Open Rates I know that the targeted segment performance is better. For my scoring I am using the following:

- Recency, last email responded to, and

- Frequency, number of emails where an action (a click-thru) was taken

So the question is when trying to apply an Recency / Frequency (RF) score to the entire database, do you / can you use all 5 email programs? Would Recency include the email to the specific segment in August? Would frequency include the segment that received the email in August?

A: Wow! The fact you are asking this question tells me you understand the methods better than you think you do. The correct answer is yes, and no, depending on the objective of the scoring. As long as you **understand** that there is the potential for the marketing to the target segment to skew the scoring of the overall group, then you are thinking about the problem correctly. Whether you decide to do the scoring as "everybody" or you score the targeted segment and "everybody else" separately really depends on what you are trying to accomplish or the objective.

Q: Wouldn't the folks in the targeted segment potentially have a higher RF score than the general population?

A: Absolutely. But this is not bad, I mean, a bunch of them responded, so they "deserve" a higher RF score, yes? Isn't response good, and so they should have higher scores overall?

If you look at the case for scoring the entire database, it generally tells you who is most likely to respond to **any** campaign. If you know a lot about your customers, you probably will not send them all the same campaign, but create different campaigns for different customer segments and hope to generate sales (or sign-ups, or downloads, or whatever). What you are really getting from scoring everybody together is identifying specific individuals or groups who:

1. are most likely to respond, and

2. appear to be defecting so you can be proactive and go after them with a specialized campaign addressing the potential defection.

You can either decide to attack certain groups or not spend the money because they are "already gone" and there will be no ROI. This doesn't have anything really to do with any specific campaign, it is the more about the aggregate, overall decision to spend on any specific customer or group of customers. The fact you did a campaign to a certain segment has no bearing on this, because if you are successful with your campaign, those targets will have higher RF scores - and quite frankly, that is what you want, right? The higher the RF score, the more likely they are to respond and the less likely they are to defect.

Now, that said, the business of database marketing is about creating test programs, looking at the results, and realizing that certain segments respond better than others to certain campaigns. A classic example is the "discount ladder," where you set the discount by RF score in order to maximize response and ROI. It is certainly OK and desirable to break the customer base into sub-segments and score these segments against themselves as well as against the overall population.

For example, score everybody who bought a lamp as their first purchase by themselves and everybody who bought a chair as their first purchase by themselves, or everybody who came from Google as a group and everybody who came from MSN as a group.

What you get from this approach is new insight and uncovery of new, profitable segments. So, for example, you find a customer segment with an average RF score of 35 (middle of the pack) in the overall scoring of the entire customer base, but it has a score of 55 (highest) when just scoring people who came from MSN. Though these people are not a "best customer" segment overall, they are "best" within the MSN segment and through testing you find they are generally responsive. They are best customer segments in terms of all segments from MSN, and as such, are probably worth targeting.

Another common use of multiple scoring groups comes into play for 1x buyers (see the RFM Toolkit chapter titled "The Commerce and Content Examples: Turning Scoring Data into Profits"). One-time buyers by definition all have a Frequency of "1," and online the percentage of 1x buyers in the database tends to be huge. So if you score the whole database together you get a very warped view of the world - if 80% of the database is 1x buyers, some of these poor quality customers will get fairly high scores.

A better approach is to split the database in one-time and multi-buyers and score each group individually. This way, you have created segments which have very similar members, and a relative ranking score like RF becomes much more meaningful. When scoring the one-time buyers, you dump the frequency variable since it is the same for all, and use just Recency or perhaps Recency and Monetary. Then you test and see which approach is the best predictor of response and defection.

Your ability to formulate this question means you are on the right track. It's not an either / or situation, it's more like a "both" depending on what you are trying to do with the scoring.

Jim

Professional Services

More on Scoring Time Frames; "LF" Scores

Q: I stumbled across your Web site some time ago and have been a regular visitor since. I receive your regular emails and find your information very useful. You will be pleased to know that I purchased your book (Drilling Down) just before Christmas and have just finished going through it. It all sounds so easy! Your explanations and examples were wonderful and easy for me to understand.

A: Well, thanks for the kind words. Would you mind if I used the paragraph above as a testimonial on my web site?

Q: Now I will attempt to put it all into practice for two businesses - a Natural Healing Centre (massage, natural medicine etc.), and an Accounting practice.

A: The healing centre is a pretty straight-up situation; should work very well for them just as described in the book. The accountant, as a service business with a built-in "forced" cycle (the tax year), a little more complex. More on this below.

Q: I have 2 questions though, if I can.

A: Sure! The two questions below are related, so I will answer them as one. Only one to a customer! Just kidding...

Q1: Neither business has a Web Site, so a visit to the workplace, usually means a purchase. I was intending to have R = last visit, and F = visits over past 12 months. Will this work?

Q2: Should I put a timeframe on F? The way I see it, if I don't, F will continue to grow for each customer as long as they are a customer. Whereas if I put a timeframe it will give a better picture of behaviour patterns.

A: The RF behavior scoring model described in the book was developed offline first, so yes, it works very well offline using visits to a store, or deposits at a bank, or for that matter, to predict the likelihood of someone to commit a crime! The likelihood of any human behavior to occur again can be predicted by past Recency and Frequency. The very first studies of this effect: it was used to predict the likelihood of a man to stand when a woman entered the room! And it worked. Goes all the way back to Pavlov and those drooling dogs of his.

Putting a time frame on F is a more advanced application of the RF idea; usually you would only do this after you proved to yourself that customers who have not visited in over a year were not worth scoring. This may very well be the case for many businesses. It will indeed give you a more focused picture of behavior but may also eliminate desirable data on customers with last visit > 12 months.

Remember, the RF scheme is a ranking, comparing customers to each other. So even though the raw number of visits (F) continues to grow as long as they are a customer, the ranking will always be a 5, 4, 3, 2, or 1 as you are comparing customers to each other. The customer with the very most visits, even if there are 1000's, will have a rank of 5, and the customer with the least visits will have a rank of 1, no matter how long a time period you are measuring. This is the benefit of using a "relative" rather than "absolute" system; it "self-adjusts" to any kind of business because it's based on comparing customers to each other, not to fixed external benchmarks.

So bottom line - if it was me, I'd score all of them first, then score just past 12 months, and test your marketing to see if you get a better result with one or the other. Unless of course you are already sure (and you may be) that customers who have not been customers for over a year are not worth marketing to. As I said, for many businesses, this is true.

Now, with the accounting business, you have "interference" in terms of behavior. Very strong external forces - the tax year, monthly financial statements - dramatically impact customer behavior. I don't know what kind of business it is (are customers businesses or consumers? Do they engage in non-year-end tax business?) but you have to consider these forces when looking to predict customer behavior.

A specialized version of Recency - called Latency - is often more appropriate in an environment where there are powerful external forces like mandated cycles. Latency is about "how long it has been," usually relative to a fixed date or fixed length of time.

For example, if someone has their year-end taxes done every year for 5 years in February and always makes an appointment by February 15th, and then the next year has not called by February 25th, the customer in "Latent" or their Latency has exceeded the norm for the customer. This tardiness is a signal something may be wrong, and the customer is in fact lost.

Can you see how Latency is more important than Recency for this business? So what if you have a bunch of customers who are Latent (and probably in danger of defection), which ones would you concentrate on? The most valuable ones, the high "F" customers probably. So you can set up an "LF" rather than "RF" type score and still rank customers by how Latent and how Frequent they are. The more Latent they are, the less likely they are to respond or be "recaptured" by any marketing effort.

It is much easier to ring up the guy in the above example on Feb 25th and perhaps get the business before he defects than it is to ring him up a month (or a year!) later and ask for the business - he has probably already switched accountants, right?

If you haven't seen these articles on the site, more on behavioral scoring in a service biz: Utilities, Telecom, Insurance - Behavioral and LifeCycle Profiling in Service Businesses

http://www.jimnovo.com/Utility-Profiling.htm

Hope the above answered your question!

Jim

Ad-Supported Content / Subscription Models

Optimizing Ad Sales and Subscriptions

Q: Should we use:

RFI - Recency, Frequency, Intensity
RFM - Recency, Frequency, and Monetary
or
RF - Recency, Frequency

to measure visitor value, and what should these terms ideally mean? Total Sessions, Total page views, etc. Also, when you measure Frequency, do you only include the Frequency during a specific period of time (i.e. one month, or one week), or do you include total lifetime activity per user?

A: On the advertising side of the business, I think the page views/session stat is probably the best to use. The reality of the ad-based business is it doesn't matter if they come back, you are selling impressions, not people. I don't think you have to overcomplicate it with formulas like RF or RFM, because you are primarily dealing with audiences, not individuals. RF and RFM are about predicting individual behavior - if they will come back.

For the ad biz, you want to know which visitor sources generate the highest page views per session. But for the subscription business you want to know what parts of the site create the most loyal visitors - those who will pay for content. These are two different issues. More on this below. If you decide to track pure Frequency, yes, it is Lifetime activity, but I don't think you need that.

Q: It's interesting. There seems to be 2 major "customers" for your systems at my company: Marketing and Product groups. What are the most powerful deliverables, in your experience, that we can give to each?

A: I am guessing Marketing has to do with getting people to come to the web site and Product is the people developing the site content.

For Marketing, the most important thing you can do is to track source, because none of these other metrics will do you any good if you can't actually do something with them. For any given metric, ask yourself this: If I knew this metric, what would I change to improve the business? If you don't know "source" of the customer (which ads, search engines, etc. are the visitors coming from?) then you can't change your marketing strategy to attract the visitors with highest page views / session.

You want to know "original source," as in when you set the first cookie, what was the referring URL or Ad?

Visitor source is very powerful, because it is largely responsible for the long-term quality of the visitor, and it is something you can often control or influence.

You don't have to report on source at the individual level, report on it at a meaningful level that you can use to make changes - again, if you can't use the info to do something then it is not worth tracking. So for ads where you are paying money for visitors, you would track by ad or by network or whatever control point you have. For search, you track at the engine level - Google, MSN, AOL, etc. When you find the average visitor from Google does 8 pages/session, and the average visitor form MSN does 2 pages/session, now you have information that is actionable and used to optimize campaigns and search.

For Product, I would also track Recency in some aggregate form, say "30 day Recency" - what percent of visitors have visited at least once in the past 30 days? You will find that your different "products" have different levels of 30 day Recency, and the ones with the highest percent Recency are the ones where your customers are most loyal - this is the true definition of "stickiness," if you think about it. This information will help guide product design - which products are the most satisfying to customers? The above approach is what I call Hurdle Rate Analysis - it's in the book or you can read some about it on the site.

And, by measuring it this way, you really have a yes / no type tracking - either they came back within 30 days or didn't, you can use a simple "switch" that will be easy to implement on the IT side, rather than tracking the actual Recency by number of days. You have to decide how you handle visitors using multiple products - they could be 30 day Recent on weather but not on news, for example, you can have multiple product flags.

You can also use source for Product. Even though the average 30 day Recency for a Product may be 30%, you find that for Visitors from Google have a 60% 30 day Recency and visitors from MSN have a 10% 30 day Recency - for the same particular product. Knowing what you know about these different audiences, which one is more desirable, and what does this mean about the product and audience?

This intersection of "visitor quality" with "product quality" creates a grid you should be able to use to tweak both ad and site effectiveness. It will show you where the very highest and very lowest quality combinations are. The highest quality visitors to the highest Recency area of the site are the most likely to pay for the content. You should be able to optimize both ad revenue and subscriptions using this matrix.

Q: Also, given the fact that we will most likely use a "phased" implementation, what do you think are the logical steps to take in phase I, II, III, etc?

A: 1. Get your source tracking down.

2. Figure out how you will aggregate users - what will be the most meaningful way to understand the source data, how will you use source, where are the control points? Don't bother aggregating unless you can do something by knowing the result.

3. Track page views/session, and aggregate by source for reports.

4. Track 30 day Recency as a measure of the visitor loyalty to each product.

With just these 3 metrics - source, views / session, and 30 day Recency across each product, you should have enough intelligence to keep you busy for several years figuring out how to optimize the business.

The next step would be to figure out who converts to paid subscribers - where do they come from, and what products do they use and stick with? Then you can refine your products and advertising to attract visitors most likely to convert to paid. I just did a study on this for another site, and found of the 38 ads they were running, a lot of them got high click-through to the site, but only 2 ads resulted in people becoming paid subscribers - and those two ads had the lowest initial click-through rates, an effect very common in direct marketing.

Jim

Predicting Subscription Defection and Non-Renewal

Q: My boss (VP of phone sales) is really looking to try out some new ideas and RFM is one he has latched onto. He actually has explored this concept for a few years but never acted upon it. Anyway, he just purchased your book and after finding that he did not have time to read it he gave it to me. My job was to read and understand at a high level and to lead a discussion with the marketing group to get them excited about the concept. I am a finance guy by trade so this concept was very interesting.

A: That's funny; the people who really "get it" the most are finance people and IT people, because modeling is kind of "black and white," very numbers driven. Stuff either works or it doesn't - did you make money or not? ROI is the name of the game.

Q: Obviously, I either did not do a good enough job explaining RFM, Latency, tripwires, etc. or they just are unwilling to have someone from their team tackle the concept. The question they always wanted answered was "We don't know why the customer behaved as they did. Thus a sales call needs to be made not a marketing campaign."

A: "Why" is not really the issue; defection is happening. Depending on the biz, a sales call might be exactly what is needed. These models are always about allocation, putting scarce resources to the highest and best use. Per customer, sales calls are expensive; direct mail is not. If you have a formal "wall" between sales and marketing, usually the "whose responsibility is it" issue is decided by "degree of pain" e.g. how valuable is the customer to the business overall?

For example, if you have a small number of very high value customers who look to be defecting according to RFM then a sales call is triggered. If you have lots of medium to low value customers who look to be defecting, then a direct mail or telephone campaign is what you need, which is probably marketing. Match the value of the effort to the value of the customer; this is how you get gigantic ROI's (or since you are a finance guy), more accurately something like ROME's - Return On Marketing Expense, or ROAS - Return on Advertising Spend.

Q: We are a subscription service in which customers pre-pay for the service they expect to use. Our sales (and I guess marketing to some extent) are responsible for driving customers to use their service throughout the year. Usually if a customer uses more than they committed to then they raise the commitment the following year. So I guess my question is this: Can RFM be used for a pre-paid subscription service?

A: Sure, perhaps not in the "classic" sense. For many service biz, particularly subscription ones (telco, insurance, etc.) you profile activity other than billing. Sounds to me like what you want to profile is usage - the more Recently and Frequently a customer has used the service, the more likely they are to continue using it. So you could rank customers by likelihood to "continue using the service." High value customers with low likelihood (low or dramatically falling RF score) to continue to use the service get a sales call, mid to low value customers with low likelihood to continue get a direct mail piece from marketing. Dramatic changes in score require the most urgent attention, in terms of allocating resources to the effort. To the extent these subscriptions are fulfilled on the web, it is quite easy to identify future defectors who will not renew, since they will be paying for the subscription but visits / log-ins show low or falling Recency. I personally know someone who predicted the demise of the dot-com he was working for using this method.

Q: As an FYI, we have customers who pay as they go and customers that sign a yearly commitment. Would it be best to segment the two groups when developing the RFM model and tripwires? As we have different size customers some spending more than $10K/year and some $1K, should we segment based upon dollar values as well?

A: Absolutely, both these segmentation approaches would help you. More on this below. Payment method is a huge behavioral clue; there will be significant differences in behavior. With a service, you hopefully know why people stop using it. Find defected best customers (high value cancels) and look at why they stopped using it (or interview them if you don't know, offer a free month or whatever to get them to talk to you), and create sales / marketing - pitches / materials to address the issues they have. Then when you see a client engaging in a defection pattern on usage (drop in RF score), engage the appropriate response (sales or marketing) based on customer value.

And sure, the more you segment your customer base, the better it works. You should start at the bottom, however. Don't "out-think" the segmentation; let the data speak to you. Try something at a very basic level and look for the hands to be raised; this will tell you what works and put you on the right track.

For example, let's say (and I imagine it would be true) that SIC codes play a role in the quality / value of a customer. So you do a campaign (sales, marketing, or both) to all customers who used to access the database Recently and Frequently, but have dropped off (RF score is lower).

What you see when the data comes back is certain SIC codes had a very high response and "activation" and start using your database again, and others do not. The data has now spoken; it has told you where it is worth spending time / money on this particular idea.

Perhaps you look at bit deeper, and find that an SIC code that looks to be a "bad idea" overall actually generates activation for you as long as the offer is made by direct mail in the South. So you keep this particular segment of the "direct mail" campaign and reject the rest.

You can look for other segments by value, by region, by services subscribed to, by average transaction value, by location of their customer, whatever. As you subdivide segments, you will find new pockets of profitability. You could spend a LifeTime chasing down all the segments - I have never, ever finished this task on any particular engagement. Clients call me years after they have stopped using my services to tell me they have discovered unique new segments that are extremely profitable and I appreciate that, because it adds to the knowledge base for everyone involved.

Jim

Advanced Defection Models for Subscription Businesses

Q: Jim, first let me say that I am enjoying your book VERY MUCH!! Nicely done, and a nice job of integrating it with the CRM paradigm, 1-to-1 etc. I'm reading very slowly and finished the Latency Metric Toolkit.

A: Great! Thanks for the kind words.

Q: I had a couple of questions on the Latency toolkit and the Latency tripwire, especially as it applies to environments with built in cycles for repeat purchases.

I am in a business where our resources are quarterly based, i.e. customers purchase our resource use them for a quarter and re-purchase the next quarter's resource. That is, we have a built in pattern, where customers would purchase our resources each quarter. I was wondering how well I can use Latency with this type of built in cycle or if I would have any problems applying your Latency concepts to it, maybe they apply that much more readily? In our case we try to call most folks who haven't purchased within 2 weeks of a new quarter (purchase cycle) beginning.

A: Right, a subscription-type business. This is also an issue with utilities and other like businesses that bill about the same amount each month or have contracts for service (like wireless). The answer is if the revenue generation really doesn't represent anything to do with the behavior, then you simply look for other parameters to profile. For example, a friend of mine was responsible for analyzing the likelihood of subscription renewal in a business that provided the content online. Increasing Latency of visit was a warning flag for pending defection, and they triggered their most profitable campaigns based on rising visit Latency. In wireless, the correlations are found in rising payment Latency – the longer someone goes past due, the higher the likelihood of defection.

Q: Also, we have actually built a model with only 3 behavioral variables in it to predict those who would leave before they had actually left so we could do something about it. The difference here from just calling folks would be that we are predicting who is at risk of leaving (defined by someone who hasn't purchased 2 consecutive quarters).

From the score, the model lets us sort our customers from hi to low and then we usually take the first 6 groups out of 20 to actually run our test groups (we do use our control groups!). We usually run the model about 4 weeks prior to a quarter starting to flag the at risk customers, and then run our campaign. One of our questions is timing our use of this where we have a built in cycle of purchasing behavior already present.

A: Well geesh, what are you asking me questions for? You already built it! And where models are concerned, simple is good - you obviously have learned some things from the book!

Q: One of the variables was a Latency measure, but instead of looking at the overall customer average and comparing variations from that, we measured each customer's history of purchasing and created a cycle-percent variable that in essence measured what percent they were over their expected time to buy and thus the model incorporated this "customized measure" for each person. I was wondering your thoughts on this type of measure, compared to the overall customer average of buying cycles in your "Hair Salon" chapter, and also any thoughts on running an anti-defection campaign like this in an environment where we have a built in cycle for repeat purchasing?

A: Sounds like a good model to me, a bit more advanced than the average person could swallow but you're essentially using the **customer's own behavior** to set the Latency tripwire for the specific customer, rather than using average customer behavior to set the trip wire. Perfect for this kind of business, as long as you have enough behavior history on a customer to be predictive. If you don't (first subscription), you could always default to the average.

As far as campaign timing / anti-defection goes, if I understand the situation correctly, you probably want to time it back from the renewal event, e.g. test dropping the campaign 1 week before renewal, 2 weeks before renewal, 3 weeks before renewal, etc. Once you get baseline for this, then matrix against "persistence" or your likelihood to renew model and try different offers.

So, for example, you will probably find out that people who are highly likely to renew require less lead time and perhaps no discount to encourage renewal; conversely, the less likely someone is to renew, the more lead time they need and the higher the discount. And likely to renew probably roughly correlates with the number of past renewals. So you end up with some kind of Frequency / Latency matrix that drives campaign timing and offer.

But don't try to guess, test.

Q: Thanks for any thoughts and input! I've mentioned your book in a lot of circles as a must read, even before any Peppers and Rogers stuff.

A: Well, that's pretty good company to be in, though I don't know that P & R ever showed anybody **how** to do something, I believe they usually tell people ****what**** they should be doing and charge fees to do it for them. Nothing wrong with that, I guess that's why they make the big bucks and got bought out!

Online / Offline Retailing and Catalogs

Using Hurdle Rates to Optimize Merchandising (Product Placement)

Q: Hi Jim,

I am here choosing all the metrics I will use in the coming days to evaluate the health of my business and learn a little bit more about it. I will begin analyzing some basic metrics and then (just after being completely comfortable with the "basic metrics" I will do some more sophisticated analyses like LTV and LifeCycle Grids (Jim's Note: LifeCycle Grids are the advanced customer LifeCycle tracking tools described in my book).

Now I am trying to decide which is the best metric to measure my site's ability to retain customers. There are three metrics that come to my mind: Customer Retention Rate, Customer Churn Rate, and Hurdle Rate.

Customer Retention Rate would be the easiest to measure but the least precise. I could be doing a great job retaining customers but if I am attracting a lot of new customers this metric could give the wrong impression that we are doing more poorly than the last time we measured.

Customer Churn Rate is very easy to calculate when you have a "subscription model business." If the customer cancels the contract it means a defection. But in my case there is no contact. We sell products. If the customer does not purchase in 30 days it doesn't mean necessarily that he defected.

The Hurdle Rate based on Recency (45 days for purchase seems to be a good number for the products we sell - natural supplements, based in Brazil) seems to be the best metric I can choose to measure our ability to retain customers over the longer term. What metric do you think I should be using to measure our ability to retain customers?

A: I think you are one of the smartest IT guys on the subject of database marketing that does *not* do database marketing for a living I have ever met (?)! Where did you learn this stuff? Did you read a book or something? ;)

Your analysis is absolutely correct on every point, and the approach is on target. If you start simple and work towards more complexity, you will learn more about your customers. And assuming most of your products are roughly a 30-day supply, 45 days is an excellent cut-off for a Hurdle Rate analysis. Simply track the percentage of customers who have made a purchase in the past 45 days over time, perhaps monthly to start. If the percentage is rising, you are getting better at retaining customers. If it is falling, you should be looking for reasons why this is so.

Once you establish this metric, the second "cut" I would take is by product. What percentage of customers have made a purchase in the past 45 days - by product category or product line? This will be very revealing to you, and will suggest which products you should put the most marketing effort into and which products perhaps you stock but don't "market." For example, all other considerations equal, the product you should feature on the home page is probably the one that has the highest 45-day repeat purchase percentage; no point in wasting home page real estate on products that create 1X buyers.

By including this tracking by product, when your overall percentage of 45-day buyers drops or rises, you can tell why. For example, if you sell a lot of products in one month that have a low 45 day repeat percentage, in the following month, you can expect your overall 45 day repurchase rate to drop, which means sales will drop in the next month.

With a system like this, you are now into forecasting sales, and can do the appropriate promotions to make sure you hit sales targets. For example, you promote products with high 45-day repeat in the following month to counteract a lot of sales in products with low 45 day repeat prior month.

You may find that when setting up to track the overall Hurdle Rate, it's easy or convenient to do this same tracking by product category or line, depending on how your systems are organized. If so, it might be worth the extra effort, because it can be frustrating to see the 45 day percent buyers drop but to not have any idea why.

Q: Setting Hurdle Rates for each product and product category is an excellent idea. If we notice that the "muscle mass" category has a higher Hurdle Rate than the "fat loss" category, we would advertise the muscle mass category more that "fat loss"?

A: Absolutely. Now you have both the response rate to ads *and* the longer term Hurdle metric to help you decide where you are really making the most money. Make sure you keep track of the source of the customer on first purchase, because the next level down is looking at Hurdle Rate by product category by ad source. You will find different ads generate different Hurdle rates for the same products.

Q: Before this idea my partners and I were always "arguing" which products should be advertised on the index page and the main category pages. Now we will have a scientific approach to choose the products!

A: Yes, no question. When you start to operate the business using these kinds of measurements you can spend more time on running the business to make the most money and less time arguing about "feelings" people have about which products or design changes will create the most sales.

Q: This metric is so important that I will ask my programmers to create an automatic Hurdle Rate for each product and category so I will not have to analyze the database every time I need this information (I will need this information very frequently). For most of the other information I will analyze them using a spreadsheet (like it's explained in your book). I will copy the SQL tables and paste them into the spreadsheet. I did some tests and it worked.

A: Yes, these are longer-term ideas that don't need to be visited as often. And when you execute promotions based on them, you will see your other, more short-term Hurdle metrics move, allowing you to measure the success of the promotion by category, for example. You might see the 45-day Hurdle percentages jump, say from 30% to 40%, but there would be a wide variation among categories. This in itself tells you which buyer categories are most profitable to promote to.

Q: Thanks a lot for your great advice...

A: No problem - you're a customer now!

Jim

Tracking and Using Promotional History; Sequential Campaign ROI

Q: I've really enjoyed your book and software. I'm a business consultant with the University of (deleted). I'm in the process of developing a Continuing Education class (2 1/2 hour program) on Customer Database Management. I plan to reference your book extensively and show off your software. I will be sure to provide attendees your web address where they can order your book.

A: Well, I'm thrilled you like the offering and thanks for the promotion!

Q: One of the areas I'm working on now, and would appreciate your input (perhaps a future newsletter topic), is what is the best way to organize data (target / control lists) for calculating ROI on promotions.

A: Typically this is done with what is called a "promotional history table," which can either be part of the customer record or a unique table keyed by customer ID. Each promotion has an "ID" and if the customer is selected for the promotion, the promotion ID is placed in the table with customer ID. So you end up with (to use a spreadsheet analogy) for each row with a customer ID a list in the columns of the row flagging promotions the customer has been a target in. This approach, of course, can create a non-symmetric table and can lead to issues down the line.

Another way to do it, which is more difficult to execute but sometimes preferred depending on what you are doing, is to have (to use a spreadsheet analogy) each row represent a customer and each column represent a promotion. If the customer was in the promotion, the intersection of customer and promotion is "Y." If the customer was not in the promotion, the intersection of customer and promotion is "N." This keeps the table symmetric and can make querying easier all the way around.

Q: I am trying to put together one promotion (for the client I mentioned above) and realized they have to track their promotion target list and control list. If they begin doing a promotion every month, or every week, that's going to grow into a large number of lists.

A: Yes, if you use lists. I can't imagine weekly promotions for this kind of (offline jewelry store) biz....unless they are going to different people each time... Using the table approach described above might be easier.

Q: Also, how do you handle a case where a customer was targeted for a promotion, does not respond, and it's time to do another promotion? Wouldn't that customer be included in the next promotion (assuming that you have not given up, or written off the customer as gone), and if so, how would you handle the ROI calculation(s) if that customer responded to the next promotion?

A: As soon as you mail to that customer again you have "poisoned" the ROI measurement of the original mailing; you would have to cut off your measurement period before the second mailing if you wanted ROI on the original mailing. But I doubt you will ever be able to measure the true effectiveness of the promotion with such short (weekly) time frames, because you cut-off any of the Halo Effects the initial promotion may have generated by stomping all over it with the results of the next promotion.

You might not care about that, and I don't really know what the objective of the campaign is. But if the objective is to maximize ROI, you won't be able to measure it if you poison the control group so quickly. Wait 30 days if you are just looking to measure the ROI of the promotion itself; wait 90 days if you are looking at the dynamics and ROI of customer retention campaigns overall.

Now, if your plan is to sequence mailings, that is, "the promotion" is actually 4 successive weekly mailers, and you are measuring that effort against control, then you can mail every week and mail to whoever you want, as long as it isn't people in control. You can set up a "decision tree" if you want that says "if they don't respond to #1, send #2 the next week; if they do respond to #1, skip a week and send #3 in week 3, that kind of thing.

Realize this though:

1. You will not be able to measure the effect of any one mailer or decision tree sequence, only the effect **of the entire sequential promotion**. So you end up with a lot of work and you don't know what was effective.

2. You **can** measure the effectiveness of an individual piece or sequence, you just have to set up control for it at each new branch or step, for example:

Mailer #1: Initial mailer, total = 1000
Test: 900 are mailed
Control: 100 are held back

You get results of: Non-responders: 500 Responders: 400

Mailer #2: Re-mail non-responders = 500
Test: 450 are mailed
Control: 50 are held back

Mailer #3: Re-mail responders = 400
Test: 360 are mailed
Control: 40 are held back

So for a simple 2-step mailing, you have 3 control groups and 3 test groups, and you can measure the effectiveness not only of the total campaign, but each piece of it. If you don't set up control at each step, if the overall campaign is successful, you won't know if it was because of the initial response or the re-mails of responders or non-responders.

The ROI you asked about above would be the ROI of Mailer #2 - did not respond to initial mailer and were mailed again. As long as control is composed of other people who received the first mailing and did not respond, you should be able to measure ROI very accurately for this sub-segment.

Jim

Selling Educational Courses Online; Latency-based Promotions

Q: Hi Jim, I was wondering if your book could help increase the percentage of visitors who buy from us. We sell educational materials.

A: Can you give me a more specific definition of "educational materials"? Are we talking pens and notebooks, books, courses? And which book are you asking about? There are two, the Marketer's Guide to E-Metrics book:

http://www.cafeshops.com/futurenowinc.8103777

 and Drilling Down:

http://jimnovo.booklocker.com/

Q: For different IT Technologies like Java there are certification exams offered by vendors like Sun. We provide software which helps people prepare for these exams. Like Kaplan's GRE prep on CD-ROM.

A: Got it.

Q: Our pricing per product ranges from $60 - $90. Our visitor to conversion ratio at present is around 0.6% and we see a GREAT scope in improving this. Are there any standard industry conversion ratios? Preferably in a domain related to ours? Any idea of Amazon's visitor to buyer conversion ratios?

A: A "domain like ours"? I take it you're an IT person, marketing people would call it a category...

Well, for retail, here are the latest stats I have seen:

Retail Entry-to-Sale Conversion Rates

0-1% conversion   7%
1-2% conversion   15%
2-3% conversion   17%
3-5% conversion   19%
5-10% conversion   16%
11-20% conversion   6%
20+% conversion   3%
Didn't know conversion   14%

Source: E-Tailing Group's 1Q 2003 research of 200 online commerce sites

I have a new client, a major name brand retailer in the US, which averages .51% conversion on visits. One of my first clients, a small specialty retailer, now averages 9.1% on visits. So the averages are all over the map, and tend to increase as the niche you are playing in gets smaller. More competition, lower conversion. There are always exceptions. Amazon's conversion rate was reported in 2001 to be near 15%. Another report in 1999 said 8.3%.

The exact nature of how Amazon conversion was measured in these cases is unknown; it probably was estimated from public records. Obviously, if you measure conversion rate using unique visitors instead of visits (I prefer visits because they are more accurate), the rate goes higher because the base you start from is lower.

My guess is that the 15% number is on unique visitors and the 8.3% number is on visits. But to really understand these numbers, you have to get into a long discussion on defining a "visit" and "unique visitor." What is the time period for defining unique, the past year? Does entering an affiliate store where the book art / description is pulled from the Amazon site count as a visit, even though the "visitor" is not at the Amazon site? Etc.

So the best thing to do is pick a measurement that makes sense for your site, stick with it, and use your own data as a benchmark, rather than comparing it to anyone else. The combination of your products, web site technology, and traffic streams are most likely unique to you and the best measure of success is your own benchmark. The E-Metrics book covers the measurements and techniques you can use on a website which are most likely to lead you to converting visitors into buyers at a higher rate; it's all about the "front end" of the customer conversion issue.

None of the stats above break out new versus repeat customers, and this can obviously make a big difference. You want your first-time buyer customer to come back and buy again; these "back end" kinds of issues are covered in the Drilling Down book. You can't manage this issue unless you measure it, and my guess is that for your business, the primary repeat purchase metric you should start with is Latency.

Latency triggers off the time between customer events, so for example, the number of weeks between purchasing the first sim and the second sim, the second sim and the third sim, etc. Look at your multi-buyers and measure the average time between purchases; this is where you start.

Let's say it is 8 weeks. Set up a "sniffer" or report run that looks at every customer each week, and flags those customers whose last purchase was 9 weeks ago; send these people a promotion (1 extra week for "slippage"). If you send the promotion before this, you risk giving discounts to people who would have bought anyway. If you send it too long after this threshold, you risk the customer has already defected and is no longer interested.

The above is a very "blunt force" example of Latency; it doesn't take into account different "pacing" by different customer segments. So for example, customers on the "Cisco track" might have an average Latency between courses of 6 weeks; customers on the "IBM track" might have an average Latency of 10 weeks between courses. You don't have to figure out why this is true; it's enough to know it is true.

So the second step is to look at multi-buyers by segment to determine Latency, and proceed as above. If you choose a segmentation scheme like "track" and you don't see any clear patterns, you may have the wrong segment scheme. You should see a "bell curve" around the average Latency if you are segmenting by a predictive behavior. If there are a too many "outliers," or the bell curve is lopsided, you have a piece of it but there is something else going on.

For example, the truest segment might be "track by price." If you now look at Latency that way and get a near perfect bell curve, you nailed it. Other variables might be occupation, country of origin, and age.

The third major behavior model is called RFM, and then there is a hybrid of all these models I developed called LifeCycle Grids. Those two are covered only in the Drilling Down book (hey, I can't give it all away free, I'd have no business!) but you can read an overview of these models on my web site.

Hope that helps!

Jim

Use F or M or Gross Margin or What for Current Value?

Q: I've used your site a lot and found it to be very informative.

A: Thanks for the kind words!

Q: I have a question about the use of RFM analysis for a low margin, eCommerce business. I read that for a relatively small customer list (<50k) using just the "RF" of the RFM analysis would be preferred since the "M" tends to hide shifts in behavior.

A: Well, the M tends to smooth shifts regardless of the size of your list. In addition, if you have a small list, having 125 segments could be too many to be really useful, so RF at 25 segments in more intuitive. The real issue with M or Monetary Value is up and coming, accelerating customers. If you use total spend (M), it will "punish" these customers with a lower rank. But the fact is they have more future potential because Recency is low and Frequency is ramping. Inversely, M tends to reward customers who have spent a lot in the past with a higher rank, though they may actually be declining or defected customers. Predicting the future is more profitable than reporting on the past, so given a choice, I would drop "M." This is especially true on the web, where communication costs are low and changes in behavior very rapid. M is really more relevant in the offline catalog context where RFM was born, because you are spending big money to communicate with the customer and the LifeCycle is much longer than online.

Q: My question to you is, since I'm talking about a low margin business, wouldn't "M" actually be more valuable than "F" for the analysis? For example, if 40% of my customers are driving 70% of my sales and 100% of my profits, that says that 60% of my customer base is losing me money. I don't want them to be given a higher value rating because they're placing MORE unprofitable orders than someone placing fewer but profitable orders. Do you see what I'm saying here???

A: Absolutely, and you have just proven to me you really understand the concept. It's a tool. The more you can customize it to your situation, the better. There is actually some discussion of this situation in the book, the idea of "M" as a "check digit" on profitability rather than using F, if the business is low margin or certain very popular items are "loss leaders."

Q: Does that then support my belief that an "RM" analysis would be more appropriate in this situation?

A: Well, I'm not sure I understand your situation completely, but if I'm getting it I would be more likely to use Recency-Gross Margin because if I'm hearing you correctly, you sell some (perhaps many) items at a negative profit. However, some of those customers may go on to buy profitable items, and I would want to consider that. So I wouldn't use sales, it could be deceiving; I would use cumulative Gross Margin.

In the end, there are 2 components to this model: Recency / Latency, which predict likelihood to buy or visit again (potential value to you in the future), and the "Money" variable, which indicates how profitable the customer is to you now (current value). You can plot the two variables on a two-dimensional space and literally "map" the current and future value of your customer base, and then use this knowledge to make marketing or service decisions.

You should design the money variable to be the one that makes the most sense for your business, according to your model and available data. If total page views are your measure of the value of a customer (ad supported site), you use total page views for current value (Frequency). If you are selling products with an evenly distributed price scale and roughly the same profit margin, you can use M. Recency, or sometimes Latency, are used to measure the potential value of the visitor or customer.

Frequency is actually a "tweener" variable, it has implications for both current and potential value. But the largest predictive power of Frequency is really in the distinction between one-time and multi-buyers.

So, as I suggested here, if you have a small list you might want to score one-time and multi-buyers each by themselves. This will buy you a lot of the power of the Frequency variable without having to mess with 3 variables and the 125 segments in the traditional RFM model. The one-time buyers you can simply score on Recency and the rest you use RF, R-GM, or whatever financial metric makes sense for the biz.

If I have failed to explain this sufficiently, please let me know!

Jim

Scores and LTV for Budgeting; Offline versus Online Business Models

Q: You'll be pleased to know that your book has been the catalyst for setting up a user forum on RFM, which now has around 30 actively contributing members. Not many, but not bad considering the only way the word was spread is by word of mouth among friends!

A: That's great! We're a small voice crying in the wilderness… but we know the future of this direction, and it is powerful indeed.

Q: We operate a retail stores, a catalog, and web site. I want to make sure I understand how LTV tables help in drawing up your budget and marketing plan. Obviously in the context of my assignment I make a few assumptions, because hardly any data is given. My take on the process is as follows:

- Work out rough average customer spend

- Work out how much I want to increase my sales in FY 2004

- Work out how many customers I need to get me to sales budget
- Now split the overall number of customers by distribution channel (distribute customer spend through each as I think appropriate)

- Work out an LTV table for retail Shop, Print Catalogue, and web site

- Take a percentage of the 'LTV at Net Present Value' figure for 2004 (say 20%) that will give me the amount of money I can afford to spend on my total marketing budget across all channels

- Create a budget and campaign for shop, catalogue and website for 2004 only

- Write analysis

Is this process correct?

A: Well, it's hard to define "correct" not knowing the specific requirements of the task, but I think you are generally on track. A couple of comments:

** "How much I want to increase my sales by in 2004" is a retail concept you may find difficult to crunch into the direct methodology. Remember, direct is much more focused on profits than sales. In retail, you follow a standard "percentage of sales" model and as long as sales go up, profits are expected to go up. Not so with direct. For one thing, in direct, actions you take today have value in the future. If you want, you could say, "OK, I know a direct customer will spend $100 first year, $80 second year, and so forth, and crush direct into a retail model, but to me this defeats the beauty of direct, because now you are using a "periodic financial accounting" system rather than a "customer accounting" system. More on this idea in the Advanced Toolkit chapter titled "LifeTime Value, I'd Like to Introduce You to the CFO."

** In fact, I'm not sure what the value is of including "the stores" in the online budgeting process, other than to determine what gross revenue needs are overall. The stores involve a completely different model than catalog and web, and I think down the line you are going to get to a place where it is hard to "force" the stores into the direct model. Now, if you are assuming that these stores possess some way to behave like a direct operation - that is, they always have customer-level knowledge of all customer transactions - then maybe it works.

But in the stores, if you have walk-in traffic that transacts anonymously, then you bust the direct model, you can't track LTV and so on. So retail is much more like a "snapshot" idea (activity today has value today) than a "movie" idea (activity today has value in the future over time). Offline retailing is generally managed in the aggregate, not at the customer level. Database marketing is almost always managed at the customer level. These two models will "collide."

For example, you do newspaper ads for the store and you see a boost in traffic. You have sales - (product costs + ad cost) = variable profit in the aggregate, forgetting overhead for the moment. There is no measurement at the customer level, no LTV involved in this, no tracking a future profit stream. In direct, you know who you attracted and can measure future profits. In direct, a campaign that looks like a loser today can be a winner in 2 months. From a management perspective, to try and "force" the retail store manager to operate under the direct model would often result in sub-optimal performance.

Q: My second question draws on your experience of the catalogue market. I need to make an assumption on costs versus profit. So, what I intend to do (presuming this is correct) is to take a percentage of the 'LTV at Net Present Value' figure for 2004 (say 20%) which will give me the amount of money I can afford to spend on my marketing budget.

Question is, what should this percentage cost be for the shop, catalogue (print) and website distribution, bearing in mind that they have relatively little experience in catalogue / web marketing and already own three shops.

A: Umm, do you see where this is leading? 20% NPV (Net Present Value) of LTV (LifeTime Value) is OK for direct marketing folks, 3% of retail sales is what is typically spent in retail on marketing. How do you reconcile these different approaches? You can't. This is what I mean by the models colliding. If you went to a retail store manager and told him he could spend 20% of the

NPV of the LifeTime Value of the average customer on marketing, he / she would at the least be a bit confused, at most think you're totally bonkers.

Put another way, retail operates on a single transaction basis (snapshot), direct takes into account transactions over time (movie). Retail cannot afford to pay more than 3% of sales because they cannot target and cannot track. In direct, you generally lose money on the first purchase from the customer. Retail management could not tolerate that approach; they try to make money on every sale. It's simply a different operating model, and this difference is driven by the difference in cost components. Retail is a high fixed, low variable cost model; direct is low fixed, high variable cost model. The seeds of "model collision" are planted in this fundamental difference between the two cost structures, and to try to "blend" them in a budget may be a futile exercise. Do each budget as a unique business model and then roll them up, if need be.

Jim

When is a Customer No Longer a Customer?

Q: I'm a "long time listener, first time caller," and a big fan of your site and your approach to data-driven marketing. I also have two copies of your book - one was not enough.

A: Well, thanks for your kind words. I love the talk radio reference, that is so funny. Never though about it like that, but it makes perfect sense! Glad to know I'm actually helping people with the book too. In the early days at Home Shopping Network, we used to think of ourselves as most like talk radio from a behavioral perspective, and the web also has many similarities, e.g. most people on a discussion list never say anything, they just lurk, as is true in talk radio.

Q: I have a question relating to some work I am doing now with our best customers that other users of your site may also have.

I work for a medium sized mail order company selling skincare products (high margin) via space ads and direct mail. Our best customer "Gold Club" has about 8000 members at the moment, although members are being promoted and demoted all the time.

According to my initial analysis, if a member does not purchase a product for more than 60 days, the chances are that they are defecting. I would like to attempt to bring them back with an offer, and leave those that don't reply for at least 6 months for a deeply discounted "kickstart" offer (although the logistics of sending out very small mailings are a pain.)

A: This is a common and logical approach, particularly for "renewable products." You don't say what the product is, but if it is "typical" skincare product, it has a sales cycle very tightly tied to product use. In this case, Latency usually makes more sense to use than Recency as the primary trigger for a campaign, since the usage cycle is highly defined.

If you have people on different "supply amounts" (some get 30 day, some 60 day, some 90 day) then it can get confusing and be ineffective to just say, "60 day Latency gets mail." 30 day should get 30-day mail, 60 day should get 60-day mail, etc. in the optimum scenario. You have to, obviously, understand what the costs are to do that and optimize around the schedule with the most bang for the buck overall.

Q: I am having some problems convincing management that these former best customers are a lost cause, they don't like the idea of "losing contact with our customer base" and want to prolong the contact longer to see if we can bring some of these customers back. In fact, when I first looked at the data around 2000 people hadn't purchased for at least 6 months, and were receiving mail from us every month at $1 US a pop.

A: Well, this is a very typical attitude in small mail order companies, particularly high margin ones. But what they don't realize is there is tremendous leverage in there, absolutely tremendous. The question for the owner is something like this: would you give up 10% of annual top line sales for a 30% improvement in annual profits? That should get their eyes sufficiently bugged out to listen a bit more.

Q: Is there any sense in the "losing contact" hypothesis or is it best to let customers go without undue struggle and prevent them from getting to the defection stage in the first place? What about a short "grace period" that includes customers a bit longer than necessary? There may be a situation in which a certain RF group is unprofitable for a DM, but the few people that do repurchase buy again, thus coming into the black again (keeping in mind the high margins). Any insight you have would be greatly appreciated.

A: Look, most mail order companies blast mail to people up to 2 years after the last purchase. I think that's silly and wasteful, and you are on the right track. They have to learn to "let go." The grace period idea is a bit unclear to me, but in general, there is some "optimized" grace period, yes. For example, a customer on a 60-day supply cycle might most profitably be approached 10 days before it runs out, 5 days before it runs out, or 5 days after it runs out, or 10 days after it runs out. When your are talking profit (as opposed to response), there is no way to know without a test of the concept.

My suggestion would be do what I call a 30-60-90. This idea is very similar to the "LifeCycle Grid" from the Drilling Down book in nature:

1. Segment by supply cycle, if there is one. Don't mix in "90 day supply" people with "60 day supply people" - if it is efficient to mail them separately. If not, well, this will still work, but won't be as profitable.

2. Take a 10% random sample of the population by Latency - 30 days before supply runs out (if applicable), 30 days after, 60 days after, 90 days after, 90-120 day after, 120-180 days after, etc. if applicable. Execute mailing the segments.

3. There should be a 30 day (or larger, depends) window where it is the most profitable to mail based on supply run-out date. It should be very clear how much money is wasted "chasing" dead customers in say, the 120-180 day Latency window from the stats.

Use this as ammo with management. If they still don't want to let go, say you'll reallocate the money to really work on the "windows" (for example, even though 120-180 day is not profitable, 120-150 might be) and then you'll do a bi-annual or annual postcard to "the dead" to keep in touch with them.

That way you efficiently "scrape" the dead for the few you can get back for very little cost, and focus the majority of the resources where the profits are.

Hope the above helped. Thanks again for the kind words, and good luck with it. Any questions, let me know!

Jim

When the Same Target Gets Different Offers

Q: Hi Jim! I purchased the Drilling Down book and just love it.

A: Well, thanks for your kind words! Always good to hear from people out there who are "getting it."

Q: We're a lab supply company. I'm getting ready to do a web promo based on Recency ratings (we're starting with just doing Recency ratings until we get our feet wet). What we plan on doing is to rank our web customers based on Recency and put them into quintiles as you suggest. We will then offer a sliding discount promo and will then measure the ROR and ROI versus the customer Recency score (Recency-based Discount Ladder).

A: I take it you mean Recency of purchase, not visit...since you're a customer now, I'll give you some background dirt on a "Recency Only" approach. Recency is about Response; RF(M) is about profit. So doing "Recency Only" on the web, where communication cost is low, probably works. If you were mailing one of those big ol' lab supply catalogs, I don't think I would drop the FM from the analysis - those catalogs are too darn expensive.

The crux of the matter is usually 1x buyers - they can be very Recent, but they are less likely to respond than multi-buyers. It would be instructional (if you can) to do a basic Frequency select by creating two groups - 1x buyers and everybody else. Score each for Recency separately and then do your sliding scale promo as planned to each group. You will probably find it works very well for multi-buyers, but results by Recency are a bit random for 1x buyers, with perhaps product of first purchase being more predictive of the discount needed to optimize profits.

Do you follow what I mean? If you divide the groups initially, it should be pretty easy to see these patterns. If you rank them all together on Recency only, your ranking will be skewed with 1x buyers and might not be optimal. This approach is discussed under the "Hurdle Rate" idea in the book pg 94 - 101.

Q: I'm concerned about the situation where several people within the same company get drastically different e-mail promotions because one person has a "5" Recency rating and another has a "2" Recency rating. Do you have any ideas on this potential problem? Of course, if a customer called and complained, we would certainly give them the higher discount, but I don't want to have to do this on a wide-scale basis. On the other hand, maybe most customers within the same company won't notice and I'm worrying about nothing at all...

A: Well, you've got your thinking cap on, and it is a minor concern. Two areas:

1. My experience is this: it is much more of a concern in the contact center than with the customer. It is critical all customer service agents understand what is going on and understand the policy of granting the discount a "buddy" is offered. If you keep track of who gets what discount, you can audit on the back end to see how much "noise" gets into the system. It is typically quite low, maybe 1 - 3% of total response (not of total mailing), and with e-mail being such a personal thing, it's even lower.

E-mail is different than dropping catalogs with a "15% off any order over $500" dotwack on the cover into the same place you mail catalogs with no offer. If the customer is treated "matter of factly" and given whatever discount they have a code for, they really don't care and the issue disappears. If they are treated to a "hell no, that's not the discount code we issued you" experience, then they start talking about it with other people in the lab and then you get them all on alert to share info and all of them order using the best offer.

2. It really is more of a concern when you have duplicate customer records and the same customer gets two different offers. So to the extent possible, try to de-dupe the list. But it really isn't a big deal. I get two catalogs from Dell Computer every few weeks and they both have different offers, one better than the other. I buy from the one with the better offer - but I still buy. Then I become more Recent with the one catalog and the offers get better in the other. But I still buy - from Dell.

Ultimately, that's the mission, and if you consider the "company" as a customer, this kind of stuff evens out in the end. After all - they could buy their equipment elsewhere, and as long as you are making money on the promotion, I wouldn't get too wrapped up in the dynamics of offer profitability at the individual buyer level, especially when you are just starting out.

Get the "gross" picture moving in a positive direction, then go back and see if maybe you can tweak for specific situations. In other words, this modeling stuff really works on the "aggregate" level. There will always be individual customers who you lose out on and beat you on the offer, it always happens. But in the aggregate, you make a lot more money than without the models.

Just make sure your customer service people understand the game - which does NOT mean giving away the **best discount to every caller**, it means giving the customer the **discount they ask for** with the promo code.

Let me know if I have explained this well enough for you to execute!

Jim

LifeTime Value and Retention in Continuity Clubs

Q: I just ordered the book too, so I am eager to learn more about SIMPLE ways to implement RFM-based strategies.

A: Well, thank you for ordering! I hope it fulfills your expectations.

Q: In the continuity club business (Jim's Note: flower of the month, book of the month, beer of the month, in this case wine) though, a little of the RFM process looks tricky because everyone has a certain Frequency built-in, because of the "repeat" nature of clubs. Also, we're starting to see a phenomenon where customers that drop out of our club continue to order from us.

A: This is quite normal, depending on how the club is set up and whether or not you make it "easy" for people to continue. In some clubs, you are either in or not (books, CD's, credit cards). Most catalog-type clubs (pay a fee in exchange for ongoing discounts / added services) see continuation beyond club membership. It's a volume-based thing and a "rational" decision by the consumer - if you need to buy a lot of stuff, joining the club makes sense, because the discount pays for the membership. As you fulfill your demand, volume drops and the club membership fee is not worth it.

In your case, it might be more attached to education, for example - you join the club to educate yourself about the products, and then quit when you can "do it on your own." Or, you get lots of product to experience the variety, and settle into a specific usage pattern. This is the customer LifeCycle at work. If you can recognize these patterns, you can use them to predict what customers are likely to do next. If you can predict behavior, you can create very high ROI customer marketing programs.

Q: This challenges our traditional thinking that club-lapse is the end of the LTV contribution. It leaves me wondering what really is the end of the LTV for any given customer. The end-all goal for me is to learn everything possible about customer lapse and how to influence it. I've been given explicit responsibility just recently to take charge of customer lapse and influence it to our advantage. I'm analyzing the scope of the problem and putting together a plan of attack.

A: Well, somebody has their thinking hat on at that company! In your environment (if I understand it correctly from a brief review of the web site), I don't think the "club" really defines long-term behavior, it could be seen simply as a customer acquisition tool, which is also true of the catalog-type clubs I referred to above. You have to be careful with this kind of club, because you can end up creating negative value customers if they buy a lot of low margin goods with a membership discount and then just simply abandon you.

The bottom line is this: you probably should not define LTV by club membership length. It may be convenient to look at membership as the definition of a "customer," but being a "member" is probably **just the first stage** of the customer LifeCycle. There is then a transition period where some stay members, some reject membership but remain customers, others quit entirely. You need to find out what variables - media source of customer, creative / offer used, first product purchased, etc. cause customers to end up in these buckets and optimize for highest value.

If you want to be proactive on this LifeCycle transition, you need to predict which members will transition and remain customers, which ones need promotional "help" doing this, and which ones you should not bother spend on. How? You can check out how we did this at Home Shopping Network in the book, it's quite simple and works like a charm. Track the customer LifeCycle using simple metrics like Recency or Latency and act only when you have to, and when you do act, always act at the point of maximum impact.

Q: What sort of work have you done on customer lapse studies, retention marketing, or in club environments like mine?

A: I've done 100's of customer retention programs over the past 20 years. Every one is different based on the industry, the business model, and the constraints of the specific business. You will find many examples in the book, and more recent case studies are on the web site. Unfortunately, companies are not very willing to let me talk openly about solving their customer retention problems; they consider this info a "trade secret" because of the financial implications and competitive issues involved.

If you are interested in using my services, the most cost-effective solution I can suggest is to read the book first; it provides a ton of "how to" information and could keep you busy for quite some time. If you want to accelerate the learning process, I'd be glad to talk with you about this. I have to tell you something first though - all my current clients read the book first, did some of the work outlined in the book, and then engaged me to help them push it forward. Ask any questions as you review the book - you're a customer now!

Jim

Scaling the Scoring Models to Database Size

Q: Thanks so much for your reply. I should have clarified that I am in catalog circulation. We currently use RFM to segment the file and then roll the RFM cells into more manageable segments (this is a new technique to me, I am new to this company, in my former company we mailed by RFM segment).

A: Hmm...this sounds like a "dumbing down" approach to it, but hey, if it works, why not. Sometimes this is done because the customer base is not really large enough to support 125 segments (RFM) or 25 segments (RF), and the differences between the segments can become unstable and less predictive unless some are aggregated together. This can also happen if you have a very large percentage of "identical" customers – for example, 1x buyers who bought the same product.

Q: Because we are in a niche market and we saturate it pretty well, I would like to see which customers are on the edge or falling off (the Latency stuff) and which ones we can "reward" for being the best. I do not think the RFM analysis shows me that amount of detail.

A: Well, it can, and that is essentially what the Drilling Down book is about. RFM as it is traditionally used - as a "snapshot" of behavior - is pretty dumb compared to how it can be used. If you start looking at scores over time, you have a much more robust kind of tool - a "movie" of the Customer LifeCycle. In this scenario, you aren't as concerned with the score at any one time, but what happens to it over time. Falling score indicates a move towards defection, rising score is an acceleration in loyalty.

Since you seem to be familiar with this area and are likely to understand this statement, the final part of the book, "Customer Scoring Grids," is where you really see the Customer LifeCycle emerge. Grids are a combination of Latency and RF(M) that produces a visual "map" of customer retention and defection.

Q: Your explanations about your books were great! I could have used the E-Metrics one in my last job.

A: At least you have a job!

Q: One other question for you. We operate our computers here at work on a shared network (where we do not have boxes at our desks). This means that I would not easily be able to load up any software that I could either download or get by disk. In my mind this simply means that I buy the book for my own personal use and use the customer scoring software at home - are the "results" I might find easily e-mailable?

A: Sure, as long as you can e-mail an Access .mdb file, you can mail it to work. One thing to note, the software produces RF scores, which may or may not be what you want. They are more "sensitive" than RFM scores when predicting behavioral change, which is really what the book is about. If you are mailing a catalog, RFM may be more important because of the cost involved. You might use them together, as in perhaps RFM says you don't mail to a certain segment, but within that segment RF has identified customers who appear to be accelerating and they should be mailed. You'd have to test it.

Q: Thanks so much! I have turned my friend (in the tennis ball machine business) on to you and we have had some great conversations based on your e-mailed chapters!

A: Well, thanks for that, and have fun Drilling!

Jim

Distribution / Operations / Channel Management

Tracking the Loyalty of Independent Agents (Insurance)

Q: Hi Jim,

I happened upon your site and found the information there very valuable - so much so that I ordered your book (customer is referring to Drilling Down).

A: Well, thank you very much for that!

Q: I'm a marketing manager with an insurance company that distributes its life, auto, home, and business insurance products through independent insurance agents. These agents represent our company as well as others.

I'm interested in techniques for measuring agent loyalty - which I think would be demonstrated by the agents choosing to place business with our company instead of another company they represent for policies.

A: I'm not sure in this case anything is too terribly different from the scenarios used in the book. Essentially, agents or consumers demonstrate loyalty though their actions, and if you can track their actions, you can spot increasing or decreasing loyalty. Your business is more complex in many ways than retail, but to the consumer (in your case agent), there are always choices to be made between alternatives, and changes in the purchase patterns agents or consumers generate often precede customer defection.

In a very simple case, let's say the average agent writes a policy every week with you. Some will write more, some less. But what you are interested in for estimating loyalty (increasing or decreasing?) is not the rate at which they write policies, but any change in rate. If you have an agent writing 3 policies a week and they drop to 1 a week, this is a significant change in behavior, and this behavior should be flagged and investigated as a prelude to agent defection.

If this agent is a "best agent," then the need to find out if there is a problem is even more urgent. The more policies the agent writes, the more imperative it is to find out if something is wrong.

In the book, the Recency (how many days since last policy was written) and Frequency (how many policies have been written in total) of writing policies is used to rank all agents against each other for "likelihood to keep writing policies." Any changes in this likelihood show up as a change in rank - called RF Score, or Recency-Frequency Score - and will alert you to high value agents who may be defecting and dropping your lines.

Depending on the data you have access to, another approach is to use Latency, in which simpler average behavior patterns rather than agent scoring are used. The example here would be the average agent writes one policy a week, and those who slide below this rate are likely future defectors. You can run these Latency numbers by line by area of the country for example, because the average Latency of writing a life policy in New England may be different than for a home policy in the Southeast or and auto policy in California.

If I am way off base in understanding how your business works, please let me know (Jim's note: she didn't, so I guess I wasn't!)

I hope I answered your question!

Jim

Tracking Defection in a Multi-Hub Distribution Chain (Manufacturing)

Q: You say your approach works for any size and any type of business. We are an audio electronics manufacturer specializing in commercial installs of professional sound equipment. Our equipment is marketed through reps (in North America) and distributors (outside North America). Neither the reps nor distributors stock our equipment. Equipment purchases are on a project basis with audio and architectural consultants releasing RFPs specifying particular pieces of equipment. Does your modeling work for such pure B2B business models with multiple hubs of distribution?

A: Sure, any business that has transactions with customers can be modeled. The question really is more like can you **do anything** with the information once you have it? If you can't "act" on the model, it won't do you much good to have one tracking the business.

Q: Our company is about $10 million in revenues. Our current database is a glorified Rolodex in ACT. I've seen cautionary notes concerning the use of models on databases of less than 2,000 customers. We have about 1881 dealers, 102 Distributors, 28 Reps, and 712 end-users who (for a variety of reasons) can purchase from us direct. We also have about 625 consultants who (hopefully) specify our equipment in projects that may require a year or two to complete.

A: Nothing wrong with ACT!, I've seen some pretty nifty stuff done with it...

Q: Which methodology should I use to uncover the behaviors of each of these small audiences and still have some degree of confidence in the results?

A: Well, in distribution networks like this, I think the primary idea would be to make sure you understand the value of each customer relative to it's own group and be prepared to take action should it look like you should.

The 1881 dealers could be ranked against each other by Recency. The rank predicts likelihood to buy again. You could then re-score them each month and see who is rising and who is falling in rank. Combined with the value of the customer, you could decide on what action to take, if any.

So for example, let's say you have two customers, and they both fall dramatically in rank. However, one has low value and the other has high value. You have a salesperson call on the high value one, you send a direct mail piece to the low value one. The cost of the retention effort is in pegged to the value of the customer; this conserves resources and ensures you get the highest ROI.

Or take the 102 distributors. A distributor (I'd guess) has more cyclical or predictable order characteristics than a dealer, as in "Distributor A orders every 30 days, Distributor B orders every 60 days," etc. This is a situation for the Latency metric. You basically set up a "trip wire" for each that says "if we don't see a new order from A 35 days after his last one, call her, if we don't see a new order from B 70 days after his last one, call him."

Once you know the average number of days between orders for a distributor, you can set something up in ACT! that at 35 or 70 days, pops up a message "check to see if distributor has ordered." If you further know the value of each, you can say "call" for the low value ones and "sales visit" for the high value ones. That way the sales force is working hardest where the money is most likely to be found.

Customer modeling work doesn't have to be complicated or use fancy software. It's a bit more manual doing it this way, but with as few records as you have, you could do all the analysis in a spreadsheet and then use ACT! as the "campaign manager" or "CRM system." All you have to do is program "reminders" in ACT!

If the above kind of system can be shown to work, then you have the justification you need to go ask for a higher level commitment to the program, in programming, people, etc. Some of the best "CRM" systems out there have been built **by the company** specifically **for the company** based on results of "skunk works" programs like the one described above.

And don't sweat the size of the populations, in the above examples, it's not like we are trying to predict the outcomes of any campaigns across the populations or do advanced statistics. We're looking at the patterns of individual behavior. And we're simply saying "Hey, there is a pattern, and if the pattern changes, we should pay attention to it."

You don't need thousands and thousands of customers to do that. In fact, you only need one. What you do need is to be able to look at the pattern of behavior of the customer over time, and be able to recognize when it changes.

Then you ACT!

Jim

Behavioral Modeling for Production Tasks / Error Forecasting

Q: Recently I had the opportunity to read your book "Drilling Down - Turning Customer Data into Profits with a Spreadsheet." It has been some time since I have come across a book of its kind. The concept you highlight is both interesting, and elegant in its simplicity.

A: Aw, shucks. Thanks for the kind words.

Q: I would like to know your opinion as to how this approach could be modified suitably for implementation in a Software Development and IT outsourcing firm like mine.

A: Generally, any transactional activity can be profiled using the RF scoring method. It is used for everything from predicting the likelihood of someone to commit another crime to predicting the likelihood of someone to make a bank deposit. RF is based on human psychology and is therefore applicable in any culture, and any part of your business where transactions are generated - medical transcription, attendance records, project tracking, and so on. All you have to do is think of situations where the prediction of the likelihood of repeat behavior is desirable for business optimization.

In some cases, frequently in service businesses, the desired outcome is inverted - that is, it is positive if people become less likely to do something. For example, in regards to attendance tracking, if you want to predict the likelihood of a person to skip or call off work, look at the Recency and Frequency of this past behavior. If you were using RF scoring, a falling score for the person would be **positive**, since they are becoming **less likely** to call off again.

In transcription, for monitoring coding errors, the higher the Recency and Frequency of past errors, the more likely they are to be committed again. A falling RF score for a transcriber would be **positive**, since they are becoming **less likely** to commit another error. A rising score, they are becoming more likely to commit an error.

The above scenarios are often part of a "Six Sigma" type process for hunting down and reducing production errors, often by retraining or reassignment.

I don't know if likelihood prediction is useful for the transcribed records themselves, but it could be. For example, predicting the likelihood of a doctor to prescribe a certain medicine or order a certain procedure. The tracking of these things might be useful to a client and you could offer this modeling and prediction sets as an added service to them.

As far as software development for clients, there are any number of situations where a simple predictive model may be useful, especially where there is transactional activity related to purchases in B2C and B2B - reordering / replenishment for trading hubs, for example. And of course, in CRM, there are many, many uses for simple predictive behavior models.

Generally, one should try using the RF scheme for prediction before any more complex modeling operations are carried out. Often, after a long and torturous data mining project is completed, one finds Recency and Frequency to be the primary variables predicting the behavioral outcome; much time and effort could have been saved by using the simple RF scoring process detailed in my book in the first place!

Jim

Data Aggregation: Cost Reduction, Cycles and Modeling Approach

Q: Hi Jim, I've been reading the content on your website and so far it has been very useful.

A: Well, that's good! I was starting to wonder if maybe I was wrong about the whole thing... Just kidding, thanks for the compliment.

Q: I do have one question. You mention that if a company has less than 65,000 transactions Excel can be used to measure customer Lifecycle metrics. What was the time frame for the transactions? Was that 65,000 per year, month, etc.? Can you still use Excel if you have more transactions by "aggregating" the data? How would you go about doing this aggregation?

A: Oh sure, you've got "one question." Good thing I don't have a limit on the number of questions per customer around here...

It's 65,000 total transactions, the number of "rows" in an Excel spreadsheet (there are actually a tad more). Access can become unfriendly over 100,000 rows or total records I'm told by some IT people, but I have seen evidence to the contrary. It seems logical if you have this many transactions, you would probably be using SQL Server, Oracle, or something else more robust than Excel to hold your customer data.

That said, you can always aggregate data to keep it under 65,000 rows and still use Excel - just be careful what and how you aggregate. Generally, the lower the economic value the transaction has, the more OK it is to aggregate. So if you had a choice, you would aggregate page views, but not purchases.

For example, you could aggregate an entire day's page views into one record, instead of keeping them as unique records. Or a whole week's worth. Instead of having individual page views, you would have an "activity record" that would look like this:

Customer ID
Date Last Activity
Total Page Views

The "date" could be an actual date or any "cut-off" - the last day of the week, or last day of the month. You lose some useful detail (maybe) but you still retain the most important parameters - date of last activity (Recency) and total Frequency. As long as you retain these metrics, you can run any of the models in the Drilling Down method. You can run these "aggregated" transactions through the Drilling Down software and you'll end up with customer scores than will work just fine for LifeCycle profiling.

With purchases and other direct revenue items, I always try to keep as much data as possible, because there are other things you will want to do down the line with the detail once you see how powerful LifeCycle profiling can be. That said, people are running into "resource limitations" these days, so here is what I would do: prove it out and then beg for money.

In the beginning, you could aggregate purchases, let's say monthly. Run these aggregate transactions through the software and create your LifeCycle models, which will be of "aggregate buying behavior." With an eye towards proving out ROI, track your marketing and show how you can double or triple response while lowering costs using LifeCycle profiling. Then say to the appropriate penny pincher, "This is what we can do with aggregate purchase behavior. If we could keep more details on each transaction, we could run these LifeCycle models based on category of product purchased, average price paid, time of day or day of week - any piece of data we can afford to store without aggregation. If we do that, we can begin to really see which products, prices, times of day or days of week create the most valuable, long LifeCycle customers and correctly target our promotions for highest ROI."

The next sound you hear should be the cash drawer opening...ka-ching!

Aggregation can also be thought of as relative to the frequency of profiling. If you want to profile customers intra-day (why?), then you need all the individual page views. But if you are only going to profile customers once a week, you could use daily totals, or once a month, use weekly totals. Whatever the next smaller logical unit is relative to the profiling cycle is a good place to aggregate.

Since what is most important is not a customer's LifeCycle score, but a change in LifeCycle score, you have to pick a time frame that makes sense for the natural cycle of your business to profile customers.

A lot of times biz owners have a pretty good feel for this. If it "feels like" (or you know for sure) your best customers buy 2x a month, then run profiles 2x a month. If they buy 2x a week, running profiles every 2 months may not help you much. You want to try to synch up your profiling with what you perceive to be the behavior, or better yet, measure the behavior first. If you synch to your best customers, you'll be on top of the rest of your customers, because their behavior is not likely to change as rapidly as it might among best customers. And after all, you want to be paying the most attention (from a tracking standpoint) to your best customers. Whatever changes you may implement based on LifeCycle Tracking for them should "trickle down" to the rest of your customers in a positive way.

Hope that answers your question; feel free to continue asking until it makes sense to you. And thanks again for the kind words on the site - be sure and tell your friends!

Jim

Operational versus "Marketing" Databases (POS Network)

Q: As of today, I am in the early planning stages of an Operational database. This Operational database communicates with merchant terminals. Loyalty cards will be distributed to merchants' customers. The loyalty and gift card functions are not problematic, but the expense to track migration of customers at the Operational database level is questionable. With a marketing database created using the software that comes with your book...

A: Ummm... I don't know how many customers you are talking about, or what kind of operational systems you have, but the scoring application that comes with the book is just a Microsoft Access application. My application doesn't "create a marketing database"; it runs on a database you have already created. You probably know that, but just to make sure...

Q: Can various reports be made on the Marketing database that track: who (of a particular segment) had a particular offer (specific to their buying behavior) and report the redemption or non-redeemed offers in a specific duration of time? Can I avoid this expense on an Operational database with a Marketing database?

A: Well, you can report on anything that makes it into the database. As long as you can get "who the offer was made to" and "who responded" data into the Marketing database, yes, you can report on it, and use it to create new offers.

Q: The programmers of the Operational Database encourage using a Marketing Database for various reasons. First, the specific offers made to particular customers at a particular merchant will be communicated to the merchants' terminal using the Operations database. This protects merchants from customer fraud or abuse of repeat redemption. Second, they want to make more money. What do you recommend?

A: I'm not sure I am following this completely, but I think the situation is this: your ops people don't want you running marketing stuff on their database, because they are afraid it will slow down performance, and that is bad for them. So they want all the coding, scoring, tracking, and development of offers to take place "offline." This is quite typical and pretty much standard procedure.

Usually the marketing database doesn't have to be "real time" where the operational database does. So each night, the operational database updates the marketing database with transactions and you do whatever you want on the Marketing database - analysis, scoring, creation of promo codes, and so forth - without slowing down operations. You get the update, then do all your analysis work outside the operational system.

Now, if you want the ops database to be able to respond in real time based on customer scores and provide promotional codes or other data, what you do is send "customer codes" back to the ops database from the marketing database after you run your scoring.

For example, you get data from ops at 1 am, run scoring until 2 am, then send promotional codes back to the ops database at 3 am. So the next day, the operational database can respond to customers in real time based on scores and codes but it doesn't have to do any calculations because it has the scores and codes already. This dramatically reduces the "load" on the operational system, while still allowing it to be "smart" in real time.

Scoring of transactional data for real-time use in operations is a classic benefit of RFM, because the scores are "standardized" and are the same format each time. Since the scores rank likelihood to purchase and customer value, it is fairly easy to set up a rules-based system to make offers accordingly.

Am I understanding the question correctly? If not, feel free to clarify!

Jim

Customer Interaction Scores

Q: We were preparing customer profiles for our company and I happened to search your website. Is there any format that we could follow? Please let me know. We need to prepare profiles that will speak to / show / identify the nature of a customer at a glance and that all employees can relate to.

A: Well, that's a pretty broad question and difficult to answer without more information. Assuming the reason you want this "employees can identify the nature of a customer at a glance" profile is so you can differentiate the profitability of customers and potentially treat them differently based on this profile, I would use a 2-digit score, based on Value to Date and Potential Value. This allows you to hide the actual data from employees but provides a very specific view of the Current and Future value of the customer.

For example, take your customers and sort them by Total Sales, Net Profit, Number of Visits / Downloads, or whatever Current Value financial metric you have. The top 20% of customers get a score of 5, the 2nd 20% get a score of 4, etc, down to the bottom 20% who get a 1. This is the first digit of the 2-digit score and represents Current Value.

Create the second digit of the score using a Potential Value metric you feel is appropriate, probably something to do with either Recency or Latency. Generally, this would involve the amount of time that has passed since the last event contributing to the current profitability metric created above - Total Sales,

Net Profit, Number of Visits / Downloads, etc. If you are using Total Sales, it would be Days since last Sale. If you are using Number of Visits, it would be Days since Last Visit.

Then sort and score customers as above. For example, last event less than 30 days ago gets a 5, last event 61 - 90 days ago gets a 4, last event 91 - 120 days ago gets a 3, etc. This score represents the Potential Value of the customer. The lower this Potential Value number, the less likely it is the customer is going to engage in profit generating activity or events in the future.

A customer with a 55 score is a very best customer; they have high current value and high potential value. A customer with a 52 is a current best customer with low likelihood to create value in the future - a customer who is defecting. A score of 35 is a customer with medium current value but high potential value - an "up and coming" best customer. You can establish interaction rules for employees based on these scores and manage customer relationships based on the scores. For example, an employee interacting with a 52 customer (defecting best customer) might be given the authority to grant special discounts or otherwise treat this customer uniquely. Likewise, a database with these scores available can drive automated interactions and customized content on a web site.

Hope that answers your question!

Jim

RF Modeling when "Revenue" is Not Predictive: Utilities, Telco

Q: We are a technology based Call Center company with over 70 clients - we do a lot of the "operational" CRM stuff you refer to - Siebel, Onyx, Kana, Webline, etc., as well as a lot of custom developed SFA solutions and data warehousing solutions we developed - mostly the premise of investing to collect enough information to do the 360 view of the customer across communication medium (email, chat, phone, fax) and reason for calling (campaign, sales, orders, info, customer service....).

We have a good mix of B2B as well as B2C. We already do a lot of the demographic modeling for list acquisition (SIC codes, size, number of computers, Geo ....). One thing I noticed is that we do a lot of lead generation based upon list acquisitions along with inbound marketing campaigns that seem to address one shot Sales, not recurring sales.

For example, we sell and service de-regulated energy for one client - this is sell once, then service. Since they pay every month for the service, how do you suggest the RFM model be used for service-based sales since there is not really an R or an F??? We still have acquisition and retention problems, but we mainly focus on operational efficiency through technology, not strategic use of CRM data. I would really like to be able to add real value based upon the transactional data collected from the customer.

I know this is not your forte, but I was just curious if you had any opinions using CRM data in an RFM model when the product is basically recurring service.

A: Thanks for the compliments on the site, book, and newsletter. I hope they will be helpful to you as we try to get a firmer grasp on these subjects this year!

It's a little tough to provide you a direct answer to such a broad question without more details, but in general, R and F are highly predictive of **any** action-oriented behavior. In a "billing / service" business like a utility, you sometimes have to hunt a bit harder for the action you want to model as predictive.

For example, at Home Shopping Network, use of the automated ordering process (touch-tone interface to the ordering system circa 1990) was very highly correlated with Future Intent to Purchase. Not exactly a traditional RF action, to be sure, but a falling RF score on use of the interface was very highly predictive of a defecting customer.

In interviewing customers with falling RF scores on the interface, we found what this really meant to them was "the thrill is gone," meaning they felt no urgency to order anymore so used the interface less - the "hard" data point representing the "soft" feelings of the customer expressed through their behavior. In other words, the beginning of the end of the LifeCycle.

How'd we figure that out? It took a long time, and we used some advanced modeling techniques to locate the correlation. Once found, it became part of the RF modeling process and put into a "LifeCycle Grid."

If you have a website or telephone "self service" interface, falling use of it might mean customers are getting ready to defect, or it might mean they are satisfied and are going to stay long term. There's no way to tell in advance, but the customer behavior will "speak" and tell you which it is.

Here's what you might be able to do:

1. Make sure you understand all the data points available to you

2. Isolate "best customers" - those who signed up and stayed signed up for the longest time, with the least cost (variable cost to you - installation, marketing etc., **not** in terms of total calls to the center).

3. Run RF profiles over time (LifeCycle) on each piece of "action-oriented" data available to you, and determine which provides the highest correlation to "best" or most profitable customer behavior.

For example, high RF of calls to the center might be highly positively linked (good service leads to better customer) or might be highly negatively linked (billing problems create repeated calls = mad customers who disconnect).

A falling RF score might be good - less recent and frequent calls = higher satisfaction - or may be bad - less recent and frequent calls = customer "apathy" or indicates they are looking for an alternative service.

In service businesses, you generally look for sharp changes in behavior - a drop of 30% in usage, and increase of 50% in calls. These are good targets for automation since they're quite clear-cut.

Also, as you probably know, bundling, if available, usually results in longer-term customers. The reverse is also true - customers who reject bundling tend to be short-term customers.

And finally, source of customer is absolutely critical in this kind of business, especially since your "markets" may be geographically constrained. Since you are an electronically driven, data-dependent acquisition shop (SIC codes, size, number of computers, Geo....) you have the luxury of looking at RF by customer acquisition source. Good customer retention **starts** with smart customer acquisition, and it should be relatively easy to look at LTV by customer source (even without using any RF, at a simple level - a "quick take").

Here's what I mean. Pick a start date, say one year ago, and take a quick look at your highest value customers (gross billings?) over this time and see where (what campaign, data element, etc) they came from. Then look at lowest value (disconnected?) customers from the same start point, and see where **they** came from. If there are differences, you're on your way to finding the answer you're looking for. In addition, once you determine there **is** a difference, survey a subset of each group and try to find the commonality in the groups and differences between the groups. This links the data to the emotions and provides a backdrop for improving acquisition technique.

Don't try to do this starting from a "micro" level and looking up. Start with macro ideas (geography?) then "drill down" (couldn't resist) a layer, then another. When you get down to the level where there appear to be no sizable differences between groups anymore, you're done. Going down any lower with the segmentation begins to create "noise."

Hope this was helpful!

Jim

RF Modeling when "Revenue" is Not Predictive: Enterprise Software

Q: I read your section about how "R" and "F" are better indicators than "M" which I agree. But for the problem I face, do you have any ideas on how I can redefine "F" for my purpose? If not, I can always use RM, but will face the drawbacks you mentioned in the book, which I think, are legitimate concerns for predicting potential value.

A: Just to ground this discussion, I assume you are talking about (a major enterprise software company with many products).

You should look for R and F in other places, if "short term" prediction is what you are after (I'll discuss long term in a minute). Long cycle businesses like enterprise software can be more difficult to model because the variables you are looking to do an RF scoring on are not as obvious. The sales activity may not be particularly predictive of customer behavior because the nature of the business precludes frequency of purchase.

For example, think customer service. Where in your organization would you see RF show up relative to customer satisfaction? Perhaps at the call center, help desk, or "outstanding issue" logs of the implementation team? There could certainly be other areas, depending on how customer care is set up. The question is: how does the Recency and Frequency of customer care predict the likelihood of customer defection?

Despite the fact you sell a "product," one could imagine you are really in the service business. This type of product sets up (hopefully) a very long Customer LifeCycle and ongoing service relationship with upgrades, add-ons, customization, and so forth. Perhaps most of the profit is really in the ongoing relationship, not the initial sale. If true, this is where the focus on RF profiling should be – on the service aspects over time.

You want to go where the transactional behavior is, because this transactional behavior is predictive. So you have to find out where it is and run your profiling there. For example, once the installation is over (is it ever over?), what is the Recency and Frequency of calls for assistance? Does the RF of "trouble calls" predict the likelihood of additional sales in the future, or is it a negative predictor - the higher the score, the less likely a customer is to upgrade? Many times in a service business, high RF scores indicate negative satisfaction, as you probably can imagine.

Somewhere in the organization there is transactional data predictive of likelihood to buy additional services / likelihood to defect. Your mission (should you choose to accept it) is to figure out where it is, or if it does not exist, create a way to capture it.

Now long term. Over very long Customer LifeCycles, one simply has to extend the time horizon. Remember, RF is a relative, not absolute, scoring system, which is why it is useful across such a broad range of businesses. It compares and ranks activity between customers, not against an external benchmark. So even though "frequency" may be every 5 or 10 years, it is still predictive relative to other customers.

For example (and I certainly don't know your business, so I am making this up as I go) say there is a "base" package, an ERP Accounting / Planning / Forecasting module. It's the product you are well known for and has high customer satisfaction; the product most companies buy first when they engage in a relationship with you.

Let's say satisfied, best customers tend to add on to this base module as the years go by. They add Human Resources, Warehouse Control, CRM, e-business marketplaces, etc. This may happen every 3 -5 years. But some customers do it more quickly the others, and this is where you see high RF scores, as compared with others who do it more slowly. So you still get an RF ranking, and you still get predictive power in the model, even though the transactions are spread out over decades. Your challenge may simply be this - you don't have data that goes back over decades.

What you want to know is this: once you have identified high scoring customers, what is it about them that is similar? Is it who made the initial sale, the type of business they are in, geography? If you compare high scoring and low scoring customers, what are the differences? What kind of business adds on to the base module every 2 years as opposed to the kind of business that adds on every 5?

Plus, can you use this knowledge to predict defection, or in your case, a low likelihood of further upgrades? If the top 20% best (most profitable) customer businesses make their first add-on by year 3 after the initial install of the base module, what does it mean when a business passes by year 3 and does not add on? Is this a red flag? Should you send in a "specialist" to find out why the add-on has not happened? Are they experiencing problems with the base module that were never documented, or worse, never fixed? Setting up this kind of "early warning system" can be very helpful in a customer retention effort - the behavior of the customer is telling you, flashing a signal, that something is wrong relative to other customers.

I hope the above answers your question. Long cycle B2B is not as simple to profile as B2C, but the behavior is still there. You just have to look a little harder for it.

Good luck, and let me know if you have further questions.

Jim

The ROI of Online Branding Efforts

Interactive Media: Branding versus Direct Marketing as a Tool

Q1: When you say that the Web is a direct marketing machine, do you mean that brand doesn't count?

A: No, "brand" always counts. The term "machine" was meant to reflect the Internet as a medium is the most efficient and effective direct marketing medium, relative to all other media. Successful direct marketing depends totally on the ability to collect data and analyze behavior, and the Internet is the mother lode of this capability compared to any other medium available.

For example, look at search marketing. It's a beautiful thing, because it is based on the premise that the customer is searching for something they want. When people are searching for what they want, they are more open to ads about what they want. In fact, they don't find search ads nearly as intrusive; they actually pay attention to them rather than screening them out. This is a classic direct marketing set-up, and the usual components follow: the likelihood to respond, the value of the customer, and so on can actually be **predicted** based on the search engine and search phrase that was used by the visitor.

Q2: Do you attribute Amazon.com's success to their direct marketing efforts or to their strong brand?

That's a hard question to answer; branding is not exactly my area of expertise. I attribute most of their **awareness** to being first, and any brand success to being focused and following through with the execution of the "brand promise." There is a huge difference between awareness and "brand"; brand is the full image of the company and includes perceptions about service and so forth.

This is why personally, I think they have weakened their brand with all the new products and changes to delivery policies. Amazon's brand always meant "fast" to me. I don't think they have ever been successful "back end" direct marketers. Their attempts at it appear random and unfocused. They use their data in a very shallow fashion compared to what goes on at a catalog or TV shopping channel, for example; they are not close to really harnessing data from what I have seen.

Q3: Could you please explain to me your (and Seth Godin's) point of view on this issue of branding versus direct marketing on the web?

Well, I won't speak for him, but I'll tell you what he might be thinking, and what I am thinking. Seth is a direct marketer and he realized the same thing I did - the Internet is just a higher tech channel for what we direct / database marketers have been doing for years offline with other media, only it is faster, cheaper, and has more data. Permission Marketing has been practiced for decades by direct marketers, though in a messy way due to a lack of the proper technology. The Internet gave us the right technology. When I place a direct marketing ad in an magazine, and ask you to fill out a coupon or call a number, am I not asking for your permission? When I run an infomercial on TV and you click by and stop to watch, am I not asking your permission?

Messy, awkward, expensive technology. But the same fundamental idea. The customer self-selects what they are interested in, and this selection starts the relationship with the advertiser. That's why search marketing is so efficient and works so well for both consumers and advertisers - the customer is in control. As a marketer, you simply have to learn what this means in terms of execution and how to make the best of it, which is something direct / database marketers have been doing for decades.

Now you can put up a web site for almost nothing, get listed in search engines, and customers will come to you, just like surfing TV channels and seeing an infomercial. Then you try everything in your power to "get permission" and ease the customer into a sale, just like you do on an infomercial, or in a mail piece, where I get your permission when you open the letter (I know, a messy and annoying way to do it, but it works).

Seth's article was about this same direct marketing process, and is based on his e-book The Big Red Fez, where he explains how to take advantage of direct marketing ideas to improve the "front end" - getting the first sale. I concentrate on the "back end" - getting the next sale. Both are parts of the same direct / database marketing discipline, and depend for success on analyzing customer behavior. As usual with his books, he takes a complex idea and turns it into a simple "object" people can more easily understand.

Jim

Measuring the ROI of Branded E-Mail

Q. Jim, I send a monthly corporate custom-published magazine (content mix of product and broader lifestyle interests) via email to my house e-mail list - how do I measure ROI on what is a purely brand loyalty vehicle?

A: Thanks for sending in such an easy question - Geesh Louise, doesn't anybody have easy ones any more?

I assume you believe over the longer run, those receiving the magazine will either convert to customers, increase their level of business with you, or bring business to you through referrals.

If you have new business "source tracking" in place (where did the business come from?), it should be fairly easy to determine if the business came from someone who is receiving the magazine, or from someone not on the magazine list. Assuming you are also able to track where the non-magazine business comes from, you can look at expenses versus business generated and find out if the magazine is at least as efficient as other ways of generating business.

Hot links to product offers would be a perfect way to do this, and you can test varying offers by Recency to maximize the profit of different customer segments. Under this scenario, the magazine is not only branding, but also selling merchandise. So you don't have to worry about the "ROI of Branding," the ROI comes from sales and you can easily quantify the ROI using merchandise profit versus the cost of the magazine.

If you are looking for "hard numbers" on the pure branding issue, the only way to accomplish this is to use a control group; that is, a random sample of people on the list are intentionally not mailed the magazine. This group can be different each time you mail. If you think branding is a long-term effect, you would want to exclude the same people repeatedly over time; shorter term, rotate the control group. Then you compare the business coming from people in the control group with the rest of the list and determine if the cost of the magazine is justified.

If you were to find the control group (no magazine) generates $1 in profit per person and those receiving the magazine also generate $1 in profit per person, then the magazine is "dead cost," meaning it has no effect one way or the other - the "branding" is ineffective, from an ROI perspective. You also might find the magazine actually depresses sales, by aggravating or annoying the customer. If this scenario is true, then a survey seems appropriate to re-focus the magazine in another direction more desirable to the customer.

If you generate $1.50 profit per person from those receiving the magazine and only $1 profit per person from the control group, and the magazine costs $.25 to produce and mail, you have a profit of $.25 per person on an investment of $.25 per person for an ROI of 100%. On a per person basis:

```
   $1.50 in profit from magazine subs
 - $1.00 in profit from control group (no magazine)
 = $0.50 incremental "lift" in profit due to "branding"
 - $0.25 cost of magazine
 = $0.25 net profit
 / $0.25 in investment (cost of magazine)
 = 100% ROI per issue
```

If creating a "pure" control group is not practical because everyone **must** get a magazine, you can create two versions of the magazine and use one as control. This would essentially be a "copy test," where one magazine, in branding lingo, would be more strongly branded, whatever that means, and the other magazine would have "weak branding" or no branding at all. Success measurement would follow the formula above, except control now gets the "weak" magazine.

This test won't prove the magazine **in and of itself** has a positive ROI, but you can assume if the "strongly branded magazine" beats the "weakly branded magazine" in ROI, you have proven the creative approach does matter and branding works.

If there is no difference or negative ROI on the "branded magazine," then the magazine itself is probably generating a "contact effect." In other words, simply reminding subscribers of your business through any contact generates positive revenue effects - the creative approach used doesn't really matter. This would imply (but not prove) negative ROI for any magazine that costs more to produce and fulfill than a simple contact e-mail sent with the same frequency as the whole magazine effort.

That's the way I would look at it, because I come from the database marketing world where everything has a quantifiable ROI, and you put your money where the ROI is highest. Branding people probably see the mags as effective and would measure ROI as they normally do, typically through surveys. Are we gaining mindshare? How much is 1 point of mindshare worth? Where is likelihood to buy or recommend to friends trending when you survey customers who get the magazine versus customers who don't? These are the kinds of ideas branding people work with.

Somewhere in the middle of a nuts and bolts database marketing approach and a "pure branding" approach would be analysis of open rates and click-through on the magazine, if applicable.

I would think the fact customers actually **want** to interact would be quite telling by itself. A high open rate would be evidence of this. You could also apply survey techniques to try and link these "click-through" type of ideas to actual behavior. In other words, survey the openers and non-openers, clickers and non-clickers about brand attitude and actual purchase behavior, and attempt to make a link. Do the non-clickers buy less frequently, have they switched brands recently, etc. versus the clickers? Then you could make statements like "clickers are 40% more brand loyal than non-clickers, who are 20% more brand loyal than the average customer not receiving the magazine."

I might also try to design a tracking survey (let's say 10% of the magazine group) that you execute every 6 months and attempt to quantify the ongoing purchase behavior of clickers and non-clickers, and compare to some baseline info about the "average customer." Just track over time and see if brand loyalty, likelihood to purchase, self-reported purchase volume, etc. grows over time. I would think this information would be very powerful for a branding oriented company who has never worked with real customer interaction data before.

I will tell you for a fact customer lifestyle magazines can be profitable in a retailing environment, having run such a magazine (2.5 million "free" subs, 6x per year) for Home Shopping Network. The mag had 23 different customer versions and generated a 60-day ROI of about 200% (profits = 3x the cost) on a regular basis. This was direct mail, not e-mail, and so it was expensive yet still generated tremendous payback and increased customer value over time.

The versioning was done as a matrix of product affinity and RFM score; customers who appeared to be defecting were given larger incentives to try and nudge them into starting another purchase LifeCycle in a known crossover category (lapsing jewelry buyers encouraged to buy fashion, for example). This works like a charm; you already know there is a tendency to crossover and you are just giving the customer a gentle push to get started before they defect.

Hope this was helpful; if you have additional questions or would like to supply more information, feel free to reply.

Have a good day!

Jim

Measuring the ROI of Branded Web Sites

Q: We constantly try to quantify the value of web sites as a branding vehicle. The thing that keeps gnawing at me is we will often report the average time spent on site. This intuitively seems like it should have a value we could wrap into our ROI, but as it is, it stands largely on its own.

Are you aware of, or have any thoughts on, how we might put an actual value to this? Is it enough to show lift without respect to time, and to talk about return visits in terms of frequency models, or is there some way to drill down to a fundamental value of what a person-second on your site could be worth (obviously the content of the site will impact how much of that value you actually got)?

A: I've done a bunch of work like this and personally, I think you measure branding with branding metrics and direct with direct metrics. If the CPG people understand the value of advertising in terms of brand affinity, recall, intent to purchase, and so forth, then it seems to me that is what you measure. They have already made the "final connection" between these metrics and ROI, so it's not really up to the marketer to make those connections. They believe increasing intent to purchase = advertising worked. And I'm not sure you really can make a connection between branding and direct metrics, because the "units" you are measuring are different and the math ultimately fails.

Here's why. Traditional advertising has never been judged by the "value of the customer," it is judged by the "value of the media." The customer is "reach" and has no individual value; individual customers are totally exchangeable as long as the reach is the same. Any single person is irrelevant; it does not matter what they do or don't do. If there is no "customer" involved, I'm not sure how you would ever get to ROI from a direct perspective. It is assumed from reach comes sales, and this is proven using branding metrics, not ROI.

Q: I've gone back and forth on this and approached it from a few different angles, like the fact that, on average, 1 second of TV advertising costs about $.0003 per person. You could use this information to calculate how much it would have cost to communicate the total person-seconds you had on your site in a particular month, but this is fraught with problems as you might guess, and am looking for another point of view.

A: You see, this is a media value, not a customer value. It's all about how much it costs to communicate, not what the customer is worth. Pegging the value relative to communication costs is a non-starter, in my opinion, because to get to ROI, you need the value of the customer.

If I was going to try and "straddle" direct and brand metrics, I think I would migrate towards evidence of "loyalty." You can use Frequency of visit, but it makes more sense when combined with Recency - not only have they visited often, but they are still visiting. Since Recency predicts repeat action, you can imply this: someone who has visited in the past 7 days is more "loyal" than someone who last visited 60 days ago, because they are more likely to visit again. You can look at the average Recency of the visitors created by different campaigns and measure which campaigns generate visitors with the highest average "loyalty" (Recency).

This is in fact exactly how database marketing companies and people who know how to execute on CRM manage customer retention - falling Recency = defecting customer. Falling Recency for a brand marketer's web site could = falling loyalty, and loyalty rising or falling is a metric branders have a good understanding of.

This makes some sense if you think of it in terms of demographics, something branders are intimately familiar with. If you look at the Recency of visit by search engine, you usually see dramatic differences. Visitors coming from one engine are more "loyal" than those coming from another engine, and this generally has to do with the distribution (and thus demos) of the engine. Each search engine is really like a cable TV Channel, with it's own demos. You can further see differences within a search engine by topic, which is similar in concept to the different demos of shows on a single cable TV channel.

As for time spent on the site, it's pretty difficult to comment on without understanding the objectives of the site. In every case I have seen, longer visits = higher sales, leads, downloads, etc., because "tasks" take time to complete. But unless you are "selling time," as with traditional media, I'm not sure "time" has an economic value to the marketer.

The time-based metrics of this sort begins to sound like the PR valuation models, e.g. "it would have cost you $XX to get this coverage in an ad." But guess what? You don't control the content of PR like you do with an ad, so frequently it can be much less effective than an ad - so less valuable.

On the other hand, time sure has economic value to the consumer, in terms of opportunity costs - they could easily be doing something else rather than staring at your site. So "person-seconds" could certainly be viewed as the sum of attention people are willing to give you instead of doing something else that has value to them. You see this happening in search engine stats now - Yahoo has more visitors than Google, but the aggregate time Google's fewer visitors spend on the site is higher. In other words, Google has higher "aggregate attention" than Yahoo. This is being used to say Google users are more "loyal" than Yahoo users, or said another way, Google users are of higher quality as advertising targets. Makes some sense to me.

On the other hand, maybe Yahoo users are more responsive than Google users, and on the direct marketing side that would mean ... oh, never mind, I think I've just started looping ...

Seems to me you can choose your metrics poison, branding or direct (ROI). Every time I try to mix the two the math, or direct side, falls apart. And the reality is you use whatever the client or culture believes in, unless they don't use metrics at all, and I'm not sure there is anybody still in business that sails the ship without navigational charts of some kind.

Jim

And now, my fellow Drillers, on to predictive financial modeling.

Chapter 26
Predicting Campaign ROI: Set Up

Up until now, we have been focusing on customer tracking and measurement, the nuts and bolts of Data-Driven marketing. The next four chapters will cover how to actually predict the financial performance of your communications, and actively manage the sales and profit levels they generate. You will also learn how to measure subsidy cost – the cost incurred when you consume resources to activate people who would have taken action anyway, and Halo Effects, the actions you never knew your communications generated as a result of your programs because you did not know how to measure them. Taking both of these concepts into consideration can make a huge difference in the profitability of your communications and ROI.

Predictive financial modeling has two requirements:

1.   The customer database with RF Scores or LifeCycle Grid tags has to be put through a carefully controlled test program to determine what the actual response rate is for each RF Score or Grid Cell on any particular activity.

2.   The activity targeted for behavioral modification has to have a known profit value to the company to be used in a true financial calculation.

The first thing you need to do with the RF scored or LifeCycle Grid tagged database is lay down some baseline testing work so you can see how your specific customers will respond. Online response results should be much higher than offline, but you need to do some test marketing so you can get relevant results for your own customers, products, and media you're using. To do this, you set up a test promotion and measure the response to this promotion by RF score or LifeCycle Grid Cell.

Using the results of the test mailing, you will be able to accurately predict what the response to a specific promotion will be for a group of customers at each of the RF Score levels / LifeCycle Grid Cells. It will tend to remain the same over time for the same communication – even if all the customers in the cell are different than the ones in the cell during the test.

The response rates will generally remain the same for any given activity and RF Score / Grid Cell combination. All RF 55 customers **as a group** will tend to have the same response rate as they do in your test. Customers, as they move between the different RF Scores or Grid Cells, will generally respond at the rate determined by their score for the activity. This means the **same customer** can have different response rates at different times, depending on RF Score or Grid Cell. And you knew that right? Because as the customer moves through the LifeCycle, they pass through the different RF Scores or LifeCycle Grid Cells.

After your test, you will easily be able to decide who to promote to and who to leave out for maximum net profit based on their RF Score or Grid Cell!

This next section is a little technical, but you need to know this stuff to be a Data-Driven marketer. And regarding this test we're talking about setting up – once you do it the first time, and see how it works, it's easy to do after that. Take your time on this section; it's critical to execute this test properly. For the sake of simplicity and readability, I'm going to drop the "RF Score or Grid Cell" routine and just deal with RF Scores. You can easily substitute using LifeCycle Grid Cells for RF Scores in any of the following work, because even through the two are derived differently, **everyone in a LifeCycle Grid Cell has the same behavioral metrics, just as everyone with the same RF Score does**.

The Big Test – Establishing Response for Each RF Score

To do the test, you will need to create a random sample of your customer base. The larger the sample, the more accurate its predictive power will be. 3% will give you a pretty good shot. Larger samples will cost more to mail but will add extra stability to the predictive power of the sample; smaller samples could result in unstable predictive power and lead to false information.

If you can afford it, go to 10%; 5% is good, but 3% is OK. **The smaller your database, the higher percentage you should take for the test, in general, to even out the instability that comes from testing small databases (under 5,000 customers).** If you have only 1,000 customers, consider a 20% test, or if you can afford it, run the test to every customer. This is an extremely important event, as the information gained is used extensively down the line. Don't skimp on this test if you can help it. Also make sure the sample is truly random, and doesn't introduce any **bias,** meaning the sample is not truly random because the selection methods used have distorted the selection process. An example of introducing bias during sample selection:

Let's say you have 1,000 customers, and they were consecutively assigned customer ID's. You want a 10% sample, or 100 customers. **You sort the customers by customer ID**, and start choosing customers with customer ID 1 and select **every 5th customer.** You would have the 100 customers you need by customer ID 500. But your sample would be **biased**, because the customers you have selected don't represent your newest customers fairly.

The customer base was sorted by ID, meaning your oldest customers have the lowest ID and newest customers the highest ID. You stopped choosing at 500, instead of choosing through the entire customer base; this creates the bias towards older customers. If you had selected **every 10th** customer instead, you would have ended with your most recent customer and have an even sample with no bias against representation by a particular customer group. Bias can occur geographically, by product type, and so on.

A convenient way to generate a random sample, if you use consecutively numbered customer ID's, is to pick a digit location from the customer ID, and specify a value for it. Then choose every customer with this value at the specified location in the ID. You'll get a 10% sample. For example, "give me everybody whose customer number ends in "2" or "give me everybody having a 4 in the second to last digit location." For this to work, you have to have at least one customer in the next highest (to the left) digit location. For example, if you have 5,349 total customers, you could use any of the last 3 digit locations (left of the comma in 5,349) but not the lead (left-most) digit location. Using the left-most digit would introduce bias, since the selection would complete before a full 10% sample is taken.

You want to end up with roughly the same number of customers **for each RF score** in your sample. Because of the way the quintile process works, the total number of customers in each RF score before you do a random sample is basically the same. Just make sure your sampling process doesn't affect this balance or you might not get a good read on the test. Being off by a few customers in each RF score is not a big deal; anything over 2% difference in the size of an RF score could be a big deal, depending on your overall response rates and size of the test.

RF Score	"Make a Purchase" Response Rate	"Click a Link" Response rate
55	12.000%	86.0%
54	11.500%	83.0%
53	10.000%	79.0%
52	9.500%	74.0%
51	9.000%	66.0%
45	8.750%	48.0%
44	8.250%	41.0%
43	6.130%	32.0%
42	4.040%	21.0%
41	1.850%	17.0%
35	0.890%	13.0%
34	0.864%	11.0%
33	0.712%	9.0%
32	0.643%	8.2%
31	0.578%	7.1%
25	0.421%	6.4%
24	0.329%	5.8%
23	0.267%	4.8%
22	0.176%	4.1%
21	0.112%	3.2%
15	0.095%	2.7%
14	0.084%	1.9%
13	0.732%	0.7%
12	0.623%	0.2%
11	0.000%	0.0%
All Customers Total	3.5%	25%

Figure 54: Response Rate by RF Score

If you took a truly random sample, you should be fine. If you sorted the customers by RF score and took a **biased** sample (as with the customer ID example above), you won't have an even number of customers in each RF score.

This is a final check for you on the quality of the sample. If the number of customers in each RF score is not roughly equal, you have inserted bias somewhere. This needs to be corrected before you do your test.

Create your customer sample. Send out a marketing promotion, **making sure you know how many customers are in each RF score**, and track your responses by RF score. You can use your regular newsletter for a mailing **as long as it has a call to action,** some reason to respond by doing something. The response data you generate represents responses by RF score for the **specific "do something"** activity you are asking for. Figure 54 on the previous page shows what your completed Response by RF Score table might look like.

To build the Response by RF Score table, collect your responses by RF score and match them up with the total number of people in each RF score. Then calculate your response rate by RF score, and create a table with each RF score and corresponding response rate, in descending order by RF score. When you later ask for a different activity of the customer, like "make a purchase" instead of "click a link," you can expect the responses by RF score to be similar, **relative to each other**. But overall response will depend on the type of activity you request, and how easy it is for the customer to respond.

Figure 54 also demonstrates this idea of relative response for two different activities — a promotion to make a purchase and a promotion to click a link. The response trails off for each activity from highest to lowest. The response at each level is different, but they tend to follow the same pattern as you move down the table. In some businesses, particularly interactive ones, the top RF scores can generate 70% response rates for PURCHASE activity! Think you could take advantage of this knowledge?

If you are using LifeCycle Grids, your response rates won't be as nearly as "consecutive" as they are in Figure 54, because the LifeCycle Grids ignore the whole "sorting" thing used in RF Scoring and instead rely on the actual customer LifeCycle. You will see trending for each row or column, but it won't be consecutive or "ranked" from top to bottom.

By the way, are you relieved we did not include M, or Monetary Value when we went through all this stuff? Instead of 25 RF scores, you end up with 125 RFM scores. Ouch! Kind of stretches the notion of simplicity with a spreadsheet. But it's a valid approach, and for the 3-D guys still with us, I just wanted to make clear that you go through the same motions as described, while just adding

M to the mix. For beginners, use RF first, and when you get up to speed, add M to see if it makes any difference.

Using M, your best customer is a 555 instead of a 55, worst is a 111 instead of 11. Your RFM score groups will have response rates much closer to each other, since the customer base is divided into many more groups. And I hope you have a ton of customers, or you won't have many in a group. It's also likely your response rates in consecutively ranked groups won't be nearly as sequential as with RF; there will be more "up and down" as you go down the list from top / best to bottom / worst, because M introduces a wildcard.

Otherwise, just follow the approaches described and you'll be fine. Use average sales for a Hurdle Rate as was described with Frequency. And I don't need to tell you that a high M customer dropping in R score is a bad thing. I hope. Now that you know the response rates of your customers by RF score, we can move on to actually modeling some promotions for profitability!

Chapter 27
Predicting Campaign ROI: The Model

Let's say the Figure 54 above represents the results of your first test. The following examples are based on this table using the "Make a Purchase" response rates by RF score.

Your overall response rate was 3.5% (bottom of Figure 54) across the entire mailing but that's really a meaningless number, when you are using RF Scores and trying to maximize revenue while minimizing the cost of promotion.

The next idea is to understand the RF score level within the customer database where you begin to lose money on promotions, and **not promote to those people, based on the projected response rate**. Let's see how it's done.

You've done your test and have response rates by RF score, Figure 54 above. Now you want to do a "real" mailing / e-mailing promotion, to as many people as you can afford to mail, but you want the promotion to be profitable.

It will cost $300 per thousand customers for the promotion, or 30 cents each, a very expensive promotion. You want customers to make a purchase in this example, **but it could be any activity you can put a value on, like a survey**.

Let's say the average purchase price on the site is $40

Your margin (price - cost of goods sold) is 10%.

Each $40 sale nets you $4 in margin.

You have 1000 customers; an "All Customer" mailing will cost:
$.30 x 1000 = $300.

Figure 55 on the next page is the financial results of this promotion, based on the 3.5% response rate on all 1000 customers from Figure 54 above:

Parameter	All Customers
1. Number mailed	1000
2. Response Rate	3.5%
3. Responses	35
4. Net Margin @ $4	$140
5. Mail cost @ $.30	$300
6. Net Profit	-$160

Figure 55: Financial Performance of Mailing to All Customers

Let's go through the table. You mail all 1000 customers (line 1). At a 3.5% response (line 2), you generate 35 responses (line 3). Those 35 sales at $4 in margin generate $140 in net margin (line 4). This is not enough to cover the promotion costs of $300 (line 5), resulting in a loss of $160 (line 6). Not very good. Let's use the RF Scoring method and help out this promotion.

In order for the sales generated in this mailing to cover the costs, the **Breakeven, or point at which profits equal expenses** in the promotion would be 75 sales, because 75 orders for a $4 profit on each sale = $300, the cost of the promotion itself.

If you need 75 sales on the mailing to 1000 customers, that's 75 / 1000 = 7.5% response rate to have profits = costs.

There's an easy formula you can use to solve for this Breakeven response rate in any promotion where you can directly measure the revenue generated by an activity. It looks like this:

(Promotion Cost per Customer) divided by (Average Margin per **Activity**) = Breakeven Response Rate

For purchases, it would be:

(Promotion Cost per Customer) divided by (Average Margin per **Sale**) = Breakeven Response Rate

In the case of the promotion just defined:

$.30 / \$4 = .075$, or a 7.5% response rate

So you have to get a 7.5% response to Breakeven. Unless you get at least a 7.5% response rate, the cost of the mailing will be greater than the profits you generate from the mailing, and you will lose money. Negative ROI.

A full "rollout" of a test (your Figure 54 test mailing) generally won't pull response quite as hard as the test, so to be conservative, you might want to increase the response rate you will accept for the rollout to all customers by 10%. Taking this "safety margin" into account, that means you need a response rate of 8.25% (10% increase over 7.25%) on your promotion to breakeven "with a little cushion," meaning profits will be slightly over costs.

Look at the RF scores in the above Figure 54 and see which scores fall below the 8.25% response rate (shaded gray). Sending **this \$.30 per customer promotion** to people with these lower scores is like lighting a match to your capital. They just are not going to respond at a high enough rate to cover the costs of the promotion given the parameters we started off with (\$.30 cents each mailer, \$4 margin each sale). In the RF score Figure 54 above, this means you would mail to people with **RF scores of RF 55 down to RF 44**, and no lower.

Again, if you are using LifeCycle Grids, your response rates won't be nearly as "consecutive" in a chart but the same idea applies. Sending this promotion to any LifeCycle Grid Cell with a response rate below 8.25% is financial suicide.

If you really need the sales volume, you can make profitable sales all the way down to the 8.25% RF scores. If sales volume is not as important as profits from sales, then cut off your mailing at a higher response level than 8.25%. Since you usually don't want to just breakeven on a promotion, using a response cut-off higher than breakeven is a more common approach.

This is an important concept to understand because it will appear again and again as you become familiar with Data-Driven marketing. This approach is "scientific" enough that you have the ability to choose between driving sales and driving profits. Take some time to think about the implications. If you mail just to the very top RF scores, you're going to generate highly profitable business, but not as much of it. The deeper (lower) you go down the RF scores, the more volume you will generate, but at a higher cost, with less profit per sale in the end. In most promotional efforts, you'll want to

**balance sales volume and profits so you generate healthy sales at a decent
profit to the company.**

Let's say you choose to mail RF scores all the way down to the 8.25%. What
does the final promotional result look like, using the actual response rates by RF
score?   You chose 7 RF scores to promote, and 6 of these 7 scores have a
response rate **higher** than 8.25%.   So you have to run out the numbers and
calculate what the response rate is at each RF segment, and then sum the results,
to find the final performance of the actual promotion.

We'll use the Figure 54 data from above, the hypothetical results from your first
test mailing, where the baseline response for your RF scores was determined.
Remember that each RF score has about the same number of customers; and
there are 25 different RF scores. If the promotion were sent to 1000 customers,
there would be 40 customers in each RF score. You take the response rate at
each RF level from 55 to 44 and calculate actual responses generated, given
each RF score has 40 customers in it. The following Figure 56 is what the
calculations look like:

RF Score	Response Rate	# of Customers	# of Responses
55	12.0%	40	4.8
54	11.5%	40	4.6
53	10.0%	40	4.0
52	9.5%	40	3.8
51	9.0%	40	3.6
45	8.75%	40	3.5
44	8.25%	40	3.3
43	6.13%	The mailing	stops here….
Totals		280	27.6

Response Rate = 27.6 / 280 = 9.86%

Figure 56: Actual Responses by RF Score

The response to this promotion would be almost 3 times greater than the 3.5% (bottom of Figure 54) response you had when you mailed to all customers, and you would save money by mailing to only the most responsive 280 customers! Here's the financial model as Figure 57 (next page) – hold on to your hat:

Parameter	All Customers	Response of Top 7 RF Scores	% Change, Top 7 RF versus All
		(Figure 56)	
1. Number mailed	1000	280	-72%
2. Response Rate	3.5%	9.86% (Actual)	
3. Responses	35	27.6	-21%
4. Net Margin @ $4	$140	$110.40	-21%
5. Mail Cost @ $.30	$300	$84.00	-72%
6. Net Profit	-$160	$26.40	

**Figure 57: Financial Model using
Actual RF Score Response Rates for Each Score Level**

Let's go through this. On the left is the All Customer promotion, the same as Figure 54 above. In the middle, the **TOP 7 RF Score** promotion, with the total mailed (280), response rate (9.86%), and responses (27.6) coming from below the bottom of Figure 56 above.

In comparing the Top 7 RF scores promotion to the All Customer promotion, the number mailed (line 1) dropped 72%. The response rate almost tripled (line 2); total customer responses came in 21% lower (line 3). That's RF Score leverage working for you. Cut the mailing size by 72% and overall response only goes down by 21%!

The 21% drop in response affects the net margin to the same degree, since it is calculated at $4 per response (line 4). But the costs (line 2) dropped 72% in line with the same decrease in the mailing size. Look at what happens to Net Profit (line 6). Costs drop dramatically in relation to profits in the mailing, and a money losing promotion starts making money!

If you have 10,000 customers, you multiply the result for 1,000 customers by 10. For this 10,000-customer example, using the RF scores made the difference between losing $1600 and making $264. Pretty significant difference, I'd say. You achieved this **by not mailing** to your least responsive customers, investing instead where you generate the most revenue for the least cost. As cost drops dramatically and response almost triples, the combination drives profitability for the promotion out of sight!

Let's talk about calculating ROI, or Return on Investment, for your promotion. To determine "simple" Return on Investment, you divide your net profit by the cost of the promotion.

Simple ROI is $26.40 profit / $84 cost = 31.4%.

If you had executed the promotion to all customers, simple ROI is:

$160 profit / $300 cost = -53%.

You don't get a pretty picture with the "all customer" mailing.

In the above ROI example, we only used the cost of the promotion itself. You should include all the costs directly created by the promotion you can measure or seem reasonable to include. In small operations, it may not be worth the trouble to do this. In large-scale operations, where there are many projects competing for funding, it would not be fair to measure ROI for marketing programs and not include the other costs; inappropriate capital allocations would result — as in "dot bomb."

For example, the cost of processing the credit card, the cost of taking the phone call, the cost of handling the package, and the cost of after the sale service should all be allocated to each response in the promotion. This drives up the cost of generating responses, and lowers the ROI. But tough luck folks, you have to play fair. Capital must be allocated where it generates the highest ROI in a Data-Driven marketing world.

The element of Time is frequently mishandled when doing ROI calculations. ROI implies time, because a Return on Investment usually occurs **over time**. When large projects are considered, managers question the ROI of the project over the usable life of the equipment or software being considered. You should do the same with a marketing promotion.

In many small companies, this is not an issue, and the simple ROI calculation above can be used to compare returns on different promotions. But in large companies, one usually compares ROI to the value of sticking the cash to be used for the promotion in the bank or buying gub'mint bonds. Let's say the annual interest rate available for parking corporate cash is 6%. That means cash can have an ROI of 6% all by itself, **over the time period of a year,** since the 6% quote is based on holding for a year.

This means any marketing promotion, to be worth investing in, has to generate at minimum, a 6% ROI, on an **annualized basis**, or over a year. If you can't generate more than a 6% annualized ROI, the CFO is better off sticking the money into bonds than giving it to you for marketing, because the company as a whole is better off with the higher return on capital. And you will be looking for a new job.

Luckily though, you're a Data-Driven marketer. You're Drilling Down. Your little promotion above generated a 31.4% ROI. Is this the annualized return? No, your promotion only took 60 days to complete. That's 1/6 of a year. On a per 1000 customer basis, you took $84 dollars from the CFO and 60 days later gave back the $84 PLUS another $26.40. A 31.4% return in 60 days. Presumably, you could do that 6 times a year **with the same $84** if doing it once only takes 60 days. At the end of each of the 6 promotions, you **could** take the original $84 and repeat the promotion, generating $26.40 in extra profits **each time**. At the end, you give back the $84. So the annualized ROI is 31.4% x 6 = 188%! You're very good at this.

Or $26.40 each promotion x 6 = $158.40 / $84 invested = 188%!

And 188% is a lot better than 6%. CFO sings your praises. Drilling Down Rules! You get a huge bonus. Ok, you don't get a huge bonus.

If you are large company with many projects competing for capital, it may be a good idea to look at marketing programs this way, provided you can achieve consistent results in consecutive promotions.

I would caution you to get with the finance department (if you have one) before you start signing the praises of your 188% annualized return. Many Data-Driven marketing companies understand these types of comparisons because the concepts are ingrained into the very structure of the way the company does business. Everything, and I mean everything, goes through an ROI analysis before capital is allocated. It's just the way everybody thinks about investing resources, since everything can be measured.

If you are not in a Data-Driven marketing company, where everyone is used to measuring the results of everything, the concept of annualized ROI may be a little tough to swallow. Think about it – if you're not used to being able to measure the financial contribution an activity makes (particularly marketing), this ROI idea is going to run into some flak. Get with your finance guy and see if, where, and how ROI is used. If you can align yourself with the company policy in your promotion measurement, you may end up with a bigger budget!

Chapter 28
Predicting Campaign ROI: Fine Tuning

Our basic financial model from the last chapter is missing a key element – allowing for discounts or the cost of other incentives you provide a customer during the promotion.

You would reduce your margin by the amount you are giving as a discount. It will have the effect of raising the "depth" of the list you will be able to mail by raising the breakeven, all other things equal. The breakeven example from the previous chapter looked like this:

(Promotion Cost per Customer) divided by Average Profit per Sale = Breakeven Response Rate

$$\$.30 / \$4 = .075, \text{ or a } 7.5\% \text{ response rate}$$

If you were to give a 2% discount on a $40 product with a $4 margin, your new margin would be only $3.20 cents.

$$2\% \text{ of } \$40 = \$.80; \$4 - \$.80 = \$3.20.$$

Using the new margin in the breakeven formula provides:

$$\$.30 / \$3.20 = .0937, \text{ or a } 9.4\% \text{ response}$$

The discounts have had the effect of raising your response rate to achieve breakeven, where profits = cost, from 7.5% to 9.4%. If all customers are receiving the same discount, you use this Breakeven as the starting point for the new model and run it through as we did in the previous chapter. Don't forget a "safety margin" on response of 10% or so.

But you don't always want to give customers the same discount, I mean, Data-Driven marketing is about targeting, right? Here is another financial effect related to the use of RF Scoring. Generally, the lower a customer's RF score, the more "push" or value you are going to have to provide to get them to respond any differently than their "baseline response" in Figure 54.

High RF scores may need very little push to outperform their baseline response; low RF scores need an enormous amount of push to outperform. In terms of a straight promotional discount, you can think about it this way: As the R score gets lower, the discount has to be raised to generate an above average response rate. This is because the lower the RF score, the less likely it is people will respond to a given promotional offer.

Figure 58 below is an example of this idea:

R Score	A High Margin (40% +) Business Discount Rate	A Low Margin (10% or Less) Business Discount Rate
5	3%	1% - 2%
4	5%	3%
3	10%	4%
2	20%	5%
1	25% or more	6% or more

**Figure 58: Effective Discount Rates Need to Rise
as R Score Falls to Achieve Decent Response Rates**

This chart is not meant to be an absolute rule, but a relative example. If you have a lower or higher than average margin business, or have done some testing and have a feel for what works, you can adjust this chart. The chart really is about the **relative** boosts you may have to make to get a decent enough reaction to pay the promotional bills. They are examples of the kind of pattern you should expect. You have to test these things and see what the reactions are at various discount levels.

"I understand," you say. "But if I'm going to use different discounts for different RF scores, this breakeven formula doesn't cut it, because margin will be different at different levels." And you would be right! You **are** getting good at this. So how do you account for different discount values in the financial model? Here's how it's done. Remember the following Figure 56 (next page), response by RF code? We calculated actual responses:

RF Score	Response Rate	# of Customers	# of Responses
55	12.0%	40	4.8
54	11.5%	40	4.6
53	10.0%	40	4.0
52	9.5%	40	3.8
51	9.0%	40	3.6
45	8.75%	40	3.5
44	8.25%	40	3.3
43	7.50%	The mailing	stops here....
Totals		280	27.6

Copy of Figure 56: Response Rate = 27.6 / 280 = 9.86%

Let's modify Figure 56 a little. Since this response table was based on a low margin (10%) business, we'll use a low margin type scale from the discount Figure 58. The following Figure 59 takes the discount information from Figure 58 and combines it with the responses by RF score from Figure 56:

RF Score (Figure 56)	Responses (Figure 56)	Discount @ R Score (Figure 58)	Discount per Unit (New)	Total Discount $ (New)
55	4.8	1%	$.40	$ 1.92
54	4.6	1%	$.40	$ 1.84
53	4.0	2%	$.80	$ 3.20
52	3.8	2%	$.80	$ 3.04
51	3.6	2%	$.80	$ 2.88
45	3.5	2%	$.80	$ 2.80
44	3.3	3%	$1.20	$ 3.96
	NOTE*			
Total				$19.64

Figure 59: Discounts Applied by RF Score
Allow Calculation of Total Promotional Discount

* **Note**: for clarity of presentation, we are using the same response rates from all the previous examples we have carried through this demonstration. As was said on the previous page, you would have to create your own "discount testing" table like Figure 58 from your own "response by discount" tests. This is an example of handling the financial modeling, not creating a discount test. The creation of high ROI "Discount Ladders" is covered in the Recency Toolkit chapter titled "Turning Recency Data into Profits."

In each column of Figure 59 above, the source of the data is described. The last 2 columns on the right (New) were calculated based on data from the Figure 56 & Figure 58 data at the right of the table.

The Discount per Unit is calculated from the selling price of $40 from the (initial example x Discount). Total discount dollars is simply the (Responses x Discount per unit). The total discounts given in this promotion are $19.64 total across each of the RF scores.

Then you take this total discount and place it into your financial model. Let's first look at the "Top 7 RF Scores" financial model from above in Figure 57, with a new line "Discounts" (see under 5. Mail Cost) from Figure 59:

Parameter	All Customers	Using Response of Top 7 RF Scores	% Change, Top 7 RF versus All
		(Figure 57)	
1. Number mailed	1000	280	-72%
2. Response Rate	3.5%	9.86% (Actual)	
3. Responses	35	27.6	-21%
4. Net Margin @ $4	$140	$110.40	-21%
5. Mail Cost @ $.30	$300	$84.00	-72%
Discounts		**$19.64**	
6. Net Profit	-$160	$ 6.76	From Total Discounts, Figure 59

Figure 60: Financial Model with Variable Discounts

Simple ROI = $6.76 / $84 = 8.0%

Wow. This is a pretty tough business. It has very low margins AND a low average selling price, so I hope it's a high volume one!

In a business with higher margins, you could afford to give bigger discounts, which would drive up your response rates. The higher the discount given, the higher the response rate will be. Also, the higher discounts also raise the breakeven response rate because they lower the margin. All of these variables interact to produce the final result, and you're in control of them. You decide how to drive sales and profits in a very deliberate way. Do your financial models, and adjust the variables until they produce the desired result. Then plan the promotion accordingly and deliver it.

In the above example, the profit seems too low. You could lower the discounts, but they're pretty low already. Any lower and you might get a big shoulder shrug from the customers. Who would respond to a ½% discount on a $40 item anyway? A better approach would be to not target as deeply into the list, leaving off the lowest RF scores. The mailing costs and cost of the discounts would go way down. Once again, we see that you are in control in Data-Driven marketing. You can choose to drive volume instead of profit and / or profit instead of volume. It's up to you and your particular business situation.

Discounts are the newest variable at your disposal. By tying discounts to RF Scores you can "scale up" or "scale down" response for any RF Score, depending on your strategy.

Here's what it would look like if you took only the top 3 RF scores from the preceding examples. We're going to run through the same process we just completed, only with the "Top 3 RF Scores" instead of the "Top 7 RF Scores" to show you the dramatic difference targeting can make, even in a low price, low margin business.

The following 3 Figures 61, 62, and 63 on the next page describe the process in detail. Figure 61 is the number of responses at each of the highest 3 RF scores. Figure 62 is the calculation of the discount at each of the highest 3 RF scores. Figure 63 is the addition of the new discount information calculated in Figure 62 to the financial model we have been using.

Let's look at them all on the same page in a sequence, so you can follow how the process links together. This is the same sequence of tables we have gone through in previous examples, just displayed on the same page for clarity:

Figure 61: ROI.a

RF Score	Response Rate	# of Customers	# of Responses
55	12.0%	40	4.8
54	11.5%	40	4.6
53	10.0%	40	4.0

Figure 62: ROI.b

RF Code	Responses	Discount	Discount per Unit	Total Discount $
55	4.8	1%	$.40	$ 1.92
54	4.6	1%	$.40	$ 1.84
53	4.0	2%	$.80	$ 3.20
	13.4		Total	$ 6.96

Figure 63: ROI.c

Parameter	Using Response of Top 7 RF Scores
Number mailed	120
Response Rate	11.1%
Responses	13.4
Net Margin @ $4	$53.60
Mail cost @ $.30	$36
Discounts	$ 6.96
Net Profit	$10.64

Simple ROI = $10.64 / $36 = 29.6%

Now that's more like it. A marginal marketing program turns into a great one just by using RF scores! The higher response rate, combined with the lower costs of mailing and reduced discounts given, produces a huge pop in performance. Now we're making money in this low margin business!

For non-purchase promotions, the same "scale by R Score" idea will hold true. The lower the R score, the harder you will have to try to change the "baseline" Figure 54 behavior and get the customer to repeat an action. So try to add as much value as you can when moving down the scale. If we're talking about content and visits, minor additions or updates will get high RF customers to check it out. To attract low RF customers, a major redesign or overhaul is in order to create any pull.

Do you see why it's so critical to track RF scores and take action with customers with the "middle" RF scores? **It gets more and more expensive to retain customers the further their RF scores drop** – the "Discount Ladder" principle (see the Recency Toolkit chapter titled "Predictive Marketing." This is why the RF scores and Hurdle Rates are so important; there's a double whammy as the customer score falls lower and lower.

As customers move towards lower RF scores, their future value to your business is falling, AND it's going to cost you more to keep them interested the further they fall. There's a snowballing effect. The RF – LTV death spiral.

As the slide in RF scores takes place, your revenues start to fall. As revenues start to fall, you can't afford to spend more money to promote, so you spend less. This means the RF scores continue to slip, and it becomes a nasty, self-reinforcing cycle. I have seen it in action. Pay attention to your RF Scores, LifeCycle Grids, and Hurdle Rates, will ya?

Chapter 29
Expense and Revenue You May Not be Capturing:
Subsidy Costs and Halo Effects

Now that you're an ultra-sophisticated Data-Driven marketer, it's time for additional work at the "back of the house" on measuring the profitability of your promotions. It's sometimes trickier than you think to do it right. And yes, this is a little more finance stuff, but it's pretty light, so stop groaning. You want to drive revenue growth while decreasing cost, don't you?

Most people look at the response to communications and judge whether it's high enough to be called a success. You can compare it to industry standards or previous experience. But response is not all it's cracked up to be, and there's a danger lurking out in customer land waiting to swallow up the new Data-Driven marketer. It's called **subsidy cost** and it matters a lot, because it can kill the profit in an otherwise profitable communication to best customers. Run these kinds of programs often enough, and they can put you right out of business.

Here's the deal with high RF (or upper right-hand LifeCycle Grid) customers. They are highly likely to repeat an action again and that's a good thing. But the fact they are highly likely to act is where subsidy costs creep in. A subsidy cost occurs **when money is spent encouraging a customer to take action when the customer would have acted anyway without the encouragement.**

Think about it. If you e-mail a 10% discount to a best, highest RF customer, they're going to take it, and you will get huge response rates. But this can be bad, because you have just spent money and margin dollars you didn't have to, because it's highly likely they **would have purchased anyway**.

I know you're probably irritated with me...I can feel it. You're probably thinking, "Why the heck did we go through all this RF stuff and identify best customers if we're not supposed to promote to them?"

Calm down, I didn't say don't promote to them. I am saying you have to be careful with **the methods** used to promote to them. When promoting to your very best, highest RF customers:

1. **Use a threshold over the average behavior the customer usually engages in to be eligible for the encouragement.** For example, if the average purchase price is $40, try "$5 off anything over $50." So they get a decent discount (10%) but don't cut into your margin as much. By the way, in promotions like this, they don't usually spend $51, but more like $60 or $70, which usually puts you even on the margin dollars, and keeps the customer happy. For non-purchase promotions, this is the perfect time to "ask for something," which is the same kind of threshold idea. Ask for survey data, refer-a-friend, etc., and try to get more value out of them for the promotion.

2. **Just reach out and touch them.** Thank-you or birthday cards, "you're so wonderful and we appreciate you so much" type of promotions, where nothing is given or asked, are an absolutely powerful force with high RF customers. It costs a little, but you will see purchases or visits go through the roof. It's one of the most profitable promotion strategies I have ever used, as long as it is **targeted** to the right people at the right time in your customer database.

3. **Try heavy encouraging behavior the customer doesn't usually engage in that is related to behavior they do engage in.** For example, in retail a category should be at least somewhat related to their main interest (affinity). If a customer has a high RF score in buying garden bulbs but not garden tools, offer the big discount on tools. If the customer has a high RF score in general news content but not lifestyle content, offer an incentive to visit the lifestyle section.

All of these promotional designs are focused on the same thing – reducing or eliminating subsidy costs by encouraging the customer to engage in a behavior slightly different than they usually engage in. This includes buying at a higher price, making unplanned purchases, or purchasing in a category outside their normal choice.

If you always give the biggest discount or incentive on your most popular products to your best customers, you will erode your margins. You will kick-off an effect known as **incentive proneness**, meaning your best customers won't buy or transact with you unless you give them an incentive on their favorite products or services. Your best selling, highest margin products / services will become your worst nightmare, and your business will suffer terribly.

So a high response rate isn't always a good thing if it's coming from people who would have purchased or visited anyway. How can you measure the subsidy cost, to find out if you are creating your own worst nightmare? By using control groups to measure promotional results.

A control group is a random sample of the customers you are about to promote to. If you were going to mail to your RF 55's, or your Recency ≤ 30 days, Frequency 25+, you **would take out** a 5% or 10% **random sample** of the group and not mail to them. Then you compare this control group's behavior to the group you mailed to, and solve for the true profit generated by the mailing.

Please recall what was said about taking random samples earlier in the book (Advanced Toolkit chapter titled "Predicting Campaign ROI: Set Up"). These issues still apply:

> The smaller your database, the higher percentage you should take, in general, to even out the instability that comes from small databases (under 5,000 customers).

> Make sure the sample is truly random, and doesn't introduce any **bias**, like being sorted in some way that affects a true random select.

If subsidy costs occurred in the promotion, you would see little or no sales lift in the test group (the one you mailed to) compared to the control group **over a defined promotion time period**. The "would have bought anyway without the promotion" behavior will happen in the control group (group not mailed), and they will purchase just as much as the test group (the group you mailed) over the life of the promotion.

If there is a lift in sales for the test group versus the control group, this sales lift has to generate enough profit margin to pay for the promotion. Otherwise, the promotion wasn't really worth doing, and you should have spent your money on defecting customers instead of on your best ones. The goal is allocating capital to highest ROI promotions. Success is measured by the incremental profits you generate, not the response rate to the offer.

In this type of promotion measurement, **sales are measured over a period of time after the communication was dropped, NOT from actual responses to the communication itself.** It is critical you look at all the activity generated by the people in both the control and test group, not just "responses" to the communication as tracked by coupons or other business process mechanisms.

The following Figure 64 is a financial analysis using control groups. We're using the numbers from previous examples – a $40 average price, 10% margin business, response rate of 12% (High RF customers), and a 5% discount (large, and not smart for this business with a high RF customer).

The promotion measurement is based on comparing the **average sales per customer (line 3)**, for the test and control groups, over the 60 days after the promotion was delivered to the customer. Pay attention to the line called Incremental Margin (line 5):

Parameter	Control Group	Test Group
1. 60 day Sales	$40,000	$440,000
2. Number of customers	1000	10,000
3. Avg. Sales / Customer	$40	$44
4. Margin @ 10%	$4.00	$4.40
5. Incremental Margin	-	**$0.40**
6. Cost of Promotion	-	$0.30
7. Cost of 5% Discount	-	$0.264
8. Net Promotional Margin per Customer	$0.00	-$0.164

**Figure 64: Measuring Subsidy Cost Using
a Control Group for Behavioral Comparison**

Oops. You literally lost 16.4 cents on every one you mailed, or $1,640 (-$.164 x 10,000) in the process. Let's go through this table:

The sales for the 60-day promotional period (line 1) were $40,000 for the control group (no promotion) and $440,000 for the test group (received promotion). The number of customers in each group (line 2) divided by 60-day sales (line 1) results in average sales per customer of $40 for the Control group and $44 for the Test group (line 3 in the table).

This results in a $4.40 margin per customer for the Test group compared with $4 per customer for the Control group (line 4). The incremental, or net gain in, margin between the Test and Control groups is $.40 per customer (line 5). This is the amount of margin per customer in the Test group **directly attributable** to the promotion sent. The cost of the promotion was a total of $.564 between delivery (line 6) and discounts (line 7). The net of these costs and incremental margin (line 5) directly caused by the promotion is a loss of $.164 (line 8).

A $4 difference in sales between Test and Control per person translates into a $.40 gain in margin per person for the Test group. You can't take credit for the whole $4.40 in margin per customer in the test group to pay for the promotion, only $.40 of it, because the Control group generated $4 in margin per customer **without a promotion over the same time period**. There wasn't enough sales lift **directly attributable to the promotion itself** to pay the promotion off. The customers in the control group bought $40 per customer all by themselves, with no promotion; only $4 of the sales in the Test group is directly attributable to the promotional effort.

By the way, the discount calculation is as follows:

10,000 mailed x 12% response = 1,200 taking discount (you would know this from actual discounts redeemed for in the commerce system)

5% of $44 average price = $2.20 per respondent x 1,200 = $2,640

$2,640 over 10,000 mailed = $0.264 per customer mailed.

It would be nice to claim the whole $4.40 per customer in margin for the test group, paying off the promotion nicely – but we're talking about **allocation** here folks, allocating money to one marketing purpose or another. And if you're managing precious marketing dollars, it makes a difference where you allocate – you need the highest return possible. The highest return is NOT in giving your best customers a discount on stuff they usually buy. Spend it on customers with falling RF scores and send your best customers a thank-you card. Then measure the thank-you promotion using a control group and see what happens. The results will blow your mind, now that you know how to measure them properly.

With control groups you don't depend on measuring a "response," like someone using a coupon or other response oriented, tracking type idea. You just measure the test behavior versus the control group.

Control groups are also the best way to track another Data-Driven marketing effect – the Halo Effect. Halo Effects occur when someone ignores your communication and doesn't take advantage of your offer. Then they decide to buy or visit anyway, probably because the promotion "reminded them" you were there, resulting in sales or activity attributable to your communication **you are not measuring**. Most people tracking response rates would never realize the customer responded, because they did not get a coupon or click back through their systems. By using control groups, you capture the Halo Effect by comparing profits in the test group with profits in the control group over time. This approach is perfect for testing the profitability of non-incentive "soft" promotions like thank-you cards or enhanced service levels. The contribution of Halo Effects to ROI can be quite significant, so they are worth measuring.

A few more words about control groups and related issues:

Be careful not to "poison" your control groups, that is, select people in a control group for one promotion to be in the test group in a second promotion running at the same time. The second promotion will drive up sales or visit behavior in the now "poisoned" control group and you won't be able to properly look for incrementality in the first promotion.

It's no fair if you look for Halo Effects "forever." "Hey Boss, we're still getting Halo Effects in June from the promotion we did in January!" Nothing doing. Anything longer than 60 days (in retailing) would be suspect to me, 90 days at the outside, unless you can demonstrate a clear reason for looking out further by looking at your "normal" purchase or activity cycle (Intra-Activity Latency). If you are seeing effects far beyond the normal Latency for the segment, there's a good chance something else is causing the effect you're seeing. A 30 to 45 day period is probably pretty fair for purchases, probably 2 – 3 weeks for visits. Decide on a standard for each type of activity and stick to it.

It's difficult to quantify **incentive proneness** at the individual level without a pretty fancy model. At the group level though, you could use a Hurdle Rate to at least track it. Take the average redemption of your customer base (number of purchases sold on deal / total items sold) and watch that as a Hurdle for the overall incentive proneness of your business or segments of customers. If this ratio consistently moves up, your customers are becoming increasingly incentive prone. Proneness is an **end of LifeCycle behavior**; look for these customers to drop in RF score if you don't keep giving your product / service away to them.

Chapter 30
Some Final Thoughts: Seasonality, CRM, Behavioral Inertia, Data-Driven Program Outlines

Well, you made it. I'm proud of you. You now know the mechanics of what goes on behind Data-Driven marketing programs like personalization, 1-to-1, relationship marketing, loyalty marketing, and so forth. You're a profiler, a modeler, and THE big cheese on the block with the answers to mystical marketing questions. You know how to allocate your marketing budget towards more profitable marketing activities and customers, and to allocate away from those with low value. And you know something about predicting behavior, like when a customer is about to defect or stop visiting.

Of all the web sites selling products out there, the catalog and TV shopping companies are doing the most consistently profitable business. Do you know why? One reason is they invented this stuff — they live and breathe it, and it works like a charm! Once you gain experience with RF techniques, you can then move on to more advanced modeling approaches.

Up next are a couple of general comments on further tweaking of Data-Driven techniques, some thoughts on using RF in the large-scale CRM (Customer Relationship Management) engines, and some definitions of the marketing programs you always hear about.

Seasonal Adjustments to Marketing Promotions

Once you start getting some experience with behavioral targeting, you will notice the response for any particular RF score or LifeCycle Grid cell can change in response to external events. One of the most powerful external events is seasonality; it tends to exaggerate or depress response to any given marketing promotion. Two identical promotions carried out during different seasons of the year can generate very different financial results.

For example, let's say you learn from experience and testing the need to hit the RF 44 customer with a "$5 off anything" coupon if the customer doesn't make a purchase for a 60-day span. If you don't do this, the customer defects and you can't drag them back no matter what you do. In the summer, when buying and visiting activity (in general) drops off, you may have to bump that to $7.50 to get the same level of response. During holiday season, you can back it off to $2.50 and get the same response. The point here is the willingness or likelihood of the customer to respond at a certain level can be depressed in summer, and exaggerated in the fall. The entire population of customers can become more likely to respond and have higher Potential Value at certain times, even though they retain their **relative** rankings to each other.

My personal classic blunder on this issue was one of my first promotions based on LifeCycle Grids, run in the summer. It was a huge financial success, generating over $1 million in profit in just 60 days! It was targeted at best customers who were slightly distant, that had not made a purchase within the past 30 to 60 days. Then I ran the exact same promotion in the fall and it was a financial disaster. Lost over $1 million in the blink of an eye.

The reason for the difference? Customers in general were more likely to buy in the fall holiday season, and I gave them a discount financially designed for the summer, when customers need a larger "push." Even though this discount was not very large (less than 5%, targeted to high RF customers), it was enough to tip the balance. The summer discount was too high to use in the fall, when customers did not need as much of a push, and created very little incremental behavior – a classic example of our old friend subsidy cost.

So be careful out there. Large external events, like seasonality, world events, elections, deaths of Hollywood stars, (or anything that focuses or diverts people's attention) can raise or lower response, generating unpredictable financial performance.

CRM Software and Customer Scoring

I hope I'm not the only one confused by all these CRM (Customer Relationship Management) offerings from companies like Broadvision, E.Piphany, Kana, Vignette, Art Technology Group, Retek Direct, Clarify, Blue Martini, Siebel Systems, Oracle and so on. Man, what a pile of software! They each have overlapping functionality, but not one of them does the whole job completely. There's "operational CRM" and "analytical CRM" and who knows what else to come down the line

Some of these packages work across multiple channels so the company can see the customer with a "360 degree" view. Some of them also have extensive promotion management capabilities so you can target specific customers with specific offers, either with e-mail or customized web pages, and track results. Sounds like a good idea.   Also sounds a little familiar to the Data-Driven marketer, doesn't it?

A few of these companies talk about using RF at a simplistic level, like the very first scoring example we went through. How much more advanced they have become is not clear. Many of these applications use rules-based engines to drive the output or results of the system. "If customer has purchased X but not Y, offer them Y at a discount " and so forth. But it's not really clear what drives these engines, where does the data come from, are analytics included?

You know what the most difficult part of using this great software is? Coming up with the rules. I mean, where do you start? You have to know a lot about customer behavior to really make CRM work in the Data-Driven marketing sense. The fact is, rule-based engines present the perfect opportunity to use RF or LifeCycle analysis. Think of all the wonderfully complex rules you could generate with a comprehensive RF scored database or LifeCycle Grid!

Remember, as much as things can change, they tend stay the same when it comes to human activity-based behavior. On the face of things, the activity might look different, but the driving force behind the activity remains the same. Regardless of whether you have a machine blindly following rules, or a human looking at the LifeCycle Grid, it's about customer behavior. And that behavior doesn't change. It may happen over a shorter time, or from a new location, or at a faster rate, but the basic underlying behavior described in this book is still there when you look at activity-based behavior on a **relative basis** – comparing each customer to all the rest of the customers.

Customers who have bought (visited) Recently and Frequently will tend to continue to buy (visit). And if you use systems of behavior analysis based on **comparing customers to each other**, much of the noise created by shifts in technology will be canceled out.

As new technology is implemented across a customer population, this technology affects all customers equally. So comparing customers to each other is the best way to "control" for changes in behavior brought on by the use of new technology. All the customers may modify their behavior in reaction to the new technology, but this only creates a new "baseline" you can use to evaluate each customer against all the others.

These CRM programs need a heavy dose of RF built right into them. What they are doing now is an excellent start. But "If customers have purchased X but not Y, offer them Y at a discount " would be so much more powerful with RF built in. Try it this way: "If customers have purchased X but not Y, offer them Y at a discount. If the customer is RF score > 45, discount = 2%. If the customer is RF 33 to 45, discount = 5%. If the customer is.... " And so on. The process would be so much more effective and profitable if the CRM machines used RF techniques in all their decision-making.

Perhaps it will become popular some day soon. I have heard whispers of it being done, but have seen no examples. If anyone out there is using RF techniques with the big CRM packages, e-mail jim@jimnovo.com, will ya?

Don't Fight Behavioral Inertia

Don't fight the flow of customer behavior; it's too hard, there are too many of them, and they don't want to change the way they do things. They're in control now, and they don't like to give up control.

Instead, find ways to use the flow to your advantage. If the customer wants to go left, don't try to get them to go right; put something on the left they will find interesting or desirable. If your highest site traffic is in the mid-afternoon, then schedule your best events or products for that time slot. Don't schedule them for the evening and then try to promote "come see us this evening" to everybody who comes in the afternoon. They don't want to. They are in charge. Do what they want you to do.

If your best customers insist on spending all their time in chat, and ignore your great content after multiple promotional attempts, find a way to make chat better. Don't try to force them to look at content if they really don't want to. Use the content to attract new customers, and then migrate them to chat when it is appropriate to do so.

Concentrate on predicting behavior, and taking advantage of it, rather than trying to make big changes to it. **You can nudge and tweak behavior when it's on the edge, while a change in behavior is already taking place.** Once the change has happened (the customer has already defected, for example), it's done. Don't waste a lot of time and money chasing "too late" situations or trying to "force" customers into a certain kind of behavior. You will always lose money fighting behavioral inertia; find a way to take advantage of it.

Data-Driven Marketing Program Outlines

Let's talk a little about each of the Data-Driven marketing approaches, and make sure we understand them and how RF fits into them.   We'll take them in increasing levels of sophistication, simplest to most complex.   In well-run programs, all of these approaches use RF to some extent to track behavior, create offers, target customers, and generally make marketing decisions.

The following is not an attempt to dissect all the nuances of each approach or all the sub-cultures inside each of them.   There is some overlap across all of them. Let's try to wrap each one up in a summary:

Database Marketing

Using the customer database to market to customers.   Hmm.   It can mean you have a list of customers and mail stuff to them, without doing any profiling or RF at all.   Frequently uses characteristics of customers to customize promotions, but not always, depending on the business.   If you follow the techniques described in this book, you <u>are</u> doing database marketing, because you are using the customer database to make marketing decisions.

Frequency Marketing

"Punch card" marketing.   If you buy 6 sandwiches, you get the 7th free.   Buy $100 worth of stuff and we'll send you a $10 coupon.   Here you are using the database to figure out who isn't buying enough and try to get them to buy more. OK, I get it.   It's really a crippled version of RF, F without the R, if you will. Concepts like LTV and subsidy cost don't matter as much; you just want them to buy more.   These programs tend to generate HUGE subsidy costs, because you're always giving the most discounts to your best customers.   They are very common in offline retail, where the effects on customer valuation and behavior are difficult to measure. Yuck.

Relationship Marketing

Database marketing with a friendly, more intelligent face.   Many database marketing types just use the database as a list and mail things to it; relationship marketing implies a deeper knowledge of the customer and some kind of give and take.   In relationship marketing, there is acknowledgement of a customer

LifeCycle, and marketing is viewed as a **process** rather than a series of seemingly unconnected events for the customer.

The process is usually defined as a series of customer stages, and there are many different names given to these stages, depending on the marketer's perspective and the type of business. For example, working from the beginning of the relationship to the end of the relationship:

Interaction > Communication > Valuation > Termination

Awareness > Comparison > Transaction > Reinforcement > Advocacy

Suspect > Prospect > Customer > Partner > Advocate > Former

During this process, you try to customize programs for individual customer groups and the stage of the process they are going through; as opposed to some forms of database marketing where everybody would get virtually the same promotions, with perhaps a change in offer. The stage in customer LifeCycle determines the approach used in marketing. A simple example of this would be sending new customers a "Welcome Kit." And in relationship marketing, you listen to the data and try to hear what it's telling you. OK, if you follow the techniques in this book, you **are** doing relationship marketing. In fact, the relationship marketing umbrella is where the original RFM approach was amplified and expanded.

Loyalty Marketing

Relationship marketing with a currency, a store of value that tries to keep the customer "locked up" with a company. In well-run loyalty programs, RF is used extensively to promote to customers, except points are used instead of discounts as the incentive for activity. Loyalty programs are expensive and difficult to do right, but can be effective, as long as these things are true:

> The rewards are desirable to the specific customer base. Generic loyalty programs with blah awards almost always fail. If you're doing a sports loyalty program and you offer tickets to great games instead of over-priced cameras for rewards, you'll do OK.

> The program is kept fresh and exciting, with a constant variety of things to involve the customer with, including refreshing of the rewards catalog.

The marketing does not focus on ideas creating subsidy costs among best customers. In the ideal world, you want to use points to generate activity from low RF customers, and you don't want your high RF customers spending down their points to zero all the time. Some marketers encourage the opposite and bankrupt their programs.

Permission Marketing

Relationship marketing with a gentler hand on the communications issues. It's a superb idea, and concerns the protocol of communication between a business and their customers **over the LifeCycle**. Permission marketing states when communicating with customers, you should be anticipated, be personal, and be relevant. The customer's definition of these three ideas would naturally change over time, so you have to listen to the customers and engage in dialogue.

This has the effect of upgrading the quality of your customer base, because in theory, only the people who really want something from you grant permission. This is definitely solidly in the RF camp, where the focus is on improving the value of customers and not spending money on customers who are not interested. Other than communication protocols, RF techniques would apply, as long as you make sure you refresh and keep the permission.

1 to 1 Marketing

Outlined in a 1993 book *"The One to One Future"* by advertising guru Don Peppers and marketing scholar Martha Rogers, Ph.D. The following 2 blurbs are from the book promotion:

"Most businesses follow time-honored mass-marketing rules of pitching their products to the greatest number of people. But selling more goods to fewer people is more efficient / more profitable. Welcome to a radically different business paradigm of 1 to1 production, marketing, and communication."

"The One to One Future" gives the best description yet of life after mass marketing. A "1 to 1" competitor focuses on share of customer — one customer at a time — rather than just share of market, which is the Holy Grail of the mass marketer." Hmmm. Selling more goods to fewer people is more efficient. Sounds like focusing your resources on your highest potential customers, and customizing your approach based on their profiles. Sort of like what we've talking about in this book all along.

Additionally, this original idea is much bigger than just marketing; it is about the entire business process. They would like companies to literally design products and service for specific customers, instead of creating a product and then trying to find people who want to buy it. As a customer of a true 1 to 1 company, you would let the company know what you need and they would provide it. This is the "share of customer" idea in action.

In practice, the concept at this time, for most companies, comes down to understanding what people want and marketing to them in a customized way. RFM is right up the 1-to-1 alley because it involves understanding customer behavior and reacting to it as an exchange between the business and the customer to the benefit of both.

So there you have it. You're ready to go. You understand the basic forces driving all these types of marketing approaches, and what goes on in the back room where the analysts who make these programs work hang out. And you know all the dirty little secrets.

You can profile customers with the best of them. The fundamental building blocks of all these approaches, and the marketing decision making driving them, are now firmly in your hands.

So go forth, and conquer customer behavior. Allocate your resources where the best returns are. Focus on retaining your highest value customers, and growing your middle value customers. And don't waste a lot of money on low value customers. Be a Data-Driven marketer.

Now go do some Drilling Down, will ya?

http://www.jimnovo.com

APPENDIX:
Software Download and ReadMe

For those who purchased a hard copy of the book or for some other reason need access to a hard copy of the software related documentation, the following is provided. This information was last updated June 2004; more current information may be available at http://www.jimnovo.com/download.htm, including the most recent software ReadMe.

The software can be accessed for download at:

http://www.jimnovo.com/home/ddsoft.htm

Point your browser there and follow the instructions on the page.

THE DRILLING DOWN SOFTWARE
END USER LICENSE AGREEMENT

Use of The Drilling Down Software (hereinafter 'SOFTWARE') is contingent on your agreement to the following terms:

1. GRANT OF LICENSE

The Drilling Down Project grants you a limited non-exclusive license to use the SOFTWARE free of charge.

You are using the SOFTWARE free of charge under the terms of this Agreement, and are not entitled to any support whatsoever. Support may be available from other users at the Drilling Down Software Community: http://www.jimnovo.com

2. DISCLAIMER OF WARRANTY

THE SOFTWARE IS PROVIDED AS IS WITHOUT WARRANTY OF ANY KIND. TO THE MAXIMUM EXTENT PERMITTED BY APPLICABLE LAW, The Drilling Down Project FURTHER DISCLAIMS ALL WARRANTIES, INCLUDING WITHOUT LIMITATION ANY IMPLIED WARRANTIES OF MERCHANTABILITY, FITNESS FOR A PARTICULAR

PURPOSE, AND NONINFRINGEMENT. THE ENTIRE RISK ARISING OUT OF THE USE OR PERFORMANCE OF THE PRODUCT AND DOCUMENTATION REMAINS WITH RECIPIENT.

TO THE MAXIMUM EXTENT PERMITTED BY APPLICABLE LAW, IN NO EVENT SHALL The Drilling Down Project BE LIABLE FOR ANY CONSEQUENTIAL, INCIDENTAL, DIRECT, INDIRECT, SPECIAL, PUNITIVE, OR OTHER DAMAGES WHATSOEVER (INCLUDING, WITHOUT LIMITATION, DAMAGES FOR LOSS OF BUSINESS PROFITS, BUSINESS INTERRUPTION, LOSS OF BUSINESS INFORMATION, OR OTHER PECUNIARY LOSS) ARISING OUT OF THIS AGREEMENT OR THE USE OF OR INABILITY TO USE THE PRODUCT, EVEN IF The Drilling Down Project HAS BEEN ADVISED OF THE POSSIBILITY OF SUCH DAMAGES.

3. SCOPE OF GRANT

You may not reverse engineer, decompile or disassemble the SOFTWARE. The Drilling Down Project shall retain title and all ownership rights to the SOFTWARE.

4. COPYRIGHT

This SOFTWARE is protected by copyright laws and international copyright treaties, as well as other intellectual property laws and treaties.

5. MAINTENANCE

The Drilling Down Project is not obligated to provide maintenance or updates for the SOFTWARE. However, any maintenance or updates provided by The Drilling Down Project shall be covered by this Agreement.

6. DISTRIBUTION

The SOFTWARE may be freely distributed provided that it is not modified and the original archive remains intact with all accompanying files, and provided that no fee is charged (except for any reasonable fees necessary to cover costs of distribution media).

Drilling Down Software 1.4 ReadMe

Note: Download the most current Readme file at: http://www.jimnovo.com/download.htm

Note: This latest version of the software runs on Access 2000 (or later). The Access 2000 version can accept any standard keyboard character in the Customer ID field, including "@", "-", "_" and so on, so that e-mail addresses or even URLs can be used as Customer ID. Other characters may be accepted, but have not been tested.

An older version running on Access 1997 is available, but this version only accepts numeric characters in the Customer ID field. No improvements, fixes, or changes will be made to this version.

The software is provided as a free download, and instructions for this download are on the first page of the Appendix to the Drilling Down book and at the end of the Introduction.

Note: There is another file, dao2535.tlb, included with this download package. Your computer may not have this file and the Drilling Down software requires it to run. If you receive a message like "Compile Error. Can't find project or library" when trying to run the program you are missing this file. Copy the file into the directory

C:\Program Files\Common Files\Microsoft Shared\Dao

If you don't have this directory, you should create it.

Note: The software is designed to handle the scoring of larger groups of customers, avoiding the manual method used in the book. The software scoring method may become unstable when used with a customer base of less than 5000 customers, particularly if a large portion of the customers have identical behavior metrics. See the Drilling Down book for more details on this subject; the spreadsheet method is generally preferred because of the ability to include data on the customer other than transactions (demographic, location, etc.)

Note: The application has no onboard help. This readme document is the help documentation for the application.

Note: This software provides the "base case" behavior analysis you can do with a spreadsheet. If you appreciate the concepts and functionality demonstrated in this software, get the companion book:

Drilling Down: Turning Customer Data into Profits with a Spreadsheet

The book expands greatly on the types of behavior profiling you can do once you have the "base case" spreadsheet generated by this software.

The book is available at: http://www.booklocker.com/jimnovo

SHORT DESCRIPTION

Creates RF (Recency / Frequency) Quintile Customer Grids

DESCRIPTION

Drilling Down Software 1.4 provides the capability to score each individual customer in a file of customer transactions against all the other customers based on the Most Recent Date of Activity (Recency) and the Highest Total Activity (Frequency) on a scale from 55 (Highest) to 11 (Lowest). Any activity transaction with a Customer ID, number of units, and date of activity can be scored, for example, orders, visits, items, or page views. Customers with the highest ranking tend to be best customers and have the highest response rate to promotions. Customers with the lowest scores tend to be customers in the process of defecting and have the lowest response rate to promotions.

Customers are divided into five equal groups called "quintiles"; a quintile represents 20% of the customer database. The Recency and Frequency attributes of each customer are assigned a score between 5 and 1, where 5 is the highest (top 20%) and 1 is the lowest (bottom 20%). This score or rank assigned represents the customer's Recency and Frequency attributes relative to all the other customers. The combination of the Recency and Frequency scores results in a 2 digit score where Recency is reflected first.

For example, the RF (Recency/Frequency) score of 45 means the customer has a 4 Recency, or is in the top 40% of all customers as far as most Recent activity, and a 5 Frequency, or is in the top 20% of all customers, as far as the most total activity engaged in.

There are 25 possible combinations of Recency (R) and Frequency (F) scores, resulting in a 5 x 5 RF score table. The application displays the total customer count at each RF score within a cell of the RF table format, with Recency on the x-axis and Frequency on the y-axis. Totals for each level of Recency and Frequency are provided. Users can then view and export a table of all customer ID's and their individual RF scores in preparation for a marketing campaign.

The aggregation of multiple transactions for a unique customer ID is derived by selecting the Most Recent Activity Date (Recency) and totaling the Units of Activity (Frequency) from all the imported activity transactions.

PREPARING DATA FOR USE IN THE APPLICATION

The Drilling Down application can import Fixed Width, Comma Delimited, Space Delimited, Tab Delimited, and SemiColon Delimited files. If your customer data is not in any of these formats, it needs to be formatted into one that is compatible with the Drilling Down application.

THE APPLICATION IMPORT READS IN ONLY 3 DATA FIELDS AND THEY MUST BE IN THIS ORDER: CUSTOMER ID, UNITS OF ACTIVITY, AND DATE OF ACTIVITY. WHEN YOU PREPARE YOUR DATA FOR USE IN THIS APPLICATION, MAKE SURE THESE 3 FIELDS ARE THE ONLY FIELDS IN THE FILE AND THEY ARE ORGANIZED IN THE RIGHT ORDER! CUSTOMER ID FIELD CAN CONTAIN ANY ALPHANUMERIC COMBINATION.

In the Access 2000 version, any standard keyboard character is allowed in the Customer ID field. Other characters may be accepted, but have not been tested.

In the Access 1997 version, NUMERIC DATA ONLY IS ALLOWED IN CUSTOMER ID FIELD. No improvements, fixes, or changes will be made to this version of the software.

NOTE: If your file format is fixed width, field sizes should be set according to the following sizes: Customer ID = 20, Activity Units = 20, Date = mm/dd/yy (time stamp is optional). Even if your Customer ID is only 10 digits long, the field size should still be set to 20.

Multiple imports can be performed before the first report is run, or a report can be run after each import. If you have monthly or weekly data and want to see the progress over time, run the report after each import.

NOTE: Each time you run a report, refresh the results in the pivot table by clicking on the "!" icon in the floating toolbar. If you do not have a floating toolbar, then choose Data > Refresh from the Access menu. Failure to do this will result in viewing the previous report results.

USING THE APPLICATION

Double-click the executable to open the application. The About screen with start button and URL http://www.jimnovo.com/ for the Drilling Down website appear.

Click start button to start. Click OK on the pop-up. On the next page, the sequence of operations is labeled 1 - 4.

1. Locate the folder and file for import.

2. DOUBLE CLICK on the file format being used.

3. Click ONCE to import each file. NOTE: A DOUBLE CLICK MAY CAUSE THE DATA TO BE IMPORTED TWICE. Press OK on the Import Complete pop-up.

4. Click ONCE to run the report.

You will see a form with the RF Score table and 4 buttons. To see the whole report, click the "Edit Pivot Table" button, which will open up an Excel pivot table. This spreadsheet can be used to print or export your results.

NOTE: You should see the floating toolbar with the "!" symbol at this point. Remember to press this after each report is run to view the most recently imported data. If you do not have a floating toolbar, then choose Data > Refresh from the Access menu.

REPORTS

Close the pivot table spreadsheet. You will see the report form again, with the "Edit Pivot Table" button and three buttons below it.

If you click once on the left-most button, "Customer Scores," you will see a table with each customer ID and the customer's RF score.

If you click once on the center button, you will see a table with each customer ID, the number of days between the customer's last Activity date and the current date (system date), and the Recency Quintile Score.

If you click once the right-most button, you will see a table with each customer ID, the total units of customer activity, and the Frequency Quintile Score presented.

All 3 of these tables can be printed or saved / exported just like any Access table. NOTE: To save / export a file, choose File > Save As from the Access menu, then enter the name and file type to Save / Export the file.

Closing any of these tables brings you back to the form with the "Edit Pivot Table" button and 3 Reporting buttons.

For FAQ, Help, Support, and User Community, visit:

http://www.jimnovo.com/

Printed in the United States
33830LVS00002B/36

9 781591 135197